Gateway to Reading

Library of Congress Cataloging-in-Publication Data

Polette, Nancy.
Gateway to reading : 250+ author games and booktalks to motivate middle readers / Nancy J. Polette.
      pages   cm
   Includes bibliographical references and index.
   ISBN 978-1-61069-423-0 (pbk.) — ISBN 978-1-61069-424-7 (ebook)
   1. Middle school libraries—Activity programs—United States.   2. Middle school students—Books and reading—United States. 3. Children's stories, American—Study and teaching.   I. Title.
   Z675.S3P565   2013
   028.5—dc23   2013008684

ISBN: 978-1-61069-423-0
EISBN: 978-1-61069-424-7

17 16 15 14 13   1 2 3 4 5

This book is also available on the World Wide Web as an eBook.
Visit www.abc-clio.com for details.

Libraries Unlimited
An Imprint of ABC-CLIO, LLC

ABC-CLIO, LLC
130 Cremona Drive, P.O. Box 1911
Santa Barbara, California 93116-1911

This book is printed on acid-free paper ∞

Manufactured in the United States of America

Gateway to Reading

250+ Author Games and Booktalks to Motivate Middle Readers

Nancy J. Polette

LIBRARIES UNLIMITED

AN IMPRINT OF ABC-CLIO, LLC
Santa Barbara, California • Denver, Colorado • Oxford, England

Contents

Introduction

We are living today in a media age in which to all appearances individuality is numbed, imagination is throttled, and the vulgar and base are exalted. Simplified communication is through e-mail. Our children spend countless hours on Facebook, Twitter, and other social networks. They are bombarded with deadening TV commercials whose credo seems to be "and a little child shall lead them—to our product!"

Unfortunately the overuse of electronic media, including multiscreen motion pictures, video games, cell phones, digital cameras, iPods, and a host of ever-changing technology, has left little time for the reader or the book.

Startling statistics come from The Thorndike Center for Visual Literacy:

- In 1950 the typical 14-year-old had a language storehouse (words stored by the brain for reading, writing, and speaking) of 25,000 words.
- In 1990 the typical 14-year-old had a language storehouse of 10,000 words.

Totalitarian governments burn books to simplify language and thought. The media age has unfortunately accomplished the same thing. Words are the cash value of language, but if not cashed in and traded for the ideas they represent, they are meaningless drivel. The challenge for librarians, teachers, and parents today is to find ways to lead children to authors and books that reveal the wonder, mystery, delight, awe, and compassion found in the printed word. *Gateway to Reading* will help in meeting this challenge.

Gateway to Reading: 250+ Author Games and Booktalks to Motivate Middle Readers introduces 40 well-known juvenile authors whose books range from humor, to mystery, to fantasy, and beyond. Ideal for book clubs in the public or school library or for use in the classroom or by homeschoolers, *Gateway* presents fun activities to lead young readers to the best in juvenile literature.

In playing the "I Have/Who Has" games, young readers will learn about the lives of authors who have a proven track record for excellence. Titles are also hidden in clever stories. Booktalks are provided for three or four of each author's books in the "Name That Book!" activities, and young readers are challenged to come up with their own titles after hearing or reading the description of each book before discovering the author's original titles. Children are then asked to find titles of each author's books hidden in an original story. A repeated challenge is to find which titles are available in the library.

Books that are worth reading are bursting with the passions that concern us all. One never knows which book can bring about a child's mental awakening and true growth. Hence it is necessary to share a vast variety of books and authors. *Gateway to Reading* is a first step in helping librarians, teachers, and parents do just that.

LLOYD ALEXANDER (1924–2007):
THE I HAVE/WHO HAS GAME

Cut the cards apart. Each player gets one card. The player who has the card with the asterisks (****) on it reads the "Who has" question. The player who has the answer card reads the answer and then the next question.

I HAVE: *The High King,* the final volume of The Chronicles of Prydain, won the Newbery Award. **** **WHO HAS:** At what age did Lloyd Alexander decide to become an author, and how did his parents feel about it?	**I HAVE:** In Wales he was trained in counterintelligence, and he was sent to Paris at the end of the war. **WHO HAS:** When he returned home and began writing, how long did it take before his first novel was published?
I HAVE: Lloyd Alexander was 15 when he decided to become an author, and his parents thought it was a foolish decision. **WHO HAS:** Who were his favorite authors, and what subject fascinated him the most?	**I HAVE:** It took 7 years before his first novel was published. **WHO HAS:** How many years later did he start writing for children, and what was his first children's book?
I HAVE: His favorite authors were Charles Dickens, Mark Twain, and Shakespeare. He was fascinated by mythology. **WHO HAS:** Because there was no money for college, what was his first job?	**I HAVE:** Ten years after his first novel for adults was published, he wrote *Time Cat* for children. **WHO HAS:** What caused him to write *The Book of Three*, the first volume of The Chronicles of Prydain?
I HAVE: Lloyd's first job was as a bank messenger. In World War II, longing for a life of adventure, he joined the army. **WHO HAS:** What job did the army train him for in Wales?	**I HAVE:** Research for *Time Cat* led to information on Welsh mythology, the basis for The Chronicles of Prydain. **WHO HAS:** Which book in The Chronicles of Prydain series won the Newbery Award?

From *Gateway to Reading: 250+ Author Games and Booktalks to Motivate Middle Readers* by Nancy J. Polette. Santa Barbara, CA: Libraries Unlimited. Copyright © 2013.

LLOYD ALEXANDER:
MYSTERY TITLES

Some words in these titles of books by Lloyd Alexander have been replaced with Dewey Decimal numbers. Go to the shelf with the Dewey number. Find the subject of the book(s) with that number. Fill in the missing word in each title. The first person to finish all the titles correctly is the winner!

1. 728.8 _____ _____ _____ _____ _____ _____ of Llyr

2. Dream-of-Jade: The Emperor's 636.8 _____ _____ _____

3. How the 636.8 _____ _____ _____ Swallowed Thunder

4. 546 _____ _____ _____ _____ Ring

5. 529 _____ _____ _____ _____ Cat

Some words in these titles of books by Lloyd Alexander have been replaced with synonyms. Put the letter of the actual title after each synonymous title.

6. Mendicant Female Monarch _____

7. Volume in Triplicate _____

8. Elevated Male Monarch _____

9. Ruse with a Thick Cord _____

10. Future Speakers _____

ACTUAL TITLES
A. *The Beggar Queen*
B. *The Fortune-Tellers*
C. *The Book of Three*
D. *The Castle of Llyr*
E. *Dream-of-Jade: The Emperor's Cat*
F. *The High King*
G. *The Rope Trick*
H. *The El Dorado Adventure*

Which titles are available in your library?

The key to Mystery Titles is on page __5__.

From *Gateway to Reading: 250+ Author Games and Booktalks to Motivate Middle Readers*
by Nancy J. Polette. Santa Barbara, CA: Libraries Unlimited. Copyright © 2013.

LLOYD ALEXANDER:
NAME THAT BOOK!

What title would YOU give each of these books by Lloyd Alexander?

1) In the imaginary kingdom of Prydain, Princess Eilonwy must leave her friends and go to the Isle of Mona for training as a proper princess. Because Eilonwy has magical powers, she is sought by Achren, the most evil enchantress in the land. Shortly after her arrival on the Isle of Mona something sinister and secret befalls Eilonwy. Her friends—Taran, the assistant pig-keeper; Fflewddur, the bard; and Prince Rhun, her intended husband—realize her peril and set out on an exciting and terrifying mission to rescue her. They encounter great forces of evil as well as private—sometimes painful—revelations in the course of their journey.

Your title _____

2) Eighteen-year-old Vesper Holly has just learned that she owns a volcano in the tiny republic of El Dorado, and Vesper being Vesper, she and her guardian respond to the mysterious telegram by sailing to Central America. Almost as soon as they arrive, Vesper and Brinnie are thrust into danger. Someone wants her property, and they will stop at nothing to get it, even if it means destroying an entire tribe of Chirica Indians and Vesper herself.

Your title _____

3) When Vesper Holly is invited to the tiny kingdom of Drackenberg's Golden Jubilee, she and her guardians find themselves involved in an attempted overthrow of the government and the disappearance of a priceless painting. Vesper saves the day by trickery with the help of a train's baggage handler, at the same time rescuing her kidnapped aunt from the evil Helvetius.

Your title _____

4) Vesper Holly has foiled murderers, crossed mountains, and narrowly escaped earthquakes. Now she is home in Philadelphia, where she can relax—until President Ulysses S. Grant asks for her help. She is to protect the children of a foreign head of state. The Centennial Exposition of 1876 is about to begin, and luminaries from around the world will be there. But so will Vesper's archnemesis, the evil Doctor Helvetius. There's only one person who can thwart his evil plans: Vesper Holly!

Your title _____

5) Meet the Arkadians—a young bean counter turned hero, a poet turned jackass, a girl of marvels, a king disguised as a peasant, and others—who play across an epic stage, firmly connecting the quest of a young protagonist to those of classical heroes and heroines of ancient Greek storytelling, reminding readers that danger, daring, and romance are still the most thrilling of literary devices.

Your title _____

See the author's titles on page __5__.
Which titles are available in your library?

LLOYD ALEXANDER:
CIRCLE THE HIDDEN TITLES

The gypsy Rizka was the beggar queen of the Arkadians, a tribe of fortune-tellers. She wore an iron ring in her nose, cooked up spells in her black cauldron, and had a feline she simply called Cat. "It's time, Cat," she said, "for our annual visit to the king in the castle of Llyr. I want to teach him a new rope trick." Rizka's cat went along to play with Dream-of-Jade, the emperor's cat.

Every year Rizka visited the high king of the House Gobbaleen and taught him a new trick. This year he wasn't interested in tricks. He was worried about his son, Prince Jen, who was off on a Xanadu adventure searching for a magic book. Of three previous trips, none had been successful. His servant, Gawgon, and the boy Taran, had accompanied him on this fourth trip, but he had been gone many months.

"I will find Prince Jen for you," Rizka said, and she stirred her black cauldron. In the dark waters she saw the remarkable journey of Prince Jen. She gave a spoonful of the liquid to her cat and watched how the cat swallowed. Thunder boomed and lightning flashed.

"The prince will return soon," she said. "It seems that the boy, Taran, wanderer that he was, got lost, and it took the prince several months to find him."

The high king was so grateful to Rizka for this good news that he had her iron ring covered with gold, a gift she would treasure always.

From *Gateway to Reading: 250+ Author Games and Booktalks to Motivate Middle Readers*
by Nancy J. Polette. Santa Barbara, CA: Libraries Unlimited. Copyright © 2013.

LLOYD ALEXANDER:
KEYS

Answers to Circle the Hidden Titles

The **gypsy Rizka** was **the beggar queen** of the **Arkadians**, a tribe of **fortune-tellers**. She wore an **iron ring** in her nose, cooked up spells in her **black cauldron**, and had a feline she simply called Cat. "It's **time, Cat,**" she said, "for our annual visit to the king in **the castle of Llyr**. I want to teach him a new **rope trick**." Rizka's cat went along to play with **Dream-of-Jade, the emperor's cat**.

Every year Rizka visited **the high king** of the **House Gobbaleen** and taught him a new trick. This year he wasn't interested in tricks. He was worried about his son, Prince Jen, who was off on a **Xanadu adventure** searching for a magic **book. Of three** previous trips, none had been successful. His servant, **Gawgon, and the boy** Taran, had accompanied him on this fourth trip, but he had been gone many months.

"I will find Prince Jen for you," Rizka said, and she stirred her **black cauldron**. In the dark waters she saw **the remarkable journey of Prince Jen**. She gave a spoonful of the liquid to her cat and watched **how the cat swallowed. Thunder** boomed and lightning flashed.

"The prince will return soon," she said. "It seems that the boy, **Taran, wanderer** that he was, got lost, and it took the prince several months to find him."

The high king was so grateful to Rizka for this good news that he had her **iron ring** covered with gold, a gift she would treasure always.

Answers to Mystery Titles

1. Castle
2. Cat
3. Cat
4. Iron
5. Time
6. *The Beggar Queen* (A)
7. *The Book of Three* (C)
8. *The High King* (F)
9. *The Rope Trick* (G)
10. *The Fortune-Tellers* (B)

Answers to Name That Book!

1. The Chronicles of Prydain
2. *The El Dorado Adventure*
3. *The Drackenberg Adventure*
4. *The Philadelphia Adventure*
5. *The Arkadians*

AVI (1937–):
THE I HAVE/WHO HAS GAME

Cut the cards apart. Each player gets one card. The player who has the card with the asterisks (****) on it reads the "Who has" question. The player who has the answer card reads the answer and then the next question.

I HAVE: Avi won the Newbery Award for *Crispin: The Cross of Lead* and a Newbery Honor Award for *Nothing But the Truth*. ******** **WHO HAS:** Where did Avi get his name?	**I HAVE:** Avi did not do well in the public high school he attended but learned to write in a smaller private high school. That was when he decided to become a writer. **WHO HAS:** How long has Avi been writing books?
I HAVE: Avi was given his name by his twin sister, Emily. He was born five minutes before her, so he was the older brother. **WHO HAS:** How was Avi exposed to books as a child?	**I HAVE:** Avi has been writing books for more than 40 years. His first book was published in 1970. **WHO HAS:** Did Avi have any jobs other than writing?
I HAVE: As a child Avi was read to every night, taken to the library weekly, and received books for his birthday. Reading was one of his greatest pleasures. **WHO HAS:** Where did Avi go to school?	**I HAVE:** Avi worked as a librarian for 25 years, first at the New York City Public Library and then at Trenton (New Jersey) State College. **WHO HAS:** What is Avi's goal as an author of more than 30 books for young people?
I HAVE: Avi went to public school in Brooklyn, New York, and was in the same class as his twin sister for the first 8 grades. **WHO HAS:** How successful was Avi as a high school student?	**I HAVE:** Avi's goal as an author is for his readers to "enjoy the sheer pleasure of a good story." **WHO HAS:** For which books has Avi won the Newbery Award?

AVI:
MYSTERY TITLES

Some words in these titles of books by Avi have been replaced with Dewey Decimal numbers. Go to the shelf with the Dewey number. Find the subject of the book(s) with that number. Fill in the missing word in each title. The first person to finish all the titles correctly is the winner!

1. Christmas 599.35 _____ _____ _____

2. Good 636.7 _____ _____ _____

3. Midnight 793.8 _____ _____ _____ _____ _____

4. 577.4 _____ _____ _____ _____ _____ _____ _____ School

5. 599.77 _____ _____ _____ _____ Rider

Some words in these titles of books by Avi have been replaced with synonyms. Put the letter of the actual title after each synonymous title.

6. Fleeing from One's Abode _____

7. A Paucity of Verity _____

8. Object on an Elevated Level _____

9. Altercation on Terra Firma _____

10. Termination of the Prologue _____

ACTUAL TITLES
A. *Midnight Magic*
B. *The Escape from Home*
C. *The Book Without Words*
D. *Nothing But the Truth*
E. *The Good Dog*
F. *Something Upstairs*
G. *The Fighting Ground*
H. *Murder at Midnight*
I. *The End of the Beginning*
J. *The Secret School*

Which titles are available in your library?

The key to Mystery Titles is on page __11__.

From *Gateway to Reading: 250+ Author Games and Booktalks to Motivate Middle Readers* by Nancy J. Polette. Santa Barbara, CA: Libraries Unlimited. Copyright © 2013.

AVI:
NAME THAT BOOK!

What title would YOU give each of these books by Avi?

1) In fourteenth-century medieval England, Crispin is accused of a crime he did not commit, and he may be killed on sight by anyone in the village. If he wishes to remain alive, he must flee. All the boy takes with him is a newly revealed name—Crispin—and his mother's cross of lead. His journey through the English countryside is amazing and terrifying. Especially difficult is his encounter with the juggler named Bear. A huge, and possibly even mad, man, Bear forces the boy to become his servant. Bear, however, is a strange master, for he encourages Crispin to think for himself. Though Bear promises to protect Crispin, the boy is being relentlessly pursued. Why are his enemies so determined to kill him?

Your title _____

2) I was the only passenger on an ocean voyage from England to Rhode Island in 1832 when I overheard the crew plotting mutiny. My tattling to the captain brought about the death of my only true friend on board, the ship's cook. Not every 13-year-old girl is accused of murder, brought to trial, and found guilty. But I was just such a girl, and my story is worth relating even if it did happen years ago. Be warned, however: if strong ideas and action offend you, read no more.

Your title _____

3) At the very edge of Dimwood Forest stood an old, charred oak where, silhouetted by the moon, a great horned owl sat waiting. The owl's name was Mr. Ocax, and he looked like death himself. With his piercing gaze, he surveyed the lands he called his own, watching for the creatures he considered his subjects. Not one of them ever dared to cross his path . . . until the terrible night when two little mice went dancing in the moonlight.

Your title _____

4) April 3, 1778. America is caught up in the Revolutionary War. On this warm spring morning, not far from Trenton, New Jersey, a 13-year-old boy and his father are quietly tilling the sod on their farm. But the boy can think of only one thing: he wants to fight. He knows how to use a gun; why won't his father let him go? Unexpectedly, the quiet is cut by the sound of a bell, an alarm ringing from the nearby tavern. Jonathan is sent to find out what the trouble is. What he finds in the next 24 hours, when he does fight and is taken prisoner by three Hessian soldiers, changes his understanding of war and life forever. The real war, he discovers, is being fought within himself.

Your title _____

See the author's titles on page ___11___.
Which titles are available in your library?

From *Gateway to Reading: 250+ Author Games and Booktalks to Motivate Middle Readers*
by Nancy J. Polette. Santa Barbara, CA: Libraries Unlimited. Copyright © 2013.

It was Ereth's birthday, and she was puzzled at the present given her by her friend, Crispin. The cross of lead was heavy. She preferred hard gold. "Thank you, Crispin. I shall hang the cross in the barn to keep the animals safe."

"I can tell you nothing but the truth," Crispin replied. "I gave you the cross for protection. Don't you know there's a war on? The enemy is approaching, and the fighting ground will be where the prairie school is now. We must escape. From home we must travel many miles before finding Providence, a safe area."

"What about Poppy and Rye?" Ereth asked. "Poppy is such a good dog, and Rye won't be any trouble. Rye is here with me, but we must wait for Poppy's return."

"Never mind Poppy and Rye," Crispin answered. "We must be away before midnight. Magic won't save us, nor will wishful thinking. We must flee at once like Romeo and Juliet together. This could result in murder at midnight. It could even be the end of the beginning of the world. Follow me and be as quiet as a silent movie or a book without words."

"Wait, I think I hear something upstairs," Crispin whispered.

"What shall we do?" asked Ereth. Just then a masked man raced down the stairs and out the door.

"Things that sometimes happen can be for the best," Crispin replied. "Let's follow him."

The masked man led the two through the ragweed field to the secret school on Smuggler's Island where they would be safe. Then he disappeared as if a windcatcher had caught him.

"Who was that masked man, anyway?" Ereth asked.

"Well, it wasn't the mayor of Central Park," Crispin replied. "Some call him the wolf rider, but his real name is Perloo the bold. But whatever his name, we shall be forever in his debt."

AVI:
KEYS

Answers to Circle the Hidden Titles

It was **Ereth's birthday,** and she was puzzled at the present given her by her friend, **Crispin. The cross of lead** was heavy. She preferred **hard gold.** "Thank you, Crispin. I shall hang the cross in the barn to keep the animals safe."

"I can tell you **nothing but the truth,**" Crispin replied. "I gave you the cross for protection. **"Don't you know there's a war on?** The enemy is approaching, and the **fighting ground** will be where the **prairie school** is now. We must **escape. From home** we must travel many miles before **finding Providence,** a safe area."

"What about **Poppy and Rye?**" Ereth asked. "Poppy is such a **good dog,** and Rye won't be any trouble. Rye is here with me, but we must wait for **Poppy's return.**"

"Never mind **Poppy and Rye,**" Crispin answered. "We must be away before **midnight. Magic** won't save us, nor will wishful thinking. We must flee at once like **Romeo and Juliet together.** This could result in **murder at midnight.** It could even be **the end of the beginning** of the world. Follow me and be as quiet as a **silent movie** or a **book without words.**"

"Wait, I think I hear **something upstairs,**" Crispin whispered.

"What shall we do?" asked Ereth. Just then a masked man raced down the stairs and out the door.

"**Things that sometimes happen** can be for the best," Crispin replied. "Let's follow him."

The masked man led the two through the **ragweed** field to the **secret school on Smuggler's Island** on where they would be safe. Then he disappeared as if a **windcatcher** had caught him.

"**Who was that masked man anyway?**" Ereth asked.

"Well, it wasn't the mayor of Central Park," Crispin replied. "Some call him the **wolfrider,** but his real name is **Perloo the bold.** But whatever his name, we shall be forever in his debt."

Answers to Mystery Titles

1. Rat
2. Dog
3. Magic
4. Prairie
5. Wolf
6. *The Escape from Home* (B)
7. *Nothing But the Truth* (D)
8. *Something Upstairs* (F)
9. *The Fighting Ground* (G)
10. *The End of the Beginning* (I)

Answers to Name That Book!

1. *Crispin: The Cross of Lead*
2. *The True Confessions of Charlotte Doyle*
3. *Poppy*
4. *The Fighting Ground*

From *Gateway to Reading: 250+ Author Games and Booktalks to Motivate Middle Readers* by Nancy J. Polette. Santa Barbara, CA: Libraries Unlimited. Copyright © 2013.

BETSY BYARS (1928–):
THE I HAVE/WHO HAS GAME

Cut the cards apart. Each player gets one card. The player who has the card with the asterisks (****) on it reads the "Who has" question. The player who has the answer card reads the answer and then the next question.

I HAVE:	Among the many awards she has won are the Newbery Medal for *Summer of the Swans* and The American Book Award for *The Night Swimmers*. ****	I HAVE:	The ideas for her books come from experiences she has had living in both the city and country as well as memories of her childhood and the actions of her two children.
WHO HAS:	How did Betsy Byars feel about writing as a child?	WHO HAS:	What was her favorite pet?
I HAVE:	She thought writing was boring, and none of her teachers encouraged her to write.	I HAVE:	Her favorite pet was a black snake named Moon, which bit her the first time she touched it.
WHO HAS:	Where did she grow up, and how many were in her family?	WHO HAS:	What did Betsy learn to do when she was 55 years old?
I HAVE:	She grew up in Charlotte, North Carolina. Her father was an engineer, her mother loved acting, and she had one older sister.	I HAVE:	At age 55 Betsy learned to fly a plane and got her pilot's license.
WHO HAS:	When did she begin her writing career?	WHO HAS:	How many books has Betsy Byars written?
I HAVE:	Betsy Byars began her writing career when she was 28, living in a small town with nothing to do.	I HAVE:	Betsy Byars has written 47 books for children and continues to add to that number each year.
WHO HAS:	Where does Betsy Byars get the ideas for her books?	WHO HAS:	What book awards has Betsy Byars won?

BETSY BYARS:
MYSTERY TITLES

Some words in these titles of books by Betsy Byars have been replaced with Dewey Decimal numbers. Go to the shelf with the Dewey number. Find the subject of the book(s) with that number. Fill in the missing word in each title. The first person to finish all the titles correctly is the winner!

1. Ant Plays 599.78 _____ _____ _____ _____

2. 004 _____ _____ _____ _____ _____ _____ _____ _____ Nut

3. 155.9 _____ _____ _____ _____ _____'s Door

4. Midnight 599.77 _____ _____ _____

5. 551.55 _____ _____ _____ _____ _____ _____ _____

Some words in these titles of books by Betsy Byars have been replaced with synonyms. Put the letter of the actual title after each synonymous title.

6. Feline Memoirs _____

7. Moribund Epistle _____

8. Monarch of Homicide _____

9. Twelve O'Clock Vixen _____

10. Distressed Tributary _____

ACTUAL TITLES
A. *Trouble River*
B. *The Computer Nut*
C. *The Midnight Fox*
D. *The Black Tower*
E. *Cat Diaries*
F. *Death's Door*
G. *Dead Letter*
H. *Tornado*
I. *King of Murder*
J. *Wanted . . . Mud Blossom*

Which titles are available in your library?

The key to Mystery Titles is on page __17__.

From *Gateway to Reading: 250+ Author Games and Booktalks to Motivate Middle Readers* by Nancy J. Polette. Santa Barbara, CA: Libraries Unlimited. Copyright © 2013.

BETSY BYARS:
NAME THAT BOOK!

What title would YOU give each of these books by Betsy Byars?

1) Carlie knows she has no say in what happens to her. Stuck in a foster home with two other kids, Harvey and Thomas J., she's just a pinball being bounced from bumper to bumper. As soon as you get settled, somebody puts another coin in the machine, and off you go again. But against her will and her better judgment, Carlie and the boys become friends. And all three of them start to see that they can take control of their own lives.

Your title _____

2) A tornado appears in the distance, and Pete, the farmhand, gathers everyone into the storm cellar. While they wait for the storm to pass, he tells the family about the dog dropped down by a tornado when Pete was a boy. Named Tornado, Pete's pet was no ordinary dog: he played card tricks, saved a turtle's life, and had a rivalry with the family cat. By the time Pete tells all of Tornado's lively stories, the storm has passed, and another family has been entertained by this very special dog.

Your title _____

3) The hunt is on! On Saturday, Jackson and his best pal, Goat, hide treasures for each other to find. It's the Hunt for the Secret Treasure, and it's so much fun that the boys decide to do it all over again. This time the hunts will be trickier, and the prizes will be outstanding. But everything goes wrong. The best treasure of all disappears from its hiding place. Only one person could be responsible: the ogre, also known as Goat's older sister, Rachel. Can the two friends find the treasure before she gets the last laugh?

Your title _____

4) Fourteen-year-old Sara is having a terrible summer. She is suffering from the awkwardness and mood swings of adolescence. Things are somewhat complicated by the fact that Charlie, her younger brother, is autistic. Sara takes Charlie to a nearby lake to see the swans, which have recently arrived. Charlie is fascinated and does not want to leave. That night Charlie thinks about the swans and sets out to find them on his own. Charlie gets lost almost immediately and is overcome with fear. Sara checks the lake but cannot find him, and Aunt Willie has no choice but to call the police. While searching for Charlie, Sara is joined by her classmate, Joe Melby. Sara reluctantly accepts his help, for she blames him for teasing Charlie and taking his watch. She soon comes to realize, however, that she had misjudged him. With Joe's help, Sara finds Charlie. Although he is very upset, he is safe and sound.

Your title _____

See the author's titles on page __17__
Which titles are available in your library?

BETSY BYARS:
CIRCLE THE HIDDEN TITLES

Cracker Jackson was a computer nut. He spent a lot of time in the black tower researching the burning questions of Bingo Brown, his best friend. Bingo had asked Cracker to find information on a McMummy and the Cybil War, but the computer kept asking Cracker to check his spelling. His search was interrupted when a strange message appeared:

THIS IS A DEAD LETTER FROM THE KING OF MURDER.

AT MIDNIGHT FOX WILL HOWL IN THE BLACK TOWER.

CLIMB THE DARK STAIRS

TO DEATH'S DOOR AND RESCUE THE KEEPER OF THE DOVES. ASK THE PINBALLS TO HELP.

DO NOT DELAY!

SIGNED: THE ANIMAL, THE VEGETABLE, AND JOHN D. JONES

P.S.: LIRPA LOOF

Cracker had no idea what the message meant. He wanted Mud Blossom, his other good friend, and Bingo to help him figure it out. The Pinballs were a club of roughnecks. He didn't want them. They had attacked the birds on the lake last summer. Of the swans, they flew away and never returned.

"I can't come now," said Mud Blossom. "I have to watch my brother, Ant. When Ant plays bear he could tear up the house if I don't stop him. Besides, tornado warnings are out, and we should all stay indoors."

Bingo was not helpful either. "I'd like to help," he said, "but don't ask me. Tarzan is on the TV, and he's in trouble. River rats are chasing him, and I have to see what happens."

Cracker thought about asking the Golly sisters for help. He hoped they had not pulled one of their disappearing acts. They were rarely home. Sometimes the Golly sisters go west, but they came right over when he called, even though they were busy writing their cat diaries and dog diaries dictated to them by their pets.

The sisters took one look at the strange message and laughed. "The last two words are spelled backward," they said. Sure enough, when Cracker turned the last two words around he began to laugh too. Hooray for the Golly sisters," he shouted. "Now I know what the message is all about. Do you?"

BETSY BYARS:
KEYS

Answers to Circle the Hidden Titles

Cracker Jackson was a **computer nut**. He spent a lot of time in **the black tower** researching **the burning questions of Bingo Brown,** his best friend. Bingo had asked Cracker to find information on a **mcmummy** and the **Cybil War**, but the computer kept asking Cracker to check his spelling. His search was interrupted when a strange message appeared:

THIS IS A **DEAD LETTER** FROM THE **KING OF MURDER**.
AT **MIDNIGHT FOX** WILL HOWL IN **THE BLACK TOWER**.
CLIMB THE **DARK STAIRS**
TO **DEATH'S DOOR** AND RESCUE THE **KEEPER OF THE DOVES**. ASK **THE PINBALLS** TO HELP.
DO NOT DELAY!
SIGNED: **THE ANIMAL, THE VEGETABLE, AND JOHN D. JONES**
P.S.: LIRPA LOOF

Cracker had no idea what the message meant. He **wanted Mud Blossom**, his other good friend, and Bingo to help him figure it out. The Pinballs were a club of roughnecks. He didn't want them. They had attacked the birds on the lake last **summer. Of the swans**, they flew away and never returned.

"I can't come now," said Mud Blossom. "I have to watch **my brother, Ant.** When **Ant plays bear** he could tear up the house if I don't stop him. Besides, **tornado** warnings are out, and we should all stay indoors."

Bingo was not helpful either. "I'd like to help," he said, "but don't ask **me. Tarzan** is on the TV, and he's in **trouble. River** rats are chasing him, and I have to see what happens."

Cracker thought about asking the Golly sisters for help. He hoped they had not pulled one of their **disappearing acts**. They were rarely home. Sometimes the **Golly sisters go west**, but they came right over when he called, even though they were busy writing their **cat diaries** and **dog diaries** dictated to them by their pets.

The sisters took one look at the strange message and laughed. "The last two words are spelled backward," they said. Sure enough, when Cracker turned the last two words around, he began to laugh too. **Hooray for the Golly sisters**," he shouted. "Now I know what the message is all about. Do you?"

Answers to Mystery Titles

1. Bear
2. Computer
3. Death
4. Fox
5. Tornado
6. *Cat Diaries* (E)
7. *Dead Letter* (G)
8. *King of Murder* (I)
9. *The Midnight Fox* (C)
10. *Trouble River* (A)

Answers to Name That Book!

1. *The Pinballs*
2. *Tornado*
3. *The Seven Treasure Hunts*
4. *Summer of the Swans*

ANDREW CLEMENTS (1949–): THE I HAVE/WHO HAS GAME

Cut the cards apart. Each player gets one card. The player who has the card with the asterisks (****) on it reads the "Who has" question. The player who has the answer card reads the answer and then the next question.

I HAVE:	The best advice for any writer is to get an idea and start writing, one word at a time. ********	**I HAVE:**	Andrew taught school for 7 years. He taught fourth grade, eighth grade, and high school.
WHO HAS:	What events in Andrew's childhood led to his becoming a writer?	**WHO HAS:**	Why did he leave teaching?
I HAVE:	Andrew's parents instilled a love of books and reading in Andrew and his brothers and sisters. The first step in becoming a writer is to be an avid reader.	**I HAVE:**	School enrollments shrank, and he was laid off. Then Andrew took his wife and son to New York and tried writing songs for a year.
WHO HAS:	What summer experiences as a child helped Andrew become an avid reader?	**WHO HAS:**	How successful was Andrew as a songwriter?
I HAVE:	Andrew's family spent summers in a cabin in Maine. With no TV or phone, after swimming and fishing all day, the boy devoured books at night.	**I HAVE:**	He gave up writing songs after a year and joined a small publishing company as an editor. Then a friend asked Andrew to join him in starting another publishing company, Picture Book Studio.
WHO HAS:	Did any of Andrew's teachers encourage him to become a writer?	**WHO HAS:**	When did Andrew begin writing children's books?
I HAVE:	His high school English teacher told him that his writing was good enough to be published. Until then he hadn't thought of becoming a writer.	**I HAVE:**	He wrote some picture book texts for Picture Book Studio. In 1990 he wrote *Frindle*, about a boy who makes up a new word for a pencil. It is the most popular of all his books.
WHO HAS:	What jobs did Andrew have after graduating from Northwestern University?	**WHO HAS:**	What advice does Andrew give young writers?

ANDREW CLEMENTS:
MYSTERY TITLES

Some words in these titles of books by Andrew Clements have been replaced with Dewey Decimal numbers. Go to the shelf with the Dewey number. Find the subject of the book(s) with that number. Fill in the missing word in each title. The first person to finish all the titles correctly is the winner!

1. Jake Drake, 371.5 _____ _____ _____ _____ _____ Buster

2. The Landry 050 _____ _____ _____ _____

3. Lunch 332 _____ _____ _____ _____ _____

4. 378 _____ _____ _____ _____ _____ _____ Story

5. Week in the 577.3 _____ _____ _____ _____ _____

Some words in these titles of books by Andrew Clements have been replaced with synonyms. Put the letter of the actual title after each synonymous title.

6. Outer Covering for Cold Weather _____

7. Custodian's Male Offspring _____

8. Conversation Forbidden _____

9. Grade Document _____

10. Seven Days among Trees _____

ACTUAL TITLES
A. *Frindle*
B. *Lunch Money*
C. *The Jacket*
D. *A Week in the Woods*
E. *The Last Holiday Concert*
F. *The Janitor's Boy*
G. *No Talking*
H. *The Report Card*
I. *Troublemaker*

Which titles are available in your library?

The key to Mystery Titles is on page __23__.

From *Gateway to Reading: 250+ Author Games and Booktalks to Motivate Middle Readers* by Nancy J. Polette. Santa Barbara, CA: Libraries Unlimited. Copyright © 2013.

ANDREW CLEMENTS:
NAME THAT BOOK!

What title would YOU give each of these books by Andrew Clements?

1) Benjamin Pratt's school is about to become the site of a new amusement park. It sounds like a dream come true! But lately Ben has been wondering if he's going to like an amusement park in the middle of his town. Maybe it would be nice if the school just stayed as it is. He likes the school. Loves it, actually. It's over 200 years old and sits right on the harbor. The playground has ocean breezes and the classrooms have million-dollar views. It belongs to the children, and these children have the right to defend it! Don't think that Ben, his friend Jill, and the tagalong Robert, can ruin a multi-million-dollar real estate deal? Then you don't know the history and the power of the Keepers of the School.

Your title _____

2) There's a folder in Principal Kelling's office filled with the incident reports of every time Clayton Hensley broke the rules. There's the minor stuff like running in the hallways, but there are also reports that show Clay's own brand of troublemaking, like when he decides to draw a spot-on portrait of Principal Kelling . . . as a donkey. It's a pretty funny joke, but really, Clay is coming to realize that the biggest joke of all may be on him. When his big brother, Mitchell, gets in some serious trouble, Clay decides to change his own mischief-making ways . . . but he can't seem to shake his reputation as a troublemaker.

Your title _____

3) The bad news is that Cara Landry is the new kid at Denton Elementary School. The worse news is that her teacher, Mr. Larson, would rather read the paper and drink coffee than teach his students anything. So Cara decides to give Mr. Larson something else to read: her own newspaper, *The Landry News*. Before she knows it, the whole fifth-grade class is in on the project. But then the principal finds a copy of *The Landry News*, with unexpected results.

Your title _____

4) The fifth-grade girls and the fifth-grade boys at Laketon Elementary don't get along very well. But the real problem is that these kids are loud and disorderly. That's why the principal uses her red plastic bullhorn. A lot. Then one day Dave Packer, a certified loudmouth, bumps into an idea: a big one that makes him try to keep quiet for a whole day. But what does Dave hear during lunch? A girl, Lynsey Burges, jabbering away. So Dave breaks his silence and lobs an insult. And those words spark a contest: Which team can say the fewest words during two whole days? And it's the boys against the girls. How do the teachers react to the silence? What happens when the principal feels she's losing control? And will Dave and Lynsey plunge the whole school into chaos?

Your title _____

See the author's titles on page ___23___.
Which titles are available in your library?

This is a school story about a bully and thief and all around troublemaker named Frindle. He took lunch money and a jacket from the little kids in Room One and even stole a report card or two (to get better grades).

In December the school paper, *The Landry News*, reported missing cash and many other things not seen after the last holiday concert.

Then Jake Drake, bully buster, arrived. He was the janitor's boy and knew every hiding place in the school.

"No talking," he warned the kids in Room One. "Try to be things not seen." A shadow approached. Then Frindle appeared and reached for a lunch box.

"Caught in the act!" Jake cried.

Frindle was taken to court, but the judge took pity on the boy and ordered him to spend a week in the woods at a camp for wayward boys. When Frindle returned he never bullied little kids or stole anything again.

ANDREW CLEMENTS:
KEYS

Answers to Circle the Hidden Titles

This is a **school story** about a bully and thief and all around **troublemaker** named **Frindle**. He took **lunch money** and a **jacket** from the little kids in **Room One** and even stole a **report card** or two (to get better grades).

In December the school paper, ***The Landry News***, reported missing cash and many other **things not seen** after the last holiday concert.

Then **Jake Drake, bully buster**, arrived. He was **the janitor's boy** and knew every hiding place in the school.

"**No talking**," he warned the kids in **Room One**. "Try to be **things not seen**." A shadow approached. Then **Frindle** appeared and reached for a lunch box.

"Caught in the act!" Jake cried.

Frindle was taken to court, but the judge took pity on the boy and ordered him to spend **a week in the woods** at a camp for wayward boys. When **Frindle** returned he never bullied little kids or stole anything again.

Answers to Mystery Titles

1. Bully
2. News
3. Money
4. School
5. Woods
6. *The Jacket* (C)
7. *The Janitor's Boy* (F)
8. *No Talking* (G)
9. *The Report Card* (H)
10. *A Week in the Woods* (D)

Answers to Name That Book!

1. *We the Children*
2. *Troublemaker*
3. *The Landry News*
4. *No Talking*

From *Gateway to Reading: 250+ Author Games and Booktalks to Motivate Middle Readers*
by Nancy J. Polette. Santa Barbara, CA: Libraries Unlimited. Copyright © 2013.

BRUCE COVILLE (1950–):
THE I HAVE/WHO HAS GAME

Cut the cards apart. Each player gets one card. The player who has the card with the asterisks (****) on it reads the "Who has" question. The player who has the answer card reads the answer and then the next question.

I HAVE:	Bruce Coville has written more than 70 children's books, including a retelling of some of the classics he enjoyed as a child. ****	I HAVE:	Before he could make a living writing, Bruce Coville worked as a toy maker, on an assembly line, and as an elementary teacher.
WHO HAS:	Where was Bruce Coville born, and where has he spent most of his life?	WHO HAS:	What did Bruce do in 1969?
I HAVE:	Bruce Coville was born in Syracuse, New York, and has spent most of his life in the Syracuse area and on his grandparents' farm.	I HAVE:	In 1969 Bruce married Katherine Dietz. They have three children, and she has illustrated several of his books.
WHO HAS:	When did Bruce Coville decide to become a writer?	WHO HAS:	Do the Covilles have any pets?
I HAVE:	He found a sixth-grade writing assignment to be so much fun he decided to become a writer.	I HAVE:	The Covilles had a large dog named Thor and four cats.
WHO HAS:	What kind of books did he read as a child?	WHO HAS:	What activities is Bruce involved in when he is not writing?
I HAVE:	He read *The Hardy Boys*, *Tom Swift*, and many of the classics like *Mary Poppins* and the *Voyages of Dr. Doolittle*.	I HAVE:	He is involved in the theater, writing, acting, and directing.
WHO HAS:	What jobs did Bruce have before he was able to make a living writing?	WHO HAS:	How many children's books has Bruce Coville written?

From Gateway to Reading: 250+ Author Games and Booktalks to Motivate Middle Readers
by Nancy J. Polette. Santa Barbara, CA: Libraries Unlimited. Copyright © 2013.

BRUCE COVILLE:
MYSTERY TITLES

Some words in these titles of books by Bruce Coville have been replaced with Dewey Decimal numbers. Go to the shelf with the Dewey number. Find the subject of the book(s) with that number. Fill in the missing word in each title. The first person to finish all the titles correctly is the winner!

1. Trouble 577.6 _____ _____ _____ _____ _____

2. Goblins in the 728.8 _____ _____ _____ _____ _____ _____

3. 342 _____ _____ _____ _____ _____ _____ Ate My Homework

4. 784 _____ _____ _____ _____ of the Wanderer

5. 523.4 _____ _____ _____ _____ _____ _____ of the Dips

Some words in these titles of books by Bruce Coville have been replaced with synonyms. Put the letter of the actual title after each synonymous title.

6. Unlighted Breathless Words _____

ACTUAL TITLES

7. Enter the Region of One-horned Horses _____

A. *Planet of the Dips*
B. *Oddly Enough*
C. *Goblins in the Castle*

8. Strangely Sufficient _____

D. *Dark Whispers*
E. *The Evil Elves*

9. Fire-breathing Serpent of Unhappy Fate _____

F. *Into the Land of the Unicorns*
G. *The Last Hunt*

10. Final Chase of Animals _____

H. *Song of the Wanderer*
I. *Dragon of Doom*
J. *My Teacher Is an Alien*

Which titles are available in your library?

The key to Mystery Titles is on page <u>29</u>.

BRUCE COVILLE:
NAME THAT BOOK!

What title would YOU give each of these books by Bruce Coville?

1) It's the weirdest alien invasion ever! "I cannot tell a lie," says Rod Allbright. And it's the truth. Ask him a question, and he's bound to give you an honest answer. Which is why, when his teacher asks what happened to last night's math assignment, Rod has to give the only answer he can: "Aliens ate my homework, Miss Maloney!" Of course, no one believes Rod this time, so they don't bother to ask him why the aliens are here. It's just as well, because he is sworn to silence about their secret mission and the fact that he has been drafted to help them.

Your title _____

2) Sixth grade is just out of this world! Susan Simmons can tell that her new substitute teacher is really weird. But she doesn't know how weird until she catches him peeling off his face and realizes that "Mr. Smith" is really an alien! At first no one will believe her except Peter Thompson, the class brain. When Peter and Susan discover Mr. Smith's horrible plans for their classmates, they know they have to act fast. Only they can get rid of their extraterrestrial visitor and save the rest of the sixth-grade class from a fate worse than math tests!

Your title _____

3) It's a sticky situation! Pleskit's quest to sample all things earthling—especially earthling foods—inevitably leads him to . . . peanut butter. He adores it. There's only one problem: he has an allergic reaction to the stuff that ends up making him feel incredibly romantic. Before long, the purple alien is chasing girls around the playground, trying to kiss them. He gets a slap in the face, which snaps him back to reality. But the damage has been done. The school is in an uproar, and unless Tim and Pleskit can find a way to convince Principal Grand that it's not really Pleskit's fault, the world's first alien student may be looking for a new classroom—on a new planet!

Your title _____

4) What moans at midnight in Toad-in-a-Cage Castle? Toad-in-a-Cage Castle was filled with secrets, such as the hidden passages that led to every room, the long stairway that wound down to the dungeon, and the weird creature named Igor who lived there. But it was the mysterious night noises that bothered William the most: the strange moans that drifted through the halls of the castle where he was raised. He wanted to know what caused them. Then one night he found out.

Your title _____

See the author's titles on page __29__.
Which titles are available in your library?

BRUCE COVILLE:
CIRCLE THE HIDDEN TITLES

Jeremy Thatcher, dragon hatcher who lived on the planet of the Dips, was worried. Better known as the peanut butter lover boy, for homework he was to hatch three dragon eggs, but every day another dragon egg was gone from the nest.

"Maybe aliens ate my homework," Jeremy said in dark whispers. "My teacher is an alien. Maybe she took the eggs."

Jeremy's friend, the weeping werewolf, stopped to visit.

"Have you seen some missing dragon eggs?" Jeremy asked.

"Maybe the evil elves took them on their last hunt, or the dragon of doom or perhaps the monsters of Morley Manor. I hear they are very fond of eggs," answered the werewolf.

Jeremy thought for a moment. "There are too many aliens around who like eggs. They could be the thieves, or maybe the goblins in the castle stole them. I left my sneakers in Dimension X, and I plan to look for the lost eggs while I am there."

Next to come by was Jennifer Murdley. When she heard about the missing eggs, she thought the dragonslayers might have taken them into the land of the unicorns. But she couldn't help find the eggs. Jennifer Murdley's toad was competing for monster of the year, and she had to get him to the contest in town.

Oddly enough, it was at that moment that Juliet Dove, Queen of Love, appeared. When she heard the eggs were missing, she wanted to help find them. She gave a twist to her monster's ring and produced a map of fortune's journey. "Follow the map," she said, "and you will have good fortune." Then she left singing the song of the wanderer.

Jeremy set off with the map in his hand. He saw a strange glow in the distance. "My teacher glows in the dark," Jeremy said. "Maybe she took the eggs after all." The glow was a campfire and a troop of players was acting out William Shakespeare's *Midsummer Night's Dream*.

In a pan next to the fire were the dragon eggs. When Jeremy explained that these were not the kind of eggs you had for breakfast, the players gave him the eggs. They explained that the dragonslayers had dropped the eggs chasing Sarah's unicorn through the forest.

Telling the players good-bye, Jeremy headed home, singing the song of the wanderer, with the eggs safely in his pocket. For once the world's worst fairy godmother had come through.

BRUCE COVILLE:
KEYS

Answers to Circle the Hidden Titles

Jeremy Thatcher, dragon hatcher who lived on the **planet of the Dips**, was worried. Better known as the **peanut butter lover boy**, for homework he was to hatch three dragon eggs, but every day another dragon egg was gone from the nest.

"Maybe **aliens ate my homework**," Jeremy said in **dark whispers**. "**My teacher is an alien**. Maybe she took the eggs."

Jeremy's friend, **the weeping werewolf**, stopped to visit.

"Have you seen some missing dragon eggs?" Jeremy asked.

"Maybe **the evil elves** took them on their **last hunt**, or the **dragon of doom** or perhaps **the monsters of Morley Manor**. I hear they are very fond of eggs," answered the werewolf.

Jeremy thought for a moment. "There are **too many aliens** around who like eggs. They could be the thieves, or maybe the **goblins in the castle** stole them. **I left my sneakers in Dimension X**, and I plan to look for the lost eggs while I am there."

Next to come by was Jennifer Murdley. When she heard about the missing eggs, she thought the **dragonslayers** might have taken them **into the land of the unicorns**. But she couldn't help find the eggs. **Jennifer Murdley's toad** was competing for monster of the year, and she had to get him to the contest in town.

Oddly enough, it was at that moment that **Juliet Dove, Queen of Love**, appeared. When she heard the eggs were missing, she wanted to help find them. She gave a twist to her **monster's ring** and produced a map of **fortune's journey**. "Follow the map," she said, "and you will have good fortune." Then she left singing the song of the wanderer.

Jeremy set off with the map in his hand. He saw a strange glow in the distance. "**My teacher glows in the dark**," Jeremy said. "Maybe she took the eggs after all." The glow was a campfire and a troop of players was acting out **William Shakespeare's *Midsummer Night's Dream***.

In a pan next to the fire were the dragon eggs. When Jeremy explained that these were not the kind of eggs you had for breakfast, the players gave him the eggs. They explained that the dragonslayers had dropped the eggs chasing **Sarah's unicorn** through the forest.

Telling the players good-bye, Jeremy headed home, singing the **song of the wanderer**, with the eggs safely in his pocket. For once **the world's worst fairy godmother** had come through.

Answers to Mystery Titles

1. River
2. Castle
3. Aliens
4. Song
5. Planet
6. *Dark Whispers* (D)
7. *Into the Land of the Unicorns* (F)
8. *Oddly Enough* (B)
9. *Dragon of Doom* (I)
10. *The Last Hunt* (G)

Answers to Name That Book!

1. *Aliens Ate My Homework*
2. *My Teacher Is an Alien*
3. *Peanut Butter Lover Boy*
4. *Goblins in the Castle*

SHARON CREECH (1945–):
THE I HAVE/WHO HAS GAME

Cut the cards apart. Each player gets one card. The player who has the card with the asterisks (****) on it reads the "Who has" question. The player who has the answer card reads the answer and then the next question.

I HAVE:	Sharon Creech won the Newbery Award for *Walk Two Moons* and a Newbery Honor for *The Wanderer.* ****	**I HAVE:**	No. Sharon begins with a character and setting and lets the character determine the plot as she is writing the book.
WHO HAS:	Why doesn't Sharon Creech have any pets?	**WHO HAS:**	The town of Bybanks appears in several of her novels. Is this a real town?
I HAVE:	Sharon Creech does not have pets because she travels a lot. Born in Cleveland, Ohio, she spent 20 years as a teacher in England and Switzerland.	**I HAVE:**	Bybanks is similar to the small town of Quincy, Kentucky, where Sharon spent part of her childhood.
WHO HAS:	Do any of Sharon's family members appear in her books?	**WHO HAS:**	What other real-life events appear in Sharon Creech's novels?
I HAVE:	Sharon has a sister and three brothers. This is the same family as in *Absolutely Normal Chaos.* The brothers' names are the same, but not the incidents in the story.	**I HAVE:**	Sharon's father inspired the character of Uncle Arvie in *Pleasing the Ghost.* Two years spent in Switzerland provided incidents found in *Bloomability.*
WHO HAS:	Did Sharon actually take the same trip that Salamanca takes in *Walk Two Moons*?	**WHO HAS:**	Did Sharon Creech actually sail across the Atlantic before writing *The Wanderer*?
I HAVE:	Yes, Sharon took the same trip that Salamanca took in *Walk Two Moons,* but not to find her mother. Her mother went along on the trip.	**I HAVE:**	No. Sharon did not sail across the Atlantic, but her daughter did, which inspired *The Wanderer.*
WHO HAS:	Does Sharon have the whole plot worked out before she begins to write?	**WHO HAS:**	What major book awards has Sharon Creech won?

SHARON CREECH:
MYSTERY TITLES

Some words in these titles of books by Sharon Creech have been replaced with Dewey Decimal numbers. Go to the shelf with the Dewey number. Find the subject of the book(s) with that number. Fill in the missing word in each title. The first person to finish all the titles correctly is the winner!

1. 728.8 _____ _____ _____ _____ _____ _____ Carona

2. 799.1 _____ _____ _____ _____ _____ _____ _____ in the Air

3. 612.1 _____ _____ _____ _____ _____beat

4. Pleasing the 133 _____ _____ _____ _____ _____

5. Walk Two 523.3 _____ _____ _____ _____ _____

Some words in these titles of books by Sharon Creech have been replaced with synonyms. Put the letter of the actual title after each synonymous title.

6. Running After a Scarlet-feathered Creature _____

7. Catching Aquatic Vertebrates in the Atmosphere _____

8. Deep Affection for a Canine _____

9. Satisfying the Disembodied Spirit _____

10. One Who Travels Aimlessly _____

ACTUAL TITLES
A. *Absolutely Normal Chaos*
B. *Chasing Redbird*
C. *The Castle Corona*
D. *The Wanderer*
E. *Pleasing the Ghost*
F. *A Fine, Fine School*
G. *Bloomability*
H. *Love That Dog*
I. *The Unfinished Angel*
J. *Fishing in the Air*

Which titles are available in your library?

The key to Mystery Titles is on page __35__.

From *Gateway to Reading: 250+ Author Games and Booktalks to Motivate Middle Readers* by Nancy J. Polette. Santa Barbara, CA: Libraries Unlimited. Copyright © 2013.

SHARON CREECH:
NAME THAT BOOK!

What title would YOU give each of these books by Sharon Creech?

1) "Trouble twins" Dallas and Florida are orphans who have given up believing there is such a thing as a loving home. Tiller and Sairy are an eccentric older couple who live in the beautiful, mysterious Ruby Holler, but they're restless for one more big adventure. When they invite the twins to join them on their journeys, they first must all stay together in the Holler, and the magic of the place takes over. Two pairs of lives grow closer and are changed forever.

Your title _____

2) Mary Lou Finney is less than excited about her assignment to keep a journal over the summer. Boring! Then cousin Carl Ray comes to stay with her family, and what starts out as the dull dog days of summer quickly turns into the wildest roller-coaster ride of all time. How was Mary Lou supposed to know what would happen with Carl Ray and the ring? Or with her boy-crazy best friend Beth Ann? Or with (sigh) the permanently pink Alex Cheevey? Suddenly a boring school project becomes a record of the most exciting, incredible, unbelievable summer of Mary Lou's life.

Your title _____

3) It started out as an ordinary summer. But the minute 13-year-old Zinny discovered the old, overgrown trail that ran through the woods behind her family's house, she realized that things were about to change. Right from the start, Zinny knew that uncovering the trail would be more than just a summer project. It was her chance to finally make people notice her and to have a place she could call her very own. But more than that, Zinny knew that the trail somehow held the key to all kinds of questions, and that the only way to understand her family, her Aunt Jessie's death, and herself, was to find out where it went.

Your title _____

4) Thirteen-year-old Sophie hears the sea calling, promising adventure and a chance for discovery as she sets sail for England with her three uncles and two cousins. Sophie's cousin Cody isn't sure he has the strength to prove himself to the crew and his father. Through Sophie's and Cody's travel logs, we hear stories of the past and the daily challenges of surviving at sea as *The Wanderer* sails toward its destination, and its passengers search for their places in the world.

Your title _____

See the author's titles on page ___35___.
Which titles are available in your library?

SHARON CREECH:
CIRCLE THE HIDDEN TITLES

Ruby is a wanderer. Some call her an unfinished angel. No one ever can find her. She might be chasing redbird and her flock in the fields or exploring the abandoned castle Corona. She doesn't fish in a stream; she goes fishing in the air. She sees things that others do not see. At night when she goes for a walk, two moons are in the sky rather than one. One day she found a mangy pup that didn't smell good. Ruby insisted that everyone should love that dog.

Ruby tries to stay out of trouble. There was the time when Granny asked her to watch the soup so it wouldn't boil over. She couldn't help it when a strong wind blew the soup pot off the stove. When Granny Torelli makes soup, she always leaves the door open. In a heartbeat Ruby tried to catch the pot, but she only burned her hands.

Yes, Ruby is different. Her parents don't know what to do with her. They tried sending her to a fine, fine school. She told her classmates that the school was haunted by a ghost dog and that pleasing the ghost was important. As soon as they heard Ruby holler, they were to scream, again and again, "Love that pup," as loudly as they could.

With all the pupils screaming, utter chaos followed. Teachers ran everywhere. The fire department was called. Ambulances came. But for Ruby it was absolutely normal chaos. Confusion is simply a replay of her life in general.

"After all," Ruby says, "without imagination, we would still be in a cave without fire. Imagination needs bloomability room, and I mean to make sure it gets it wherever I go!"

From *Gateway to Reading: 250+ Author Games and Booktalks to Motivate Middle Readers*
by Nancy J. Polette. Santa Barbara, CA: Libraries Unlimited. Copyright © 2013.

SHARON CREECH:
KEYS

Answers to Circle the Hidden Titles

Ruby is a **wanderer**. Some call her an **unfinished angel**. No one ever can find her. She might be **chasing red-bird** and her flock in the fields or exploring the abandoned **castle Corona**. She doesn't fish in a stream; she goes **fishing in the air**. She sees things that others do not see. At night when she goes for a **walk, two moons** are in the sky rather than one. One day she **finds** a mangy pup that **doesn't** smell good. Ruby **insists** that everyone should **love that dog**.

Ruby tries to stay out of trouble. There **is** a time when Granny **asks** her to watch the soup so it **won't** boil over. She can't help it when a strong wind blows the soup pot off the stove. When **Granny Torelli makes soup**, she always leaves the door open. In a **heartbeat** Ruby **tries** to catch the pot, but she only **burns** her hands.

Yes, Ruby is different. Her parents don't know what to do with her. They **try** sending her to **a fine, fine school**. She **tells** her classmates that the school **is** haunted by a ghost dog and that **pleasing the ghost is** important. As soon as they **hear Ruby holler**, they **are** to scream, again and again, "**Love that pup**," as loudly as they **can**.

With all the pupils screaming, utter chaos **follows**. Teachers **run** everywhere. The fire department **is** called. Ambulances **come**. But for Ruby it **is absolutely normal chaos**. Confusion is simply a **replay** of her life in general.

"After all," Ruby says, "without imagination, we would still be in a cave without fire. Imagination needs **bloomability** room, and I mean to make sure it gets it wherever I go!"

Answers to the Mystery Titles

1. Castle
2. Fishing
3. Heart (beat)
4. Ghost
5. Moons
6. *Chasing Redbird* (B)
7. *Fishing in the Air* (J)
8. *Love That Dog* (H)
9. *Pleasing the Ghost* (E)
10. *The Wanderer* (D)

Answers to Name That Book!

1. *Ruby Holler*
2. *Absolutely Normal Chaos*
3. *Chasing Redbird*
4. *The Wanderer*

CHRISTOPHER PAUL CURTIS (1953–):
THE I HAVE/WHO HAS GAME

Cut the cards apart. Each player gets one card. The player who has the card with the asterisks (****) on it reads the "Who has" question. The player who has the answer card reads the answer and then the next question.

I HAVE:	*Bud, Not Buddy* was the first book to receive both the Newbery Award and the Coretta Scott King Award. *The Watsons Go to Birmingham—1963* is a Newbery Honor book. ********	**I HAVE:**	Christopher used his grandfathers—Earl Lewis, a pitcher in the Negro Leagues, and Herman E. Curtis Sr., a band leader—as models for two characters in *Bud, Not Buddy*.
WHO HAS:	Most writers say that they were avid readers as children. Was this true of Christopher Paul Curtis?	**WHO HAS:**	Does Christopher include any of his own real-life experiences in his novels?
I HAVE:	Christopher grew up at a time when there were few books written with African American heroes. He therefore did not read as much as he might have.	**I HAVE:**	A long automobile trip Christopher took from Michigan to Florida was the basis for *The Watsons Go to Birmingham—1963*. He took the real-life experience of a long road trip and changed the destination.
WHO HAS:	What job did Christopher hold after high school?	**WHO HAS:**	How does Christopher make his characters act and sound so real?
I HAVE:	After high school Christopher worked in an auto assembly plant hanging 80-pound doors on cars for 13 years. He started writing at break times.	**I HAVE:**	Christopher researches how children talk and act for each historical period he writes about. He spends a lot of time researching details in the library.
WHO HAS:	When did Christopher begin writing seriously?	**WHO HAS:**	How have Christopher's children been helpful to his writing.
I HAVE:	Christopher took a year off building cars to write his first novel, *The Watsons Go to Birmingham—1963*, which was a big success. He never went back to building cars.	**I HAVE:**	Christopher's son Steven has taped his handwritten manuscripts, and his daughter Cydney wrote a song for *Bud, Not Buddy*.
WHO HAS:	Are any of the characters in his books modeled after real people?	**WHO HAS:**	What honors have Christopher Paul Curtis's books received?

CHRISTOPHER PAUL CURTIS:
MYSTERY TITLES

Some words in these titles of books by Christopher Paul Curtis have been replaced with Dewey Decimal numbers. Go to the shelf with the Dewey number. Find the subject of the book(s) with that number. Fill in the missing word in each title. The first person to finish all the titles correctly is the winner!

1. Mr. Chickee's Funny 332 _____ _____ _____ _____ _____

2. Mr. Chickee's Messy Mission is about an elderly man who is 362.4 _____ _____ _____ _____ _____

3. Bud, Not Buddy hitchhikes across the state of 977.4 _____ _____ _____ _____ _____ _____ _____ _____

4. The Watsons Go to Birmingham in the state of 976.1 _____ _____ _____ _____ _____ _____ _____

5. Elijah of Buxton lives in 971 _____ _____ _____ _____ _____ _____

Here is a booktalk for one of the author's most popular books. Fill in words you think belong in the blank spaces. The actual missing words are in the answer key on page __41__. How good were your guesses?

The Watsons Go to Birmingham—1963. Delacorte, 1995.

Enter the hilarious world of 10-year-old Kenny and his family, the Weird Watsons of Flint, 6._____. There's Momma, Dad, little sister Joetta, Kenny, and Byron, who's 7._____ and an "official juvenile delinquent." When Momma and Dad decide it's time for a visit to 8._____, Dad comes home with the amazing 9._____, and the Watsons set out on a trip like no other. They are heading South. They are going to Birmingham, Alabama, toward one of the darkest moments in 10._____ history.

Which titles are available in your library?

The key to Mystery Titles is on page __41__.

CHRISTOPHER PAUL CURTIS: NAME THAT BOOK!

What title would YOU give each of these books by Christopher Paul Curtis?

1) The year is 1860, and 11-year-old Elijah is a first-generation freeborn black who has had no direct experience with slavery. His Canadian town of Buxton, located just across the border from Detroit, serves as a haven for runaway slaves and their children, where blacks can live free and govern themselves away from the horrors of pre-emancipation America. When the town's corrupt preacher steals money from a citizen who has been saving to buy his family's freedom, Elijah sets off for Detroit in pursuit. But leaving behind his Canadian home and crossing into dangerous American territory, he encounters terrifying evidence of the grievous human cost of slavery. He encounters a group of captured runaway slaves; unable to save them all, he escapes with the youngest, a baby, and returns to Buxton a hero.

Your title _____

2) In 1936 in Flint, Michigan, times are hard, and Bud is a homeless boy on the run. Mistreated in a foster home, he runs away, taking only his precious suitcase with a picture of the father he hopes to find. The picture is on a flyer advertising Herman Calloway and the Dusky Devastators. He hitchhikes to Grand Rapids, where the band is supposed to be, receiving help on the way from Mr. Lewis, who sends a telegram to Herman Calloway telling him when the boy will arrive. Bud does reach Grand Rapids and the place where the band is playing. Herman, who is up in years, wants nothing to do with the boy, who is taken under the wing of the band's lead singer. When the contents of Bud's suitcase are finally revealed, Bud discovers that Herman is his grandfather, and with the help of other members of the band, he can look forward to a brighter future.

Your title _____ .

3) As president of the Flint Future Detective Club, Steven is helped in making decisions by a dictionary that throws words in the air. At this first meeting, Steven and his friends Russell and Richelle follow Russell's dog, Rodney Rodent, into a mural to chase a demonic-looking gnome, only to find the mysterious Mr. Chickee on the other side. Will Steven continue to be the club's leader, or will Richelle, the smartest girl in school, take over?

Your title _____

See the author's titles on page __41__.
Which titles are available in your library?

From *Gateway to Reading: 250+ Author Games and Booktalks to Motivate Middle Readers*
by Nancy J. Polette. Santa Barbara, CA: Libraries Unlimited. Copyright © 2013.

Mr. Chickee found some money that looked different. He showed it to his friend, Bud. Not Buddy Smith, but Buddy Watson, who lived next door. Mr. Chickee planned to go on a mission to Birmingham, but when Bud looked at Mr. Chickee's funny money, he told him to have it examined by Elijah of Buxton before trying to spend it. Elijah was a money expert and wanted to be sure Mr. Chickee's trip would not turn out to be Mr. Chickee's messy mission, especially when he was taking along the Watsons. "Go to Birmingham," Elijah told Mr. Chickee, "but do not spend any of the funny money. If you do, you could all end up in jail."

Mr. Chickee followed Elijah's advice, and a successful trip was had by all.

Answers to Circle the Hidden Titles

Mr. Chickee found some money that looked different. He showed it to his friend, **Bud. Not Buddy** Smith, but Buddy Watson, who lived next door. Mr. Chickee planned to go on a mission to Birmingham, but when Bud looked at **Mr. Chickee's funny money**, he told him to have it examined by **Elijah of Buxton** before trying to spend it. Elijah was a money expert and wanted to be sure Mr. Chickee's trip would not turn out to be **Mr. Chickee's messy mission**, especially when he was taking along **the Watsons. "Go to Birmingham,"** Elijah told Mr. Chickee, "but do not spend any of the funny money. If you do, you could all end up in jail."

Mr. Chickee followed Elijah's advice, and a successful trip was had by all.

Answers to Mystery Titles

1. Money
2. Blind
3. Michigan
4. Alabama
5. Canada
6. Michigan
7. Thirteen
8. Grandma
9. Ultra-Glide
10. American

Answers to Name That Book!

1. *Elijah of Buxton*
2. *Bud, Not Buddy*
3. *Mr. Chickee's Messy Mission*

ROALD DAHL (1916–1990):
THE I HAVE/WHO HAS GAME

Cut the cards apart. Each player gets one card. The player who has the card with the asterisks (****) on it reads the "Who has" question. The player who has the answer card reads the answer and then the next question.

I HAVE:	In many of his books Dahl punishes adults who harm children and gives adults rough treatment in general.	I HAVE:	He worked for an oil company in Africa, joined the Royal Air Force, was a fighter pilot in World War II, and crashed his plane near Egypt.
	****		
WHO HAS:	Where was Roald Dahl born, and where did he spend his summers as a child?	WHO HAS:	When did Dahl start his writing career?
I HAVE:	Roald Dahl was born in South Wales, United Kingdom, and spent childhood summers with his grandparents in Norway.	I HAVE:	While stationed in Washington, D.C., he began writing short stories for magazines and won many awards.
WHO HAS:	How successful was Roald Dahl as a pupil at school?	WHO HAS:	Why did Dahl start writing for children?
I HAVE:	Dahl, who liked to play pranks, did not do well in school. He attended 3 different schools as a child and disliked them all.	I HAVE:	Dahl started writing for children after telling bedtime stories to his 5 children.
WHO HAS:	What did Dahl say when his mother wanted to send him to the university?	WHO HAS:	What was Dahl's first children's book?
I HAVE:	Dahl told his mother he wanted to get a job to travel the world and have great adventures.	I HAVE:	Dahl's first children's book was *James and the Giant Peach*, published in 1961 and still enjoyed today.
WHO HAS:	What adventures did Dahl have as a young man?	WHO HAS:	What is it children love about Dahl's books that adults object to?

ROALD DAHL:
MYSTERY TITLES

Some words in these titles of books by Roald Dahl have been replaced with Dewey Decimal numbers. Go to the shelf with the Dewey number. Find the subject of the book(s) with that number. Fill in the missing word in each title. The first person to finish all the titles correctly is the winner!

1. Danny, Champion of the 909 _____ _____ _____ _____ _____

2. Fantastic Mr. 599.7 _____ _____ _____

3. George's Marvelous 610.9 _____ _____ _____ _____ _____ _____ _____ _____

4. 793.8 _____ _____ _____ _____ _____ Finger

5. Wonderful Story of Henry 362.1 _____ _____ _____ _____ _____

Words in these titles of books by Roald Dahl have been replaced with synonyms. Put the letter of the actual title after each synonym title.

6. The Wicken _____

7. Additional Information About a Male Child _____

8. Enchanted Digit _____

9. Noxious Rhyming Lines _____

10. Large Amiable Being of Superhuman Size _____

ACTUAL TITLES
A. *The Minipins*
B. *The BFG (Big Friendly Giant)*
C. *The Magic Finger*
D. *Charlie and the Chocolate Factory*
E. *The Twits*
F. *The Witches*
G. *More About Boy*
H. *Matilda*
I. *Vile Verses*
J. *Danny, Champion of the World*

Which titles are available in your library?

The key to Mystery Titles is on page __47__.

ROALD DAHL:
NAME THAT BOOK!

What title would YOU give each of these books by Roald Dahl?

1) Mr. and Mrs. Twit are the smelliest, nastiest, ugliest people in the world. They hate everything, except playing mean jokes on each other, catching unsuspecting birds to put in their bird pies, and making their caged monkeys, the Muggle-Wumps, stand on their heads all day. But the Muggle-Wumps have had enough. With the help of Roly-Poly Bird, they set out to get some well-deserved revenge.

Your title _____

2) Fantastic Mr. Fox is on the run! The three meanest farmers around are out to get him. Fat Boggis, squat Bunce, and skinny Bean have joined forces, and they have Mr. Fox and his family surrounded. What they don't know is that they're not dealing with just any fox—Mr. Fox would never surrender. But only the most fantastic plan ever can save him now.

Your title _____

3) George is alone in the house with Grandma. The most horrid, grizzly old grunion of a grandma ever. She needs something stronger than her usual medicine to cure her chronic grouchiness. He decides to mix up a special grandma medicine, a remedy for everything. And George knows just what to put into it. Grandma's in for the surprise of her life—and so is George, when he sees the results of his mixture.

Your title _____

4) Danny's life seems perfect: his home is a gypsy caravan, he's the youngest car mechanic around, and his best friend is his dad, who never runs out of wonderful stories to tell. When Danny discovers his father's secret, he's off on the adventure of a lifetime. Here's a story about a 9-year-old boy, his dad, and a daring and hilarious pheasant-snatching expedition. Just as important, it's the story of the love between a boy and his father, who, in Danny's own words, is "the most marvelous and exciting father a boy ever had."

Your title _____

5) "Well, first of all," said the BFG, "human beans is not really believing in giants, is they? Human beans is not thinking we exist." Sophie discovers not only that giants exist but also that there are a great many of them who like to guzzle and swallomp nice little chiddlers. But not the Big Friendly Giant. He and Sophie cook up an ingenious plot to free the world of troggle-humping—forever.

Your title _____

See the author's titles on page <u> 47 </u>.
Which titles are available in your library?

From *Gateway to Reading: 250+ Author Games and Booktalks to Motivate Middle Readers*
by Nancy J. Polette. Santa Barbara, CA: Libraries Unlimited. Copyright © 2013.

ROALD DAHL:
CIRCLE THE HIDDEN TITLES

The annual chocolate eating contest was about to begin. The grand prize would be awarded by the year's previous winner, Charlie, and the chocolate factory would be the prize. Matilda was determined to win that chocolate factory but so were the Minipins, the BFG (big friendly giant), and the Twits. Owning such a factory would be fantastic! Mr. Fox thought when he showed up at the last minute. Another contestant was James and the giant peach. He wanted a chocolate-covered peach. Everyone laughed at the last contestant to enter. Danny was so little that he could not possibly eat enough chocolate to win.

The witches were the judges. One waved her magic finger, and the contest began. Matilda ate 3 chocolate bars in 1 minute; Mr. Fox ate 4. The BFG and the Twits and James ate 6 each, but Danny managed to consume 8 in the same length of time.

Next to be eaten were enormous crocodile chocolates. Each chocolate was as big as a plate and shaped like a crocodile. Vile verses were found inside each one. Again, Danny ate more than any other contestant. Then Charlie and the great glass elevator arrived with more chocolates. Matilda and Mr. Fox dropped out of the contest. The BFG, the Minipins, the Twits, and James said they could not eat another bite. The grand prize was given to Danny, champion of the world, whose nickname was Boy.

Everyone wanted to know more about Boy and how he had managed to eat so many chocolates.

"Before I came here," Danny said, "I took a big dose of George's marvelous medicine. One dose of that medicine, and there is no limit as to what you can eat. I read all about it in the wonderful story of Henry Sugar. A lifelong reader is a lifelong learner, and it helps to win contests too!"

ROALD DAHL:
KEYS

Answers to Circle the Hidden Titles

The annual chocolate eating contest was about to begin. The grand prize would be awarded by the year's previous winner, **Charlie, and the chocolate factory** would be the prize. **Matilda** was determined to win that chocolate factory but so were **the Minipins**, the **BFG** (big friendly giant), and **the Twits**. Owning such a factory would be **fantastic! Mr. Fox** thought when he showed up at the last minute. Another contestant was **James and the giant peach.** He wanted a chocolate-covered peach. Everyone laughed at the last contestant to enter. Danny was so little that he could not possibly eat enough chocolate to win.

The witches were the judges. One waved her **magic finger**, and the contest began. **Matilda** ate 3 chocolate bars in 1 minute; Mr. Fox ate 4. The **BFG** and the **Twits** and James ate 6 each, but Danny managed to consume 8 in the same length of time.

Next to be eaten were **enormous crocodile** chocolates. Each chocolate was as big as a plate and shaped like a crocodile. **Vile verses** were found inside each one. Again, Danny ate more than any other contestant. Then **Charlie and the great glass elevator** arrived with more chocolates. **Matilda** and Mr. Fox dropped out of the contest. The **BFG**, the **Minipins**, the **Twits**, and James said they could not eat another bite. The grand prize was given to **Danny, champion of the world**, whose nickname was Boy.

Everyone wanted to know **more about Boy** and how he had managed to eat so many chocolates.

"Before I came here," Danny said, "I took a big dose of **George's marvelous medicine**. One dose of that medicine, and there is no limit as to what you can eat. I read all about it in **the wonderful story of Henry Sugar**. A lifelong reader is a lifelong learner, and it helps to win contests too!"

Answers to Mystery Titles

1. World
2. Fox
3. Medicine
4. Magic
5. Sugar
6. *The Witches* (F)
7. *More About Boy* (G)
8. *The Magic Finger* (C)
9. *Vile Verses* (I)
10. *The BFG* (B)

Answers to Name That Book!

1. *The Twits*
2. *Fantastic Mr. Fox*
3. *George's Marvelous Medicine*
4. *Danny, Champion of the World*
5. *The BFG*

CYNTHIA DEFELICE (1951–):
THE I HAVE/WHO HAS GAME

Cut the cards apart. Each player gets one card. The player who has the card with the asterisks (****) on it reads the "Who has" question. The player who has the answer card reads the answer and then the next question.

I HAVE:	Cynthia DeFelice continues to write, but the last count included 11 novels and 13 picture books. ****	I HAVE:	After college Cynthia worked on a farm, which she disliked. She went back to school to get a library degree and became a children's librarian.
WHO HAS:	Who does Cynthia say is most responsible for her becoming a reader and a writer?	WHO HAS:	What inspired Cynthia to write for children?
I HAVE:	Cynthia says it was her mother's love of language and nightly story times that led her to become a reader and eventually a writer.	I HAVE:	Cynthia wanted to write books that would bring the same amazement to children's faces that she saw when she read or told stories to children.
WHO HAS:	Where did Cynthia get her books as a child for summer reading?	WHO HAS:	How old was Cynthia when her first children's book was published?
I HAVE:	Cynthia and her brothers got their books at a nearby drugstore.	I HAVE:	Cynthia was 36 years old when her first children's book was published. She took a year off from her job to write it.
WHO HAS:	What were Cynthia's favorite books to read as a child?	WHO HAS:	Are any real-life characters found in Cynthia's books?
I HAVE:	Cynthia read *Nancy Drew*, the *Hardy Boys*, comic books, *MAD* magazine, and more.	I HAVE:	Both Mr. Henry and the dog, Hoover, really existed. Mr. Henry was Cynthia's sixth-grade teacher, and the dog belonged to her friends.
WHO HAS:	What job did Cynthia have after college?	WHO HAS:	How many children's books has Cynthia written?

CYNTHIA DEFELICE:
MYSTERY TITLES

Some words in these titles of books by Cynthia DeFelice have been replaced with Dewey Decimal numbers. Go to the shelf with the Dewey number. Find the subject of the book(s) with that number. Fill in the missing word in each title. The first person to finish all the titles correctly is the winner!

1. Dancing 611 _____ _____ _____ _____ _____ _____ _____ _____

2. Lostman's 577.6 _____ _____ _____ _____ _____

3. Mule 591.4 _____ _____ _____ _____

4. Devil's 624.2 _____ _____ _____ _____ _____ _____

5. Missing 599.5 _____ _____ _____ _____ _____ _____ _____

Some words in these titles of books by Cynthia DeFelice have been replaced with synonyms. Put the letter of the actual title after each synonymous title.

6. Cavorting Bones _____

7. Lucifer's Span Across Water _____

8. Missing Male's Tributary _____

9. Small Carnivorous Mammal _____

10. Absent Seacow _____

ACTUAL TITLES
A. *Casey in the Bath*
B. *Three Perfect Peaches*
C. *The Dancing Skeleton*
D. *The Light on Hogback Hill*
E. *Devil's Bridge*
F. *Mule Eggs*
G. *Lostman's River*
H. *Weasel*
I. *Signal*
J. *Missing Manatee*

Which titles are available in your library?

The key to Mystery Titles is on page __53__.

 From *Gateway to Reading: 250+ Author Games and Booktalks to Motivate Middle Readers* by Nancy J. Polette. Santa Barbara, CA: Libraries Unlimited. Copyright © 2013.

CYNTHIA DEFELICE:
NAME THAT BOOK!

What title would YOU give each of these books by Cynthia DeFelice?

1) It's 1849, and 12-year-old Lucas Whitaker is all alone after his whole family dies of a disease called consumption, which has swept through the community. Lucas is grief-stricken and filled with guilt. He might have saved his mother, who was the last to die, if only he had listened to news of a strange cure for this deadly disease. Unable to manage the family farm by himself, Lucas finds work as an apprentice to Doc Beecher: doctor, dentist, barber, and undertaker. Doc amputates a leg as easily as he pulls a tooth, yet when it comes to consumption, he remains powerless, unwilling to try the cure he calls nonsense. Lucas can't accept Doc's disbelief, and he joins others in the dark ritual they believe is their only hope. The startling results teach Lucas a great deal about fear, desperation, and the scientific reasoning that offers hope for a true cure.

Your title _____

2) All Skeet Waters wants is to catch a big, beautiful tarpon on his fly rod and to keep everything else in his life in Florida the way it's always been. But on his spring break from school, Skeet overhears his mother telling his father to move out permanently. Then, while riding in his boat to escape his parents' troubles, he discovers a manatee that has been shot in the head. Skeet puts aside his search for the manatee's killer when Dirty Dan the Tarpon Man offers to take him out to catch his first tarpon on a fly. Because of Dan, Skeet begins to unravel the mysteries surrounding the manatee's apparent murder and his parents' dissolving marriage. Skeet discovers that life is a lot like tarpon fishing, in which you can't look just at the surface of the water: you have to look through it, at what lies beneath.

Your title _____

3) Allie Nichols has hardly laid the last spirit to rest when she's sure that another one is trying to reach her. But how can Allie help a ghost who won't speak? All she has to go on is a sound—a sort of whine—and a smell. At the same time, a strange boy joins her sixth-grade class. Allie doesn't understand why L. J. Cutler would start a new school at the end of the year or why he's such a surly kid. She wants nothing to do with him. Then Mr. Henry, a teacher she loves, asks Allie to dog-sit Hoover, his golden retriever, while he's away and to befriend L. J. over the summer. She's delighted to spend time with Hoover, but she hardly looks forward to visiting L. J. Cutler—until she discovers a connection between L. J., the ghost, and Hoover.

Your title _____

4) While running on the trail near his house in upstate New York, Owen McGuire meets a girl with startling green eyes and bloody cuts all over her body who seems to be utterly alone. Her name is Campion, after the wildflower that is an alien species in the area—alien meaning "from someplace else"—and Campion claims to come from someplace else entirely, a planet called Home. She plans to signal her parents to come pick her up in their spaceship. Owen agrees to help, and as he does, he feels happier than he has in a long time. His mother died a year and a half ago, and now he and his workaholic father live together like two planets on separate orbits, in a new house far from his friends. What will he do when Campion asks him to come with her into outer space, away from his lonely life on Earth?

Your title _____

See the author's titles on page __53__.
Which titles can you find in your library?

From *Gateway to Reading: 250+ Author Games and Booktalks to Motivate Middle Readers*
by Nancy J. Polette. Santa Barbara, CA: Libraries Unlimited. Copyright © 2013.

CYNTHIA DEFELICE:
CIRCLE THE HIDDEN TITLES

Lucas Whitaker wanted to be a ghost hunter. But first he had to study under the greatest hunter of all, Casey. The apprenticeship of Lucas Whitaker would allow him to get rid of two ghosts, the ghost of Cutler Creek and the ghost of Poplar Point. Everyone said Willy's silly grandma didn't really see ghosts, but Lucas knew that she did. He noticed that every time the light on Hogback Hill glowed, it was a signal for Grandma to see the ghosts.

When Lucas arrived at Casey's he found Casey in the bath. "Ghost hunting is dirty business," Casey said. "I was out on Devil's Bridge last night when a dancing skeleton appeared. To get away I had to jump into the muddy Lostman's River. When I climbed out, I was muddy from head to toe."

The first ghost hunting lesson Lucas had was to find four mule eggs. Because mules don't lay eggs, Lucas wasn't sure how to do this. He tried to weasel out of the task, but Casey wouldn't let him. It was then that he found three perfect peaches. He said the ghost chant and kissed his elbow just the way Casey had taught him, and sure enough, the peaches turned into mule eggs.

Lucas went to Grandma's house to try out his new skills. The light on Hogback Hill came on, and Grandma saw the ghosts. Lucas kissed his elbow and said the chant. The ghosts disappeared. Grandma was pleased as punch. "Move in with us, Lucas," she said.

Lucas had a better idea. He taught Grandpa the chant and told him just what to do. From then on, when grandpa kissed his elbow and said the chant, the ghosts departed.

Lucas became a more famous ghost hunter than Casey. He traveled the world teaching folks how to get rid of ghosts and once helped to find a missing manatee. So if you see someone kissing his elbow and chanting strange words, you will know that Lucas has been there.

From *Gateway to Reading: 250+ Author Games and Booktalks to Motivate Middle Readers* by Nancy J. Polette. Santa Barbara, CA: Libraries Unlimited. Copyright © 2013.

CYNTHIA DEFELICE:
KEYS

Answers to Circle the Hidden Titles

Lucas Whitaker wanted to be a ghost hunter. But first he had to study under the greatest hunter of all, Casey. **The apprenticeship of Lucas Whitaker** would allow him to get rid of two ghosts, **the ghost of Cutler Creek** and **the ghost of Poplar Point**. Everyone said **Willy's silly grandma** didn't really see ghosts, but Lucas knew that she did. He noticed that every time **the light on Hogback Hill** glowed, it was a **signal** for Grandma to see the ghosts.

When Lucas arrived at Casey's he found **Casey in the bath**. "Ghost hunting is dirty business," Casey said. "I was out on **Devil's Bridge** last night when a **dancing skeleton** appeared. To get away I had to jump into the muddy **Lostman's River**. When I climbed out, I was muddy from head to toe."

The first ghost hunting lesson Lucas had was to find four **mule eggs**. Because mules don't lay eggs, Lucas wasn't sure how to do this. He tried to **weasel** out of the task, but Casey wouldn't let him. It was then that he found **three perfect peaches**. He said the ghost chant and kissed his elbow just the way Casey had taught him, and sure enough, the peaches turned into **mule eggs**.

Lucas went to Grandma's house to try out his new skills. **The light on Hogback Hill** came on, and Grandma saw the ghosts. Lucas kissed his elbow and said the chant. The ghosts disappeared. Grandma was pleased as punch. "Move in with us, Lucas," she said.

Lucas had a better idea. He taught Grandpa the chant and told him just what to do. From then on, **when grandpa kissed his elbow** and said the chant, the ghosts departed.

Lucas became a more famous ghost hunter than Casey. He traveled the world teaching folks how to get rid of ghosts and once helped to find a **missing manatee**. So if you see someone kissing his elbow and chanting strange words, you will know that Lucas has been there.

Answers to Mystery Titles

1. Skeleton
2. River
3. Eggs
4. Bridge
5. Manatee
6. *The Dancing Skeleton* (C)
7. *Devil's Bridge* (E)
8. *Lostman's River* (G)
9. *Weasel* (H)
10. *Missing Manatee* (J)

Answers to Name That Book!

1. *The Apprenticeship of Lucas Whitaker*
2. *Missing Manatee*
3. *The Ghost of Cutler Creek*
4. *Signal*

KATE DICAMILLO (1964–   ):
THE I HAVE/WHO HAS GAME

Cut the cards apart. Each player gets one card. The player who has the card with the asterisks (****) on it reads the "Who has" question. The player who has the answer card reads the answer and then the next question.

I HAVE:	*Because of Winn-Dixie* was a Newbery Honor book, and *The Tale of Despereaux* won the Newbery Medal in 2004. *The Tiger Rising* was a National Book Award finalist. ********	**I HAVE:**	As an adult Kate worked on the children's book floor of a book warehouse and fell in love with children's books.
WHO HAS:	What happened in Kate's childhood that helped her to become a writer?	**WHO HAS:**	What does Kate consider is more important than talent in a writer?
I HAVE:	Kate was a sickly child suffering many bouts of pneumonia. Time in bed was spent reading.	**I HAVE:**	Kate considers that working every day at writing is more important than talent.
WHO HAS:	What were some of Kate's favorite books as a child?	**WHO HAS:**	How did the story *Because of Winn Dixie* come about?
I HAVE:	As a child Kate enjoyed reading *The Twenty-One Balloons*, *The Secret Garden*, and *The Yearling*.	**I HAVE:**	Living in a Minneapolis apartment, Kate could not have a dog, so she invented one in writing *Because of Winn Dixie*.
WHO HAS:	What treasured companion did Kate have as a child?	**WHO HAS:**	What is the basic theme of most of Kate's books?
I HAVE:	Kate's childhood companion was a poodle named Nanette, which she dressed in a variety of costumes.	**I HAVE:**	An important theme in Kate's stories is to always have hope and never give up.
WHO HAS:	What job as an adult challenged Kate to begin writing?	**WHO HAS:**	What awards have Kate DiCamillo's books won?

From Gateway to Reading: 250+ Author Games and Booktalks to Motivate Middle Readers by Nancy J. Polette. Santa Barbara, CA: Libraries Unlimited. Copyright © 2013.

KATE DICAMILLO:
MYSTERY TITLES

Some words in these titles of books by Kate DiCamillo have been replaced with Dewey Decimal numbers. Go to the shelf with the Dewey number. Find the subject of the book(s) with that number. Fill in the missing word in each title. The first person to finish all the titles correctly is the winner!

1. *Because of Winn Dixie.* The story of a 636.7 _____ _____ _____

2. *The Tale of Despereaux.* The tale of a 599.35 _____ _____ _____ _____ _____

3. *Miraculous Journey of Edward Tulane.* The story of a china 599.3 _____ _____ _____ _____ _____ _____

4. *The Magician's Elephant.* The story of a boy who was an 362.7 _____ _____ _____ _____ _____ _____

5. A 599.75 _____ _____ _____ _____ _____ Rising

Here is a booktalk for one of the author's most popular books. Fill in words you think belong in the blank spaces. The actual missing words are in the answer key on page __59__.

How good were your guesses?

The Tiger Rising is the tale of 12-year-old Rob Horton, who finds a caged tiger in the 6._____ behind the Kentucky Star Motel, where he lives with his dad. The tiger triggers all sorts of 7._____ _____ in Rob's life; for one thing, it takes his mind off his recently deceased mother and the itchy red 8._____ on his legs that the wise motel housekeeper, Willie May, says is a manifestation of the sadness that Rob keeps "down low." Something else for Rob to think about is Sistine (as in the chapel), a new city 9._____ with fierce black eyes who challenges him to be honest with her and himself. Spurred by the tiger, events collide to break Rob out of his silent introspection, to form a new friendship with Sistine, to develop a new understanding of his 10._____, and most important, to lighten his heart.

Which titles are available in your library?

The key to Mystery Titles is on page __59__.

KATE DICAMILLO:
NAME THAT BOOK!

What title would YOU give each of these books by Kate DiCamillo?

1) India Opal and her preacher father arrive at her new home in a trailer park in Naples, Florida. Life changes for her when she saves a scruffy dog at the Winn-Dixie store. The store owner is about to call the dog pound when Opal claims that the dog is hers. The dog is perfectly content to go home with Opal, and the girl soon discovers that there are friendly people in town. She becomes friends with an ex-con pet store clerk who plays music to help the animals sleep. She discovers the neighborhood "witch," a blind woman who sees with her heart. Because of Winn-Dixie, the name she has given the dog, Opal is befriended by many unusual people, and her world changes and expands.

Your title _____

2) In the city of Baltese, 10-year-old Peter Augustus Duchene is on his way to the market to purchase a meager meal for himself and his guardian when he sees a sign advertised by a fortune teller. "The most profound and difficult questions that could possibly be posed by the human mind or heart will be answered within for a small price." He makes a decision to ask her how to find his sister. The fortune teller tells him to follow the elephant. When an elephant falls from the sky, it sets off a chain reaction of events that eventually lead to a heartwarming reunion.

Your title _____

3) Once, in a house on Egypt Street, there lived a cold-hearted, 3-foot-tall china rabbit named Edward Tulane. He was treated with the utmost care and adored completely. And then one day he falls overboard and sinks to the bottom of the sea, where he will spend 297 days. Caught in a fisherman's net, he lives with the old man and his wife and begins to care about his humans. Then their adult daughter takes him to the dump, where a dog and a hobo find him. They ride the rails together until Edward is cruelly separated from them. His heart is truly broken when his next owner, 4-year-old Sarah Ruth, dies. When his head is shattered by an angry man, Edward wants to join Sarah Ruth, but those he has loved convince him to live. Repaired by a doll store owner, he closes his heart to love, as it is too painful, until a wise doll tells him that he must open his heart for someone to love him.

Your title _____

4) Here are four stories of Despereaux Tilling, a new baby mouse who is different from all other mice. Sadly, his love for the beautiful Princess Pea ultimately causes him to be banished by his own father to the foul, rat-filled dungeon. The second story introduces Chiaroscuro, a rat who instead of loving the darkness of his home in the dungeon, loves the light so much he ends up in the castle and in the queen's soup. The third story describes young Miggery Sow, a girl who has been "clouted" so many times that she has cauliflower ears. Still, all the slow-witted, hard-of-hearing Mig dreams of is wearing the crown of Princess Pea. The fourth story returns to the dungeon-bound Despereaux and connects the lives of mouse, rat, girl, and princess in a dramatic conclusion.

Your title _____

See the author's titles on page 59.
Which titles are available in your library?

KATE DICAMILLO:
CIRCLE THE HIDDEN TITLES

This is the tale of Despereaux, a magician who lost his magic powers. The magician's elephant no longer rose in the air with a wave of his hand. Neither did audiences see a tiger rising above the stage. This all happened because of Winn Dixie, an evil sorceress who cast a spell on the magician.

Not knowing what else to do, the magician consulted a good sorceress, whose name was Mercy Watson. "To the rescue!" she shouted. "You must change your name to Edward Tulane and follow this map to the magic well. One sip of the well water and the spell will be broken."

That was the reason for the miraculous journey of Edward Tulane (formerly the magician), who found the well, took one sip of the water, and to his great joy found his powers restored.

From *Gateway to Reading: 250+ Author Games and Booktalks to Motivate Middle Readers* by Nancy J. Polette. Santa Barbara, CA: Libraries Unlimited. Copyright © 2013.

KATE DICAMILLO:
KEYS

Answers to Circle the Hidden Titles

This is **the tale of Despereaux**, a magician who lost his magic powers. **The magician's elephant** no longer rose in the air with a wave of his hand. Neither did audiences see a **tiger rising** above the stage. This all happened **because of Winn Dixie**, an evil sorceress who cast a spell on the magician.

Not knowing what else to do, the magician consulted a good sorceress, whose name was **Mercy Watson. "To the rescue!"** she shouted. "You must change your name to Edward Tulane and follow this map to the magic well. One sip of the well water, and the spell will be broken."

That was the reason for **the miraculous journey of Edward Tulane** (formerly the magician), who found the well, took one sip of the water, and to his **great joy** found his powers restored.

Answers to Mystery Titles

1. Dog
2. Mouse
3. Rabbit
4. Orphan
5. Tiger
6. Woods
7. Magic
8. Blisters
9. Girl
10. Father

Answers to Name That Book!

1. *Because of Winn-Dixie*
2. *The Magician's Elephant*
3. *The Miraculous Journey of Edward Tulane*
4. *The Tale of Despereaux*

SID FLEISCHMAN (1920-2010)
THE I HAVE/WHO HAS GAME

Cut the cards apart. Each player gets one card. The player who has the card with the asterisks (****) on it reads the "Who has" question. The player who has the answer card reads the answer and then the next question.

I HAVE:	*The Whipping Boy*, the tale of a boy from the London streets who is punished each time Prince Brat misbehaves, won the Newbery Award. **** 	**I HAVE:**	After writing numerous screenplays, he decided to write a book for his own young children to show them what a writer does. A publisher liked the book, so Sid decided to divide his time between writing children's books and screenplays.
WHO HAS:	As a child, what was Sid Fleischman's dream job ?	**WHO HAS:**	How long does it take Sid Fleischman to write a novel for young readers?
I HAVE:	The dream job he wanted as an adult was to be a magician. After high school he performed on stage in a midnight ghost-and-goblin show.	**I HAVE:**	It sometimes takes a year to write and rewrite a children's novel until he is satisfied he has done his best.
WHO HAS:	When did he decide not to be a magician?	**WHO HAS:**	Does he outline or plot out his novels before beginning to write?
I HAVE:	World War II changed his plans for the future. After serving in the Naval Reserve, he finished college and got a job as a reporter.	**I HAVE:**	He does not plot his novels before writing. He starts with a character and an idea, and the character decides what will happen next.
WHO HAS:	When did Sid Fleischman decide to become a writer?	**WHO HAS:**	What relation is Sid Fleischman to Paul Fleischman, who received the Newbery Award for *Joyful Noise*?
I HAVE:	When the paper he worked for closed, he wrote a novel that was bought by Hollywood, and Sid became a screenwriter.	**I HAVE:**	Paul is Sid's son. They are the only father and son to each receive the Newbery Award.
WHO HAS:	What caused Sid the screenwriter to become a children's writer?	**WHO HAS:**	For which book did Sid Fleischman receive the Newbery Award?

SID FLEISCHMAN:
MYSTERY TITLES

Some words in these titles of books by Sid Fleischman have been replaced with Dewey Decimal numbers. Go to the shelf with the Dewey number. Find the subject of the book(s) with that number. Fill in the missing word in each title. The first person to finish all the titles correctly is the winner!

1. Bandit's 523.3 _____ _____ _____ _____

2. 612.8 _____ _____ _____ _____ _____ Stealer

3. Giant 599.35 _____ _____ _____ of Sumatra

4. Midnight 636.1 _____ _____ _____ _____ _____

5. The White 599.67 _____ _____ _____ _____ _____ _____ _____ _____

Some words in these titles of books by Sid Fleischman have been replaced with synonyms. Put the letter of the actual title after each synonymous title.

6. Frightened Feather-covered Vertebrate _____

7. Robber of Sleep Images _____

8. Vanishing Performance _____

9. An Adult Male of Mystery Plus Cohorts _____

10. Young Male Undergoing Corporal Punishment _____

ACTUAL TITLES
A. *The Abracadabra Kid*
B. *The Whipping Boy*
C. *Bandit's Moon*
D. *Mr. Mysterious & Co.*
E. *By the Great Horn Spoon*
F. *A Carnival of Animals*
G. *Disappearing Act*
H. *The 13th Floor*
I. *Dream Stealer*
J. *The Scarebird*

Which titles are available in your library?

The key to Mystery Titles is on page __65__.

SID FLEISCHMAN:
NAME THAT BOOK!

What title would YOU give each of these books by Sid Fleischman?

1) Jemmy, once a poor boy living on the streets, now lives in a castle. As the whipping boy, he bears the punishment when Prince Brat misbehaves, for it is forbidden to spank, thrash, or whack the heir to the throne. The two boys have nothing in common and even less reason to like one another. But when they find themselves taken hostage after running away, they are left with no choice but to trust each other.

Your title _____

2) "Mark Twain was born fully grown, with a cheap cigar clamped between his teeth." So begins Sid Fleischman's ramble-scramble biography of the great American author and wit, who started life in a Missouri village as a barefoot boy named Samuel Clemens. Abandoning a career as a young steamboat pilot on the Mississippi River, Sam took a bumpy stagecoach to the Far West. In the gold and silver fields, he expected to get rich quick. Instead, he got poor fast, digging in the wrong places. His stint as a sagebrush newspaperman led to a duel with pistols. Had he not survived, the world would never have heard of Tom Sawyer or Huckleberry Finn—or red-headed Mark Twain.

Your title _____

3) Opie and Aunt Etta think there's something funny going on when Professor Pepper announces that he's going to raise the ghost of a dead outlaw—live on stage. Can Opie cut through all the fog to get to the bottom of the professor's plans? See the Ghost of Crookneck John! That's what Professor Pepper's sign promises, and Opie can hardly wait to see such a sight. But the unseen specter escapes from his coffin during the show, and as if that weren't bad enough, the town bank is robbed too! Is Crookneck John a bandit from beyond the grave, or is more than the fog being pulled over the townsfolks' eyes?

Your title _____

4) An unseen man they call the Toad is stalking 12-year-old Kevin and his older sister Holly. They flee town in Holly's beat-up old car, driving west until they reach the Pacific Ocean. They change their names and attempt to hide in plain sight as street performers in Venice, California. But have they really eluded the Toad?

Your title _____

See the author's titles on page __65__.
Which titles are available in your library?

From *Gateway to Reading: 250+ Author Games and Booktalks to Motivate Middle Readers*
by Nancy J. Polette. Santa Barbara, CA: Libraries Unlimited. Copyright © 2013.

SID FLEISCHMAN:
CIRCLE THE HIDDEN TITLES

The abracadabra kid was kidnapped on the night of the bandit's moon. His best friends were Bo and Mzzz. Mad as hornets, they shouted, "By the great horn spoon, no one can do that to our friend!"

They went searching for a midnight horse to give chase, but the woods were filled with a carnival of animals, and there was no black horse to be found.

"Where do you think they took him?" Bo asked.

"Mr. Mysterious and company might know," Mzzz replied. "They are all fortune tellers and can find lost things. But we can't stay out looking too long. If I'm out too late, I'll get a whipping."

"Boy!" Bo shouted. "You are worrying more about your backside than about finding our friend. You're nothing but an old scarebird!"

The boys made their way to the wagon where Mr. Mysterious lived. When they told him about their missing friend, he closed his eyes and said mysterious words, "Your friend was kidnapped by Jim Ugly, a dream stealer. He has him tied up on the 13th floor of the Plaza Hotel in town."

Bo and Mzzz headed for town and told the police what had happened. Their friend was found, and Jim Ugly was captured and put in jail. The Kid, however, had done another disappearing act. He had taken off for the Pacific Islands to find the giant rat of Sumatra and save the people from being eaten alive.

From *Gateway to Reading: 250+ Author Games and Booktalks to Motivate Middle Readers* by Nancy J. Polette. Santa Barbara, CA: Libraries Unlimited. Copyright © 2013.

SID FLEISCHMAN:
KEYS

Answers to Circle the Hidden Titles

The abracadabra kid was kidnapped on the night of the **bandit's moon**. His best friends were **Bo and Mzzz. Mad** as hornets, they shouted, "**By the great horn spoon**, no one can do that to our friend!"

They went searching for a **midnight horse** to give chase, but the woods were filled with **a carnival of animals**, and there was no black horse to be found.

"Where do you think they took him?" Bo asked.

"**Mr. Mysterious and company** might know," Mzzz replied. "They are all fortune tellers and can find lost things. But we can't stay out looking too long. If I'm out too late, I'll get a **whipping**."

"**Boy**!" Bo shouted. "You are worrying more about your backside than about finding our friend. You're nothing but an old **scarebird**!"

The boys made their way to the wagon where Mr. Mysterious lived. When they told him about their missing friend, he closed his eyes and said mysterious words, "Your friend was kidnapped by **Jim Ugly, a dream stealer**. He has him tied up on **the 13th floor** of the Plaza Hotel in town."

Bo and Mzzz headed for town and told the police what had happened. Their friend was found, and **Jim Ugly** was captured and put in jail. The Kid, however, had done another **disappearing act**. He had taken off for the Pacific Islands to find **the giant rat of Sumatra** and save the people from being eaten alive.

Answers to Mystery Titles

1. Moon
2. Dream
3. Rat
4. Horse
5. Elephant
6. *The Scarebird* (J)
7. *Dream Stealer* (I)
8. *Disappearing Act* (G)
9. *Mr. Mysterious & Co.* (D)
10. *The Whipping Boy* (B)

Answers to Name That Book!

1. *The Whipping Boy*
2. *The Trouble Begins at 8*
3. *The Ghost on Saturday Night*
4. *Disappearing Act*

PAULA FOX (1923–):
THE I HAVE/WHO HAS GAME

Cut the cards apart. Each player gets one card. The player who has the card with the asterisks (****) on it reads the "Who has" question. The player who has the answer card reads the answer and then the next question.

I HAVE:	Among her many awards, Paula Fox has received the Newbery Medal, the Empire State Award, and the O. Henry Prize. ****	I HAVE:	Despite having had only 3 months of high school, at age 30 Paula Fox passed the entrance exams to Columbia University.
WHO HAS:	Why would some say that Paula Fox is a woman of the world?	WHO HAS:	What jobs led to Paula becoming a writer?
I HAVE:	Abandoned by her mother, Paula spent time as a child in Cuba and as an adult in England, France, Poland, and the United States.	I HAVE:	Paula worked as a reader for film studios, as a reporter, and as a teacher. Her first novel was published when she was 43 years old.
WHO HAS:	When did Paula decide she wanted to be a writer?	WHO HAS:	Did Paula Fox marry and have children?
I HAVE:	Paula was 7 years old when she decided she wanted to be a writer like her father.	I HAVE:	Paula Fox married 3 times and had two sons, Adam and Gabriel. She gave up one daughter for adoption.
WHO HAS:	What was Paula's life as a teenager like?	WHO HAS:	Did Paula and her daughter ever find each other as adults?
I HAVE:	At age 15 Paula took care of herself working in a dress shop and a dance studio.	I HAVE:	Paula and daughter Linda did find each other, and Paula discovered she had five additional grandchildren.
WHO HAS:	How much education did Paula Fox have?	WHO HAS:	What honors have Paula Fox's books received?

PAULA FOX:
MYSTERY TITLES

Some words in these titles of books by Paula Fox have been replaced with Dewey Decimal numbers. Go to the shelf with the Dewey number. Find the subject of the book(s) with that number. Fill in the missing word in each title. The first person to finish all the titles correctly is the winner!

1. Eagle 629.133 _____ _____ _____ _____

2. 599.8 _____ _____ _____ _____ _____ _____ Island

3. One-Eyed 636.8 _____ _____ _____

4. 326 _____ _____ _____ _____ _____ Dancer

5. Western 551.51 _____ _____ _____ _____

Some words in these titles of books by Paula Fox have been replaced with synonyms. Put the letter of the actual title after each synonymous title.

6. Small Gatherer of Pigs _____

7. Simian Land Surrounded by Water _____

8. Feline with Single Vision _____

9. Captive Moving to Music _____

10. Young Male with Rock Countenance _____

ACTUAL TITLES
A. *Amzat and His Brothers*
B. *Blowfish Live in the Sea*
C. *Eagle Kite*
D. *The Little Swineherd*
E. *Monkey Island*
F. *One-Eyed Cat*
G. *Portrait of Ivan*
H. *The Slave Dancer*
I. *The Stone-Faced Boy*
J. *The Village by the Sea*

Which titles are available in your library?

The key to Mystery Titles is on page ___71___ .

PAULA FOX:
NAME THAT BOOK!

What title would YOU give to each of these books by Paula Fox?

1) One day, 13-year-old Jessie Bollier is earning pennies playing his fife on the docks of New Orleans; the next, he is kidnapped and thrown aboard a slave ship, where his job is to provide music while shackled slaves "dance" to keep their muscles strong and their bodies profitable. As the endless voyage continues, Jessie is sickened by the greed, brutality, and inhumanity of the slave trade, but nothing prepares him for the ultimate horror he will witness before his nightmare ends.

Your title _____

2) Ivan's father pays little attention to him, his mother is dead, and he spends most of his time at his home in New York, attended only by a Haitian housekeeper. His father commissions an artist, Matt Mustazza, to paint a portrait of Ivan, but he also gives his son another gift: permission to accompany Matt on a trip to paint an old mansion in Florida. Ivan, Matt, and his eccentric friend Miss Manderby and her cat Alyosha pile into a "crazy old car" and head south, where Ivan meets a free-spirited girl, Geneva, and begins the painful but rewarding process of finding himself.

Your title _____

3) Thirteen-year-old Carrie is concerned about her nineteen-year-old half-brother, Ben. She can't understand his change from the loving, funny brother she's always known to the sullen, shut-off young man he's become. When he asks her to come with him to Boston to meet his real dad, she's hopeful—maybe the old Ben isn't gone after all. But the truth Carrie uncovers in Boston isn't quite so simple. The old Ben is gone. And somehow, she's going to have to learn to accept the way things are now.

Your title _____

4) Eleven-year-old Clay Garrity is on his own. His father lost his job and left the family. Now Clay's mother is gone from their welfare hotel. Clay is homeless and out on the streets of New York. In the park he meets two homeless men, Buddy and Calvin, who become Clay's new family during those harsh winter weeks. But the streets are filled with danger and despair. If Clay leaves the streets he may never find his parents again. But if he stays on the streets, he may not survive at all.

Your title _____

See the author's titles on page __71__.
Which titles are available in your library?

From *Gateway to Reading: 250+ Author Games and Booktalks to Motivate Middle Readers* by Nancy J. Polette. Santa Barbara, CA: Libraries Unlimited. Copyright © 2013.

PAULA FOX:
CIRCLE THE HIDDEN TITLES

Amzat and his brothers were swineherds. They lived in a village by the sea. Two brothers were big and strong, but Amzat was the little swineherd. When others made fun of him for being so small, he took his only friend, a one-eyed cat, and hid out on Monkey Island.

One day when Amzat was feeling very sad, he went to the island and occupied himself by making an eagle kite. He heard a strange sound and looked up to see a large ship approaching. The sound was the tramping of slaves on deck as the slave dancer played his fife. As the ship passed, Amzat looked into the eyes of a young slave on deck. The slave stood like a stone-faced boy, knowing the terrible fate that awaited him.

Amzat's heart went out to the boy, and just as the ship passed, a western wind caught his kite and it flew into the air above the ship. The slaves looked upward. The kite was a sign of hope that one day they would be free.

Amzat might have been small, but he gave the greatest gift of all, hope for a better future.

From *Gateway to Reading: 250+ Author Games and Booktalks to Motivate Middle Readers* by Nancy J. Polette. Santa Barbara, CA: Libraries Unlimited. Copyright © 2013.

PAULA FOX:
KEYS

Answers to Circle the Hidden Titles

Amzat and his brothers were swineherds. They lived in a **village by the sea**. Two brothers were big and strong, but Amzat was **the little swineherd**. When others made fun of him for being so small, he took his only friend, a **one-eyed cat**, and hid out on **Monkey Island**.

One day when Amzat was feeling very sad, he went to the island and occupied himself by making an **eagle kite**. He heard a strange sound and looked up to see a large ship approaching. The sound was the tramping of slaves on deck as **the slave dancer** played his fife. As the ship passed, Amzat looked into the eyes of a young slave on deck. The slave stood like a **stone-faced boy**, knowing the terrible fate that awaited him.

Amzat's heart went out to the boy, and just as the ship passed, a **western wind** caught his kite and it flew into the air above the ship. The slaves looked upward. The kite was a sign of hope that one day they would be free.

Amzat might have been small, but he gave the greatest gift of all, hope for a better future.

Answers to Mystery Titles

1. Kite
2. Monkey
3. Cat
4. Slave
5. Wind
6. *The Little Swineherd* (D)
7. *Monkey Island* (E)
8. *One-Eyed Cat* (F)
9. *The Slave Dancer* (H)
10. *The Stone-Faced Boy* (I)

Answers to Name That Book!

1. *The Slave Dancer*
2. *Portrait of Ivan*
3. *Blowfish Live in the Sea*
4. *Monkey Island*

NEIL GAIMAN (1960–):
THE I HAVE/WHO HAS GAME

Cut the cards apart. Each player gets one card. The player who has the card with the asterisks (****) on it reads the "Who has" question. The player who has the answer card reads the answer and then the next question.

I HAVE:	Neil Gaiman won the Newbery Medal for *The Graveyard Book*. He won the BAFTA for best animated film based on his book *Coraline*. ****	I HAVE:	Neil Gaiman's first published books were biographies, followed by the Sandman series of comic books, which won many awards.
WHO HAS:	What were the childhood days most remembered by Neil Gaiman?	WHO HAS:	Does Neil Gaiman write in forms other than comics and books?
I HAVE:	Neil says his best days were those spent in libraries.	I HAVE:	He writes prose, poetry, film scripts, journalism articles, song lyrics, and drama.
WHO HAS:	What authors did Neil Gaiman read as a child and youth?	WHO HAS:	For what ages does Neil Gaiman write?
I HAVE:	As a child and youth Neil Gaiman devoured the books of J. R. R. Tolkien, C. S. Lewis, Edgar Allan Poe, and Ursula LeGuin.	I HAVE:	Neil Gaiman writes for all ages. In addition to Gothic horror for teens, his picture books for young readers include *M Is for Magic* and *The Dangerous Alphabet*.
WHO HAS:	What kind of student was Neil, who grew up in England?	WHO HAS:	Can we find Neil Gaiman on Twitter?
I HAVE:	He read at the age of 4 and was a good student, reading all of his school books as soon as he received them. He won both the reading and English prizes.	I HAVE:	Gaiman joined Twitter as @neilhimself and has over a million followers.
WHO HAS:	What were Neil Gaiman's first published books?	WHO HAS:	What awards has Neil Gaiman won?

Some words in these titles of books by Neil Gaiman have been replaced with Dewey Decimal numbers. Go to the shelf with the Dewey number. Find the subject of the book(s) with that number. Fill in the missing word in each title. The first person to finish all the titles correctly is the winner!

1. 634.737 _____ _____ _____ _____ _____ _____ _____ _____ _____ Girl

2. Crazy 646.724 _____ _____ _____ _____

3. Dangerous 411 _____ _____ _____ _____ _____ _____ _____ _____

4. The Graveyard 011 _____ _____ _____ _____

5. M Is for 793.8 _____ _____ _____ _____ _____

Some words in these titles of books by Neil Gaiman have been replaced with synonyms. Put the letter of the actual title after each synonymous title.

6. Instructions _____

7. Demented Locks _____

8. Parapets Containing Coyote Cousins _____

9. A Single Cemetery Volume _____

10. Perilous ABCs _____

ACTUAL TITLES
A. *Blueberry Girl*
B. *Coraline*
C. *Crazy Hair*
D. *The Dangerous Alphabet*
E. *The Graveyard Book*
F. *Instructions*
G. *M Is for Magic*
H. *Odd and the Frost Giants*
I. *The Wolves in the Walls*

Which titles are available in your library?

The key to Mystery Titles is on page __77__.

NEIL GAIMAN:
NAME THAT BOOK!

What title would YOU give to each of these books by Neil Gaiman?

1) Nobody Owens, known to his friends as Bod, is a normal boy. He would be completely normal if he didn't live in a sprawling graveyard, being raised and educated by ghosts, with a solitary guardian who belongs to the world of neither the living nor the dead. There are dangers and adventures in the graveyard for a boy: an ancient Indigo Man beneath the hill, a gateway to a desert leading to an abandoned city of ghouls, the strange and terrible menace of the Sleer. But if Bod leaves the graveyard, he will come under attack from the man Jack—who has already killed Bod's family.

Your title _____

2) When Coraline steps through a door to find another house strangely similar to her own (only better), things seem marvelous. But there's another mother there, and another father, and they want her to stay and be their little girl. They want to change her and never let her go. Coraline will have to fight with all her wits and courage if she is to save herself and return to her ordinary life.

Your title _____

3) In a village in ancient Norway lives a boy named Odd, and he's had some very bad luck: his father perished in a Viking expedition, a tree fell on and shattered his leg, and the endless freezing winter is making villagers dangerously grumpy. Out in the forest Odd encounters a bear, a fox, and an eagle—three creatures with a strange story to tell. Now Odd is forced on a stranger journey than he had imagined—to save Asgard, city of the gods, from the Frost Giants who have invaded it. It's going to take a very special kind of 12-year-old boy to outwit the Frost Giants, restore peace to the city of gods, and end the long winter.

Your title _____

4) There are sneaking, creeping, crumpling noises coming from inside the walls. Lucy is sure there are wolves living in the walls of their house, and as everybody says, if the wolves come out of the walls, it's all over. Her family doesn't believe her. Then one day, the wolves come out. But it's not all over. Instead, Lucy's battle with the wolves is only just beginning.

Your title _____

See the author's titles on page ___77___.
Which titles can you find in your library?

NEIL GAIMAN:
CIRCLE THE HIDDEN TITLES

Coraline lived on Blueberry Hill, so she was naturally called the blueberry girl. She wore nothing but blue, like blue pants and blue shirts and blue shoes. She even dyed her hair blue, so everyone thought she had crazy hair.

One day Coraline got tired of being blue and wanted to be a happier color. She purchased a book of instructions that told her how to wash the blue out of her clothes and hair, but nothing worked. She decided to visit her cousin Odd, who lived in the frozen North where everything was white. Maybe he could tell her how to turn her blue clothes and hair to white clothes and hair. Odd and the frost giants put their heads together, but all they could think of was to use magic.

Coraline bought a dangerous alphabet book and looked at the M page. She found that M is for magic, and the magic she was to perform led her to the home of wild wolves. In the walls of their cave were pictures of a graveyard. The pictures led Coraline to a graveyard book that told her to work the magic spells in a graveyard at midnight. The spells worked, and she now has no hair at all.

NEIL GAIMAN:
KEYS

Answers to Circle the Hidden Titles

Coraline lived on Blueberry Hill, so she was naturally called the **blueberry girl**. She wore nothing but blue, like blue pants and blue shirts and blue shoes. She even dyed her hair blue, so everyone thought she had **crazy hair**.

One day **Coraline** got tired of being blue and wanted to be a happier color. She purchased a book of **instructions** that told her how to wash the blue out of her clothes and hair, but nothing worked. She decided to visit her cousin Odd, who lived in the frozen North where everything was white. Maybe he could tell her how to turn her blue clothes and hair to white clothes and hair. **Odd and the frost giants** put their heads together, but all they could think of was to use magic.

Coraline bought a **dangerous alphabet** book and looked at the M page. She found that M is for magic, and the magic she was to perform led her to the home of wild **wolves**. **In the walls** of their cave were pictures of a graveyard. The pictures led Coraline to a **graveyard book** that told her to work the magic spells in a graveyard at midnight. The spells worked, and she now has no hair at all.

Answers to Mystery Titles

1. Blueberry
2. Hair
3. Alphabet
4. Book
5. Magic
6. *Instructions* (F)
7. *Crazy Hair* (C)
8. *The Wolves in the Walls* (I)
9. *The Graveyard Book* (E)
10. *The Dangerous Alphabet* (D)

Answers to Name That Book!

1. *The Graveyard Book*
2. *Coraline*
3. *Odd and the Frost Giants*
4. *The Wolves in the Walls*

JEAN CRAIGHEAD GEORGE (1919–2012):
THE I HAVE/WHO HAS GAME

Cut the cards apart. Each player gets one card. The player who has the card with the asterisks (****) on it reads the "Who has" question. The player who has the answer card reads the answer and then the next question.

I HAVE:	Before writing *Julie of the Wolves*, Jean studied wolves with scientists in Barrow, Alaska. ****	I HAVE:	Jean married a naturalist, and they lived for a time in a wilderness tent, which led to her writing about the natural world.
WHO HAS:	How did Jean Craighead George come to develop the love of nature found in her books?	WHO HAS:	How did Jean introduce her children to wildlife?
I HAVE:	Jean's father was a naturalist who took his children on many wilderness trips, where they learned to appreciate the natural world.	I HAVE:	Jean took her children on wilderness trips and brought wild animals home for the children to care for.
WHO HAS:	As a child what careers did she plan on following when she grew up?	WHO HAS:	When did Jean write *My Side of the Mountain*?
I HAVE:	As a child Jean decided she would be an illustrator, a writer, a dancer, and a poet.	I HAVE:	Jean wrote *My Side of the Mountain* while her children napped. It told of her wildlife experiences as a child.
WHO HAS:	When did Jean decide to concentrate on writing as a career?	WHO HAS:	What travels led to more books about wildlife and the natural world?
I HAVE:	Jean concentrated on writing in college and worked as a reporter on the *Washington Post* after college.	I HAVE:	Jean took her children camping on the tundra, in the mountains, and on the prairies and wrote about their experiences.
WHO HAS:	What led to Jean writing about the natural world?	WHO HAS:	What research did Jean do for *Julie of the Wolves*, a Newbery Medal winner?

JEAN CRAIGHEAD GEORGE:
MYSTERY TITLES

Some words in these titles of books by Jean Craighead George have been replaced with Dewey Decimal numbers. Go to the shelf with the Dewey number. Find the subject of the book(s) with that number. Fill in the missing word in each title. The first person to finish all the titles correctly is the winner!

1. 636.8 _____ _____ _____ _____ of Rockville Station

2. Frightful's 551.4 _____ _____ _____ _____ _____ _____ _____ _____

3. Julie of the 599.7 _____ _____ _____ _____ _____ _____

4. 628.9 _____ _____ _____ _____ Storm

5. 582.16 _____ _____ _____ _____ Castle Island

Some words in these titles of books by Jean Craighead George have been replaced with synonyms. Put the letter of the actual title after each synonymous title.

6. Conflagration with Heavy Rain _____

7. A High Precipice Grasper _____

8. Primary Feast of Praise _____

9. AM, Midday, and PM _____

10. A Large Hairy Spider in My Reticule _____

ACTUAL TITLES
A. *Morning, Noon, and Night*
B. *The Talking Earth*
C. *The Missing Gator of Gumbo Limbo*
D. *The First Thanksgiving*
E. *The Cats of Rockville Station*
F. *A Tarantula in My Purse*
G. *Charlie's Raven*
H. *Cliff Hanger*
I. *Fire Storm*
J. *Frightful's Daughter*

Which titles are available in your library?

The key to Mystery Titles is on page __83__.

JEAN CRAIGHEAD GEORGE:
NAME THAT BOOK!

What title would YOU give to each of these books by Jean Craighead George?

1) Faced with the prospect of a disagreeable arranged marriage or a journey across the barren Alaskan tundra, 13-year-old Miyax chooses the tundra. She finds herself caught between the traditional Eskimo ways and the modern ways of the whites. Miyax, or Julie as her pen pal Amy calls her, sets out alone to visit Amy in San Francisco, a world far away from Eskimo culture and the frozen land of Alaska. During her long and arduous journey, Miyax comes to appreciate the value of her Eskimo heritage, learns about herself, and wins the friendship of a pack of wolves.

Your title _____

2) Billie Wind lives with her Seminole tribe. She follows their customs, but the dangers of pollution and nuclear war she has learned about in school seem much more real to her. How can she believe the Seminole legends about talking animals and earth spirits? She wants answers, not legends. "You are a doubter," say the men of the Seminole Council, and so Billie goes out into the Everglades alone, to stay until she can believe. In the wilderness she discovers that she must listen to the land and animals to survive. With an otter, a panther cub, and a turtle as companions and guides, she begins to understand that the world of her people can give her the answers she seeks.

Your title _____

3) Liza Poole lives outdoors with her mother in the Florida Everglades. Liza feels lucky to live in her small yellow tent amid tropical birds and exotic plants. And at the center of this natural paradise lies Dajun, the majestic alligator who protects Gumbo Limbo's environment. Then one day a state official arrives with frightening orders. Dajun is scaring people nearby—he must be killed! Liza takes action to save the invaluable gator, but suddenly he is nowhere to be found. Now she must find Dajun before it's too late, and her search will lead her into the heart of an exciting eco mystery!

Your title _____

4) Borden's father, Leon, was a logger in the old-growth forests of California. That is, until the spotted-owl lovers interfered. One day, frustrated by his father's unemployment, Borden sets out on a mission of revenge against the spotted owl, but he returns home with a half-starved owlet instead. The family soon discovers that the owlet, whom Borden names Bardy, loves to take showers and watch late-night TV. Only after the whole family has fallen in love with Bardy do they realize that the conflict between nature and human industry is not so easily resolved.

Your title _____

See the author's titles on page ___83___.
Which titles are in your library?

From *Gateway to Reading: 250+ Author Games and Booktalks to Motivate Middle Readers* by Nancy J. Polette. Santa Barbara, CA: Libraries Unlimited. Copyright © 2013.

JEAN CRAIGHEAD GEORGE:
CIRCLE THE HIDDEN TITLES

Dear Rebecca,

Winter is here, but I am ready for it. I have worked morning, noon, and night freezing acorn pancakes, dandelion salad, and 38 other wild recipes. The harvest meal I cook will be very much like the first Thanksgiving, not like the day we had the fire storm.

Of course living on my side of the mountain can have its scary moments. The other day I found a tarantula in my purse, and when I went to take a shower in the creek, there's an owl in my shower! I took him home for my sister, Julie.

Of the wolves I have little to write. They have not been around for some time. My brother Charlie tamed a wild bird, and Charlie's raven goes everywhere with him. Before letting the bird fly, Charlie gives a look to the north to be sure the weather is okay.

One day in the woods I happened to be on the far side of the mountain and saw smoke. Careless campers had left a fire on Tree Castle Island that turned the woods into a fire storm. For a time it was a cliff hanger to see how far the fire would spread. The fire almost reached Frightful's mountain. You probably remember that Frightful was the bird that kept me company here. Now Frightful's daughter flies over for a visit now and then.

Both Julie and I look forward to your return. Right now we are searching for the missing gator of Gumbo Limbo. The gator has been a favorite around here for years, and I hope we find him.

Write soon and tell me all the news.

JEAN CRAIGHEAD GEORGE:
KEYS

Answers to Circle the Hidden Titles

Dear Rebecca,

Winter is here, but I am ready for it. I have worked **morning, noon, and night** freezing **acorn pancakes, dandelion salad, and 38 other wild recipes**. The harvest meal I cook will be very much like **the first Thanksgiving**, not like the day we had the **fire storm**.

Of course living on **my side of the mountain** can have its scary moments. The other day I found a **tarantula in my purse**, and when I went to take a shower in the creek, **there's an owl in my shower!** I took him home for my sister, **Julie**.

Of the wolves I have little to write. They have not been around for some time. My brother Charlie tamed a wild bird, and **Charlie's raven** goes everywhere with him. Before letting the bird fly, Charlie gives a **look to the north** to be sure the weather is okay.

One day in the woods I happened to be on **the far side of the mountain** and saw smoke. Careless campers had left a fire on **Tree Castle Island** that turned the woods into a **fire storm**. For a time it was a **cliff hanger** to see how far the fire would spread. The fire almost reached **Frightful's mountain**. You probably remember that Frightful was the bird that kept me company here. Now **Frightful's daughter** flies over for a visit now and then.

Both **Julie** and I look forward to your return. Right now we are searching for **the missing gator of Gumbo Limbo**. The gator has been a favorite around here for years, and I hope we find him.

Write soon and tell me all the news.

Answers to the Mystery Titles

1. Cats
2. Mountain
3. Wolves
4. Fire
5. Tree
6. *Fire Storm* (I)
7. *Cliff Hanger* (H)
8. *The First Thanksgiving* (D)
9. *Morning, Noon, and Night* (A)
10. *A Tarantula in My Purse* (F)

Answers to Name That Book!

1. *Julie of the Wolves*
2. *The Talking Earth*
3. *The Missing Gator of Gumbo Limbo*
4. *There's an Owl in the Shower*

PATRICIA REILLY GIFF (1935–):
THE I HAVE/WHO HAS GAME

Cut the cards apart. Each player gets one card. The player who has the card with the asterisks (****) on it reads the "Who has" question. The player who has the answer card reads the answer and then the next question.

I HAVE:	Patricia Reilly Giff received the Newbery Honor Award for *Pictures of Hollis Woods* and *Lily's Crossing*. ****	I HAVE:	Patricia began her writing career in a large closet.
WHO HAS:	When did Patricia decide she wanted to become a writer?	WHO HAS:	What message does Patricia give to children in most of her books?
I HAVE:	Patricia decided to become a writer when she read her first book. "Writing," she said, "is a way of talking to people."	I HAVE:	Patricia's message in her books is that every person has something special about him or her.
WHO HAS:	What were Patricia's favorite books as a child?	WHO HAS:	What skill does Patricia believe is most important to a writer?
I HAVE:	Patricia's favorite books as a child were *Little Women*, *The Secret Garden*, the *Black Stallion*, and the Sue Barton and Nancy Drew series.	I HAVE:	Patricia believes that the ability to observe closely is essential to any writer. She often takes a walk or visits a school to observe before writing.
WHO HAS:	What career did Patricia have before becoming a full-time writer?	WHO HAS:	How many books has Patricia written?
I HAVE:	Patricia was a reading teacher for 20 years and a consultant for Dell Yearling Books.	I HAVE:	Patricia has written more than 60 books for children.
WHO HAS:	Where does Patricia do her writing?	WHO HAS:	What awards have Patricia Reilly Giff's books won?

PATRICIA REILLY GIFF: MYSTERY TITLES

Some words in these titles of books by Patricia Reilly Giff have been replaced with Dewey Decimal numbers. Go to the shelf with the Dewey number. Find the subject of the book(s) with that number. Fill in the missing word in each title. The first person to finish all the titles correctly is the winner!

1. B-E-S-T 158 _____ _____ _____ _____ _____ _____ _____

2. 792.8 _____ _____ _____ _____ _____ with Rosie

3. Flying 612 _____ _____ _____ _____

4. Pictures of Hollis 591.7 _____ _____ _____ _____ _____

5. Watch Out! Man-Eating 597.96 _____ _____ _____ _____ _____

Some words in these titles of books by Patricia Reilly Giff have been replaced with synonyms. Put the letter of the actual title after each synonymous title.

6. Out of Control Female _____

7. A Complete Trip to One's Abode _____

8. Five Plus Six _____

9. Levitating Lower Appendages _____

10. Abode of Garment Menders _____

ACTUAL TITLES
A. *Don't Tell the Girls*
B. *Eleven*
C. *Fancy Feet*
D. *Flying Feet*
E. *Fourth Grade Celebrity*
F. *All the Way Home*
G. *Lily's Crossing*
H. *Number One Kid*
I. *House of Tailors*
J. *Wild Girl*

Which titles are available in your library?

The key to Mystery Titles is on page __89__.

From *Gateway to Reading: 250+ Author Games and Booktalks to Motivate Middle Readers* by Nancy J. Polette. Santa Barbara, CA: Libraries Unlimited. Copyright © 2013.

PATRICIA REILLY GIFF:
NAME THAT BOOK!

What title would YOU give to each of these books by Patricia Reilly Giff?

1) When her mother died, Lidie stayed behind in Brazil with her aunt and uncle. When her father sends for her and Lidie arrives at her father's house, she realizes that her father and brother think that she's still 7 years old! They don't know that she is a better horse rider than her brother, who is training to be a jockey. However, when the filly named Wild Girl arrives, things start to turn around in Lidie's life as she develops a connection with the horse. But will this newfound friendship be enough to help the skittish filly feel at ease in her new home? And can Wild Girl help Lidie show her father and brother who she really is?

Your title _____

2) When Sam discovers a newspaper clipping that features a picture of himself as a very young boy and the head-line "MISSING," he feels there must be some mystery in his past, which he soon becomes desperate to solve. Perhaps Caroline, his new partner for a school castle-building assignment, will help him. But Caroline, who's been to 3 schools already this year, has troubles of her own. Will she and Sam find the answer before it's too late? And what if the answer is what Sam fears? What if his only true family—his grandfather—isn't really his family at all?

Your title _____

3) When 12-year-old Nory Ryan's family first settled on Maidin Bay they owned the land they lived on. Now everyone must pay taxes to an Englishman, Lord Cunningham, who owns all their lands. Those that cannot afford to pay are evicted. Her father is away fishing. Nory's mother died long ago. Nory, her two sisters, and her brother rely on their elderly grandfather to help get by. Then grandfather recognizes the smell of rot from the potato fields; the potatoes are rotting while still in the ground. Even Nory knows what that means: they may actually starve to death. So begins Nory's struggle to stay alive.

Your title _____

4) Hollis Woods has been in so many foster homes she can hardly remember them all. When Hollis is sent to Josie, an elderly artist who is quirky and affectionate, she wants to stay. But Josie is growing more forgetful every day. If Social Services finds out, they'll take Hollis away and move Josie into a home. Hollis is determined not to let anyone separate them. She has escaped the system before; this time, she plans to take Josie with her.

Your title _____

See the author's titles on page __89__.
Which titles are in your library?

PATRICIA REILLY GIFF:
CIRCLE THE HIDDEN TITLES

I could tell you all about Stacy, but Rosie's story is more interesting. And it's not a big whopper. Rosie's dream was to dance. While we are B-E-S-T friends, I don't think Rosie is much of a dancer. To dance with Rosie, even though she thinks she has fancy feet, is like Lily's crossing the playground on stilts. She falls down all the time.

Don't tell the girls in the fourth grade who follow 11-year-old Rosie around all the time, but she really shouldn't be a fourth grade celebrity. The girls think she is famous because she dances at the Catfish Cafe, but she's really a wild girl.

Rosie's last name is Tailor, and the house of Tailors is a wild place. When you ring the doorbell, instead of a bell, a voice shouts out, "Watch out! Man eating snake!" The sign on Rosie's sister Maggie's door says Willow Run. I asked her what it meant, and Maggie said it was just a pretty name for a pretty room. Her walls are plastered with pictures of Hollis Woods, the famous number one kid who is a movie star.

One night we went to see Rosie dance at the Catfish Cafe. A not-so-perfect Rosie finished her dance, and everyone clapped politely, but someone else stole the show. One storyteller and eleven jugglers performed, and we talked about them all the way home.

From *Gateway to Reading: 250+ Author Games and Booktalks to Motivate Middle Readers*
by Nancy J. Polette. Santa Barbara, CA: Libraries Unlimited. Copyright © 2013.

PATRICIA REILLY GIFF:
KEYS

Answers to Circle the Hidden Titles

I could tell you **all about Stacy**, but Rosie's story is more interesting. And it's not a **big whopper**. Rosie's dream was to dance. While we are **B-E-S-T friends**, I don't think Rosie is much of a dancer. To **dance with Rosie**, even though she thinks she has **fancy feet**, is like **Lily's crossing** the playground on stilts. She falls down all the time.

Don't tell the girls in the fourth grade who follow **11-year-old Rosie** around all the time, but she really shouldn't be a **fourth grade celebrity**. The girls think she is famous because she dances at the Catfish Cafe, but she's really a **wild girl**.

Rosie's last name is Tailor, and the **house of Tailors** is a wild place. When you ring the doorbell, instead of a bell, a voice shouts out, "**Watch out! Man eating snake!**" The sign on Rosie's sister **Maggie's door** says **Willow Run**. I asked her what it meant, and Maggie said it was just a pretty name for a pretty room. Her walls are plastered with **pictures of Hollis Woods**, the famous **number one kid** who is a movie star.

One night we went to see Rosie dance at the Catfish Cafe. A **not-so-perfect Rosie** finished her dance, and everyone clapped politely, but someone else stole the show. One storyteller and **eleven** jugglers performed, and we talked about them **all the way home**.

Answers to Mystery Titles

1. Friends
2. Dance
3. Feet
4. Woods
5. Snake
6. *Wild Girl* (J)
7. *All the Way Home* (F)
8. *Eleven* (B)
9. *Flying Feet* (D)
10. *House of Tailors* (I)

Answers to Name That Book!

1. *Wild Girl*
2. *Eleven*
3. *Nory Ryan's Song*
4. *Pictures of Hollis Woods*

JAMIE GILSON (1933–):
THE I HAVE/WHO HAS GAME

Cut the cards apart. Each player gets one card. The player who has the card with the asterisks (****) on it reads the "Who has" question. The player who has the answer card reads the answer and then the next question.

I HAVE: *Do Bananas Chew Gum?* won the Carl Sandburg Award, and *Can't Catch Me* was a Junior Literary Guild selection. ***** **WHO HAS:** How does Jamie Gilson say she learned to write?	**I HAVE:** Jamie read to her 3 children and found that their favorite books were funny books. She decided to write funny books. **WHO HAS:** What was Jamie's first book, and where did the idea come from?
I HAVE: Jamie Gilson says she has always been a reader and that she learned to write by reading. **WHO HAS:** What books did Jamie read as a child?	**I HAVE:** Jamie's first book was *Harvey, the Beer Can King*. She got the idea from a boy down the street who had 1000 beer cans. **WHO HAS:** Why are most of the settings in Jamie's books small towns?
I HAVE: As a child Jamie read any books she could get her hands on. Her favorites were *Homer Price, Caddie Woodlawn,* and *The Wizard of Oz.* **WHO HAS:** What jobs did Jamie have after getting a degree at Northwestern University?	**I HAVE:** Even though Jamie's family moved a lot when she was a child, it was always from one small town to another. **WHO HAS:** What are other experiences Jamie has had that are found in her books?
I HAVE: After college Jamie taught school for one year. She then wrote scripts for educational radio and *Encyclopaedia Britannica* films. **WHO HAS:** What gave Jamie the idea to write for children?	**I HAVE:** She went on an outdoor education trip with fourth graders, watched a pie eating contest, and saw moldy bread in a locker, all incidents that are woven into her funny stories. **WHO HAS:** What awards have Jamie's books won?

JAMIE GILSON:
MYSTERY TITLES

Some words in these titles of books by Jamie Gilson have been replaced with Dewey Decimal numbers. Go to the shelf with the Dewey number. Find the subject of the book(s) with that number. Fill in the missing word in each title. The first person to finish all the titles correctly is the winner!

1. 794.1 _____ _____ _____ _____ _____ I Love It!

2. Do 634 _____ _____ _____ _____ _____ _____ _____ Chew Gum?

3. Double 636.7 _____ _____ _____ Dare

4. 796.334 _____ _____ _____ _____ _____ _____ Circus

5. Hello, My Name Is Scrambled 591.4 _____ _____ _____ _____

Some words in these titles of books by Jamie Gilson have been replaced with synonyms. Put the letter of the actual title after each synonymous title.

6. Do Yellow Tropical Fruits Masticate Chicle? _____	**ACTUAL TITLES**
	A. *4B Goes Wild*
	B. *Do Bananas Chew Gum?*
7. A Twice Canine Challenge _____	C. *Double Dog Dare*
	D. *Hello, My Name Is Scrambled Eggs*
8. Capture Exclamation _____	E. *Soccer Circus*
	F. *Gotcha!*
9. Odorous Back Street Passage Way _____	G. *Chess! I Love It, I Love It, I Love It!*
	H. *Stink Alley*
10. Freight Vehicle plus Locomotive Emergency _____	I *Wagon Train 911*
	J. *Hobie Hanson, You're Weird*

Which titles are available in your library?

The key to Mystery Titles is on page __95__.

From *Gateway to Reading: 250+ Author Games and Booktalks to Motivate Middle Readers* by Nancy J. Polette. Santa Barbara, CA: Libraries Unlimited. Copyright © 2013.

JAMIE GILSON:
NAME THAT BOOK!

What title would YOU give to each of these books by Jamie Gilson?

1) Mr. Star broke the news gently. "Well, 4B," he said, "it appears we're going to do it." It was the talk of last year's fourth, especially the part about the catfish between the principal's sheets. It is the good-behavior reward for this year's fourth grade. It is Outdoor Education: three days at Camp Trotter in Wisconsin. For Hobie Hanson it is bad news. Three days also means two nights—two nights far from home. The thought brings wooly-worms to his stomach and floods his head with what-ifs. As things turn out, however, Outdoor Education lives up to its name, and in ways that neither Hobie nor his friends expect.

Your title _____

2) Patrick is the biggest pest in second grade. He gets away with stuff other kids don't. Today he's out to get Richard. When he does something that makes him look smart or Richard look silly, he flashes a sign: "Gotcha!" Richard has been zapped, powed, and bonked. Even his friends at Table Two are laughing at him, and there's no relief in sight, because Mrs. Zookey wants Richard to be Patrick's partner for an entire field trip. But sticking with Patrick is asking for trouble.

Your title _____

3) Richard's day gets off to a bad start when he has to wear too-big purple corduroy pants to school. Although it's Richard's turn to lead the Pledge of Allegiance and to hand out the mealworms that Mrs. Zookey's class is going to study, those purple pants keep getting in his way. Richard tells his classmates that the pants are a gift from his aunt and uncle, who are space aliens from the purple planet Pluto. After he names one of his mealworms Uncle Ken, the real Uncle Ken shows up in Mrs. Zookey's classroom; knock-knock jokes, too-loud laugh, and all. Richard has some explaining to do, but a plan for Silly Clothes Day and a surprising rapport with his uncle make it a good day after all.

Your title _____

4) Some of the second graders in Mrs. Zookey's class have a new interest: chess. Vice principal Mr. E (and he is something of a mystery) has started a chess club, and Richard, Ben, Ophelia, and Patrick are all members. As usual, Patrick is a nuisance, so Richard isn't at all happy when Mr. E tells him that he and Patrick are alike. It's true that to become better chess players both of them need to learn to concentrate and to plan ahead. And Richard is determined to get better at chess, even if it means putting up with Patrick's shenanigans.

Your title _____

See the author's titles on page __95__.
Which titles are in your library?

JAMIE GILSON:
CIRCLE THE HIDDEN TITLES

When a substitute comes to school, 4B goes wild. It all started with a double dog dare to see who could think of at least thirteen ways to sink a sub. Hobie Hanson was the winner, which isn't surprising since he is pretty strange. His favorite game is "Can't Catch Me, I'm the Gingerbread Man." Kids often took one look at Hobie and said, "Hobie Hanson, you're weird."

Hobie's first idea was to give us different names. "Hello, my name is scrambled eggs," he told the substitute. His next idea was to give nothing but wrong answers. When the sub asked Hobie what kind of sound a rattlesnake makes, he said, "It goes Eeeeeeeeeeeeee!" Then he told her about the time he rescued a little kid from an attacking rattlesnake in the mall and got a citation that reads: "Hobie Hanson, Greatest Hero of the Mall."

By now the substitute was pretty sure that 4B had a plan to sink her. She was positive when Hobie told her that we were reenacting the westward movement, and the unit was called wagon train 911, which meant we had to spend all our time outside taking care of the wounded. What Hobie really wanted to do, of course, was play soccer circus.

It turned out that the substitute was no dummy. She had a list of our real names and the teacher's plan book, which said nothing about wagon trains. She followed the regular schedule and 30 minutes before the bell, "Gotcha!" she said, and gave us a one-page writing assignment. We could choose to write on the topics of Do bananas chew gum in Stink Alley? or Chess! I Love It, I Love It, I Love It! For once, we were all as quiet as a bug in a rug.

From *Gateway to Reading: 250+ Author Games and Booktalks to Motivate Middle Readers*
by Nancy J. Polette. Santa Barbara, CA: Libraries Unlimited. Copyright © 2013.

JAMIE GILSON:
KEYS

Answers to Circle the Hidden Titles

When a substitute comes to school, **4B goes wild**. It all started with a **double dog dare** to see who could think of at least **thirteen ways to sink a sub**. Hobie Hanson was the winner, which isn't surprising since he is pretty strange. His favorite game is **"Can't Catch Me, I'm the Gingerbread Man."** Kids often took one look at Hobie and said, **"Hobie Hanson, you're weird."**

Hobie's first idea was to give us different names. **"Hello, my name is scrambled eggs,"** he told the substitute. His next idea was to give nothing but wrong answers. When the sub asked Hobie what kind of sound a rattlesnake makes, he said, **"It goes Eeeeeeeeeeeeee!"** Then he told her about the time he rescued a little kid from an attacking rattlesnake in the mall and got a citation that reads: **"Hobie Hanson, Greatest Hero of the Mall."**

By now the substitute was pretty sure that 4B had a plan to sink her. She was positive when Hobie told her that we were reenacting the westward movement, and the unit was called **wagon train 911**, which meant we had to spend all our time outside taking care of the wounded. What Hobie really wanted to do, of course, was play **soccer circus**.

It turned out that the substitute was no dummy. She had a list of our real names and the teacher's plan book, which said nothing about wagon trains. She followed the regular schedule and 30 minutes before the bell, **"Gotcha!"** she said, and gave us a one-page writing assignment. We could choose to write on the topics of **Do bananas chew gum** in **Stink Alley**? or **Chess! I Love It, I Love It, I Love It!** For once, we were all as quiet as a **bug in a rug**.

Answers to Mystery Titles

1. Chess
2. Bananas
3. Dog
4. Soccer
5. Eggs
6. *Do Bananas Chew Gum?* (B)
7. *Double Dog Dare* (C)
8. *Gotcha!* (F)
9. *Stink Alley* (H)
10. *Wagon Train 911* (I)

Answers to Name That Book!

1. *4B Goes Wild*
2. *Gotcha!*
3. *Bug in a Rug*
4. *Chess! I Love It, I Love It, I Love It!*

MARY DOWNING HAHN (1937–):
THE I HAVE/WHO HAS GAME

Cut the cards apart. Each player gets one card. The player who has the card with the asterisks (****) on it reads the "Who has" question. The player who has the answer card reads the answer and then the next question.

I HAVE: *Daphne's Book* received the William Allen White Award. *Wait Till Helen Comes* received the Dorothy Canfield Fisher Award. **** **WHO HAS:** What behavior often got Mary in trouble at school?	**I HAVE:** After reading Nancy Drew and the Hardy Boys series, Mary and Ann changed from playing orphan games to playing detective games. **WHO HAS:** What job did Mary have after graduating from college with a master's degree in English?
I HAVE: Mary daydreamed at school and read library books instead of doing her homework. **WHO HAS:** What was different about the stories Mary created as a child?	**I HAVE:** After college Mary worked as a children's librarian in a Maryland library. **WHO HAS:** How old was Mary when she started writing for children?
I HAVE: Mary's stories had no words. They were told in a series of pictures. **WHO HAS:** What was important about the orphan game Mary played with her friend, Ann?	**I HAVE:** Mary was 40 years old when she started writing for children and wishes she had started much sooner. **WHO HAS:** What kinds of experiences does Mary create for the young characters in her books?
I HAVE: Because Mary's mother was a teacher, she was expected to follow many rules. In creating adventures for orphans, no rules had to be followed. **WHO HAS:** How did the Nancy Drew and the Hardy Boys series influence Mary and her friend Ann?	**I HAVE:** The characters in her books have the same kinds of experiences that Mary had as a child. **WHO HAS:** What awards have Mary Downing Hahn's books received?

MARY DOWNING HAHN:
MYSTERY TITLES

Some words in these titles of books by Mary Downing Hahn have been replaced with Dewey Decimal numbers. Go to the shelf with the Dewey number. Find the subject of the book(s) with that number. Fill in the missing word in each title. The first person to finish all the titles correctly is the winner!

1. Anna on the 630.1 _____ _____ _____ _____

2. Daphne's 070.5 _____ _____ _____ _____

3. The Doll in the 635 _____ _____ _____ _____ _____ _____

4. Following My Own 612 _____ _____ _____ _____ steps

5. Look for Me by 523.3 _____ _____ _____ _____ light

Some words in these titles of books by Mary Downing Hahn have been replaced with synonyms. Put the letter of the actual title after each synonymous title.

6. Deceased Male Native American Tributary _____

7. A Toy Baby in the Flower Plot _____

8. Mannerly Male Bandit Plus Self _____

9. Vows to the Deceased _____

10. Walking on the Sidewalk's Split Seam _____

ACTUAL TITLES
A. *All the Lovely Bad Ones*
B. *Time for Andrew*
C. *Dead Man in Indian Creek*
D. *The Gentleman Outlaw and Me*
E. *The Doll in the Garden*
F. *Daphne's Book*
G. *Following My Own Footsteps*
H. *Promises to the Dead*
I. *Stepping on the Cracks*
J. *The Spanish Kidnapping Disaster*

Which titles are available in your library?

The key to Mystery Titles is on page __101__.

MARY DOWNING HAHN:
NAME THAT BOOK!

What title would YOU give to each of these books by Mary Downing Hahn?

1) Daphne is the weird girl in Jessica's class, the one no one wants to talk to or even be seen with. But when the girls are assigned to be partners in the Write-a-Book contest at school, they find they have a lot in common and start spending time together outside of the project. As their friendship deepens, Jessica stumbles on a terrible secret about Daphne's life. Jessica promises not to tell anyone. But sometimes it takes a true friend to break a promise instead of keeping one.

Your title _____

2) When 12-year-old Florence boards the crowded horse-drawn coach in London, she looks forward to a new life with her great uncle and aunt at Crutchfield Hall, an old manor house in the English countryside. Anything will be better, she thinks, than the grim London orphanage where she has lived since her parents' death. But Florence doesn't expect the ghost of her cousin Sophia, who haunts the cavernous rooms and dimly lit hallways of Crutchfield and concocts a plan to use Florence to help her achieve her murderous goals. Will Florence be able to convince the others in the household of the imminent danger and stop Sophia before it's too late?

Your title _____

3) Twelve-year-old Molly and her ten-year-old brother, Michael, have never liked their younger stepsister, Heather. Ever since their parents got married, she has made Molly and Michael's lives miserable. Now their parents have moved them all to the country to live in a house that used to be a church, with a cemetery in the backyard. And as if that's not bad enough, Heather starts talking to a ghost named Helen and warning Molly and Michael that Helen is coming for them. Molly feels certain Heather is in some kind of danger, but every time she tries to help, Heather twists things around to get her into trouble. It seems as if things can't get any worse. But they do—when Helen comes.

Your title _____

4) When 16-year-old Cynda goes to stay with her father and his second wife, Susan, at their remote bed-and-breakfast inn in Maine, everything starts off well despite legends about ghosts and a murder at the inn. But Cynda feels like a visitor in Dad's new life, an outsider. Then intense, handsome stranger Vincent Morthanos arrives at the inn and seems to return Cynda's interest. At first she is blind to the subtle, insistent signs that Vincent is not what he seems—that he is, in fact, a vampire. Can Cynda free herself and her family from Vincent's power before it's too late?

Your title _____

See the author's titles on page __101__.
Which titles are available in your library?

From *Gateway to Reading: 250+ Author Games and Booktalks to Motivate Middle Readers* by Nancy J. Polette. Santa Barbara, CA: Libraries Unlimited. Copyright © 2013.

My name is Eli, and I want to tell you about the time a gentleman outlaw and me found a dead man in Indian Creek. Right then, knowing we hadn't done it, we made promises to the dead to skedaddle as fast as we could.

My outlaw career began when I got tired of taking orders from my sister, Anna. On the farm there's always plenty of work. Anna all year round keeps telling me what to do. My other sister, Daphne, never does her share. I was always finding Daphne's book and doll in the garden where she had been playing. And the twins were as lazy as ever. Gordy was always following my own footsteps, but wouldn't do a lick of work. I didn't have time for Andrew either. He was always wanting me to fix something. That left wanting to hide out like the ghost of Crutchfield Hall, so I left the old Willis place where we lived to make my fortune. That was why I took to crime.

The first thing the gentleman outlaw and me did was to kidnap a rich Spanish girl named Witch. Being a witch catcher was no easy job. We sent a note asking for $5,000 and told them to go to their ranch and wait till Helen comes. It turned out to be a Spanish kidnapping disaster, since her folks only pretended to be rich. They wanted us to keep her.

Since folks will think we had something to do with the dead man in Indian Creek, I think I'll give up a life of stepping on the cracks. As soon as it gets dark I'm going back to the farm. Look for me by moonlight and I'll be there, having given up the outlaw life.

From *Gateway to Reading: 250+ Author Games and Booktalks to Motivate Middle Readers* by Nancy J. Polette. Santa Barbara, CA: Libraries Unlimited. Copyright © 2013.

MARY DOWNING HAHN:
KEYS

Answers to Circle the Hidden Titles

My name is Eli, and I want to tell you about the time a **gentleman outlaw and me** found a **dead man in Indian Creek**. Right then, knowing we hadn't done it, we made **promises to the dead** to skedaddle as fast as we could.

My outlaw career began when I got tired of taking orders from my sister, **Anna. On the farm** there's always plenty of work. **Anna all year round** keeps telling me what to do. My other sister, Daphne, never does her share. I was always finding **Daphne's book** and **doll in the garden** where she had been playing. And the twins were as lazy **as ever. Gordy** was always **following my own footsteps**, but wouldn't do a lick of work. I didn't have **time for Andrew** either. He was always wanting me to fix something. That left wanting to hide out like **the ghost of Crutchfield Hall**, so I left **the old Willis place** where we lived to make my fortune. That was why I took to crime.

The first thing **the gentleman outlaw and me** did was to kidnap a rich Spanish girl named Witch. Being a **witch catcher** was no easy job. We sent a note asking for $5,000 and told them to go to their ranch and **wait till Helen comes**. It turned out to be a **Spanish kidnapping disaster**, since her folks only pretended to be rich. They wanted us to keep her.

Since folks will think we had something to do with the **dead man in Indian Creek**, I think I'll give up a life of **stepping on the cracks**. As soon as it gets dark I'm going back to the farm. **Look for me by moonlight** and I'll be there, having given up the outlaw life.

Answers to Mystery Titles

1. Farm
2. Book
3. Garden
4. Foot (steps)
5. Moon (light)
6. *Dead Man in Indian Creek* (C)
7. *The Doll in the Garden* (E)
8. *The Gentleman Outlaw and Me* (D)
9. *Promises to the Dead* (H)
10. *Stepping on the Cracks* (I)

Answers to Name That Book!

1. *Daphne's Book*
2. *The Ghost of Crutchfield Hall*
3. *Wait Till Helen Comes*
4. *Look for Me by Moonlight*

KAREN HESSE (1952–):
THE I HAVE/WHO HAS GAME

Cut the cards apart. Each player gets one card. The player who has the card with the asterisks (****) on it reads the "Who has" question. The player who has the answer card reads the answer and then the next question.

I HAVE:	Karen Hesse's books have received so many awards, it is hard to count them all. *Out of the Dust* received the Newbery Medal. ********		**I HAVE:**	Karen and her husband traveled across America for 6 months, camping in a tent.
WHO HAS:	Did Karen's childhood offer any clues that she might become a writer as an adult?		**WHO HAS:**	When did Karen decide she wanted to write for children?
I HAVE:	Karen was a shy child who spent many hours at home writing poetry.		**I HAVE:**	In reading aloud to her own 2 children, Karen discovered the world of children's books and knew this was what she wanted to write.
WHO HAS:	What else did Karen do as a child that helped her become a famous writer?		**WHO HAS:**	What reception did Karen's first book, *Wish on a Unicorn*, get?
I HAVE:	Karen says that as a child she was an observer rather than an active participant. The ability to closely observe is essential for any writer.		**I HAVE:**	Karen's first book, *Wish on a Unicorn*, was given distinctive honors by the *Hungry Mind Review*.
WHO HAS:	Where did Karen grow up and go to college?		**WHO HAS:**	What activities is Karen involved in when she is not writing?
I HAVE:	Karen grew up in Maryland and graduated from the University of Maryland, where she studied theater and English.		**I HAVE:**	Karen has served on the boards of school and public libraries and The Society of Children's Book Writers and Illustrators.
WHO HAS:	What six month journey did Karen and her husband take in 1975?		**WHO HAS:**	What other awards have Karen Hesse's books won?

KAREN HESSE:
MYSTERY TITLES

Some words in these titles of books by Karen Hesse have been replaced with Dewey Decimal numbers. Go to the shelf with the Dewey number. Find the subject of the book(s) with that number. Fill in the missing word in each title. The first person to finish all the titles correctly is the winner!

1. Lester's 636.7 _____ _____ _____

2. 816 _____ _____ _____ _____ _____ _____ _____ from Rifka

3. Light in the 551.55 _____ _____ _____ _____ _____

4. 790 _____ _____ _____ _____ _____ of Dolphins

5. Time of 235 _____ _____ _____ _____ _____ _____

Some words in these titles of books by Karen Hesse have been replaced with synonyms. Put the letter of the actual title after each synonymous title.

6. Animal of the Matren Family _____

7. Opus of Porpoises _____

8. Emerging from the Earth's Powder _____

9. Period of Celestial Beings _____

10. Beam in the Tempest _____

ACTUAL TITLES
A. *Aleutian Sparrow*
B. *Lester's Dog*
C. *Letters from Rifka*
D. *A Light in the Storm*
E. *The Music of Dolphins*
F. *Out of the Dust*
G. *Phoenix Rising*
H. *Sable*
I. *Stowaway*
J. *A Time of Angels*

Which titles are available in your library?

The key to Mystery Titles is on page __107__.

KAREN HESSE:
NAME THAT BOOK!

What title would YOU give to each of these books by Karen Hesse?

1) Amelia's own world is suddenly coming apart as the war escalates, putting her dear friend Daniel, a Union soldier, in great danger. Her Uncle Edward's store is being boycotted and vandalized by secessionist sympathizers because he is a known abolitionist. Her mother's condition deteriorates, forcing her to move to her grandmother's house on the mainland. But before the year is through, Amelia will make a powerful discovery about her own views on slavery, as she comes to the difficult realization that certain compromises can't be made, even at the risk of losing her mother's approval.

Your title _____

2) Rifka knows nothing about America when she flees from Russia with her family in 1919. But she dreams she will at last be safe in the new country from the Russian soldiers and their harsh treatment of the Jews. Throughout her journey, Rifka carries with her a cherished volume of poetry by Alexander Pushkin. In it she records her observations and experiences in the form of letters to her beloved cousin, whom she has left behind. Stronghearted and determined, Rifka must endure a great deal: humiliating examinations by doctors and soldiers, deadly typhus, separation from all she has ever known and loved, murderous storms at sea—and as if this is not enough, the loss of her glorious golden hair. And even if she does make it to America, she's not sure America will have her.

Your title _____

3) On the night of the accident at the Cookshire nuclear power plant Nyle's modest world fills with protective masks, evacuations, contaminated food, disruptions, and mistrust. Things become even more complicated when Ezra Trent and his mother, refugees from the heart of the accident, take temporary shelter in the back bedroom of Nyle's house. The back bedroom is the dying room. It took her mother when Nyle was six; it stole away her grandfather just 2 years ago. Now Ezra is back there, and Nyle doesn't want to open her heart to him. Too many times she's let people in, only to have them desert her. If she lets herself care for Ezra, she knows he'll end up leaving her too.

Your title _____

4) Mags has a lot to wish for: a nice house with a mama who isn't tired out from work; a normal little sister; a brother who doesn't mooch for food; and once in a while, she'd like some new clothes for school. When her sister Hannie finds a stuffed unicorn, Mags's wishes start to come true. She knows the unicorn can't really be magic, but she won't let anything ruin her newfound luck—even if it means telling her own sister to believe something that can't possibly be true.

Your title _____

See the author's titles on page ___107___.
Which titles can you find in your library?

KAREN HESSE:
CIRCLE THE HIDDEN TITLES

Come with me as a stowaway on a magical journey. Our destination is spelled out in big letters from Rifka, our guide: DREAMS!

You may think you are walking on a country road, but close your eyes and see that magical bird, the Phoenix, rising from out of the dust. Witness the bird that can never be destroyed, unlike the Aleutian sparrow, but rises from the ashes to fly and sing again.

Walk by the creek and close your eyes. Over the bark of your neighbor Lester's dog, you hear strange and beautiful sounds. It is the music of dolphins calling to you from the faraway sea. Dream on and feel yourself sailing away to the music.

If a storm interrupts your dream, follow the light in the storm and you will be dreaming again.

It is a time of angels with sable wings who swoop down and lift you to another place. That place is in your mind where anything is possible. It is called IMAGINATION. Use it well as every writer does!

KAREN HESSE:
KEYS

Answers to Circle the Hidden Titles

Come with me as a **stowaway** on a magical journey. Our destination is spelled out in big **letters from Rifka**, our guide: DREAMS!

You may think you are walking on a country road, but close your eyes and see that magical bird, the **Phoenix, rising** from **out of the dust. Witness** the bird that can never be destroyed, unlike the **Aleutian sparrow**, but rises from the ashes to fly and sing again.

Walk by the creek and close your eyes. Over the bark of your neighbor **Lester's dog,** you hear strange and beautiful sounds. It is **the music of dolphins** calling to you from the faraway sea. Dream on and feel yourself sailing away to the music.

If a storm interrupts your dream, follow the **light in the storm** and you will be dreaming again.

It is **a time of angels** with **sable** wings who swoop down and lift you to another place. That place is in your mind where anything is possible. It is called IMAGINATION. Use it well as every writer does!

Answers to Mystery Titles

1. Dog
2. Letters
3. Storm
4. Music
5. Angels
6. *Sable* (H)
7. *The Music of Dolphins* (E)
8. *Out of the Dust* (F)
9. *A Time of Angels* (J)
10. *A Light in the Storm* (D)

Answers to Name That Book!

1. *A Light in the Storm*
2. *Letters from Rifka*
3. *Phoenix Rising*
4. *Wish on a Unicorn*

JOHANNA HURWITZ (1937–):
THE I HAVE/WHO HAS GAME

Cut the cards apart. Each player gets one card. The player who has the card with the asterisks (****) on it reads the "Who has" question. The player who has the answer card reads the answer and then the next question.

I HAVE:	*Rip-Roaring Russell* was named a notable book by the American Library Association. *Aldo Applesauce* was a Children's Choice Book chosen by the IRA and Children's Book Council. ********	**I HAVE:**	After graduating from Columbia University, Johanna became a children's librarian at the New York Public Library.
WHO HAS:	Who introduced Johanna to the world of books?	**WHO HAS:**	What was the setting of Johanna's first books that featured Nora, Teddy, and Russell?
I HAVE:	Johanna's parents lined their New York apartment with bookshelves and her father took her with him on his many bookstore and library trips.	**I HAVE:**	The setting of Johanna's first books was the apartment house where she lived with her husband and 2 children.
WHO HAS:	When did Johanna start writing?	**WHO HAS:**	How much money did Johanna receive for her first published work?
I HAVE:	As a child she read her poems and stories to members of her reading club, The Melrose Bookworms.	**I HAVE:**	When she was 12, Johanna received 50 cents for a poem to be published in a children's magazine.
WHO HAS:	Where did Johanna as a child get information about the faraway places she wanted to write about?	**WHO HAS:**	What is the subject matter of all Johanna's books?
I HAVE:	To learn about faraway places, Johanna sent postcards to each state and received colorful brochures in return.	**I HAVE:**	Johanna writes about the everyday life experiences of herself and her family.
WHO HAS:	What job did Johanna have after graduating from Columbia University?	**WHO HAS:**	What honors have Johanna Hurwitz's books received?

JOHANNA HURWITZ:
MYSTERY TITLES

Some words in these titles of books by Johanna Hurwitz have been replaced with Dewey Decimal numbers. Go to the shelf with the Dewey number. Find the subject of the book(s) with that number. Fill in the missing word in each title. The first person to finish all the titles correctly is the winner!

1. Aldo 637 _____ _____ _____ _____ _____ _____ _____ _____

2. 796.357 _____ _____ _____ _____ _____ _____ _____ _____ Fever

3. Class 791.3 _____ _____ _____ _____ _____

4. 599.736 _____ _____ _____ _____ _____ in the Family

5. New 391.4 _____ _____ _____ _____ _____ for Silvia

Some words in these titles of books by Johanna Hurwitz have been replaced with synonyms. Put the letter of the actual title after each synonymous title.

6. Descending and Ascending Autumn _____

7. National Sport Temperature _____

8. Academic Campus Finished _____

9. Instructor's Favorite _____

10. Grade Level Group Cut-up _____

ACTUAL TITLES
A. *Aldo Ice Cream*
B. *The Down and Up Fall*
C. *Class President*
D. *School Spirit*
E. *Baseball Fever*
F. *School's Out*
G. *Teacher's Pet*
H. *Mighty Monty*
I. *Class Clown*

Which titles are available in your library?

The key to Mystery Titles is on page __113__.

From *Gateway to Reading: 250+ Author Games and Booktalks to Motivate Middle Readers* by Nancy J. Polette. Santa Barbara, CA: Libraries Unlimited. Copyright © 2013.

JOHANNA HURWITZ:
NAME THAT BOOK!

What title would YOU give to each of these books by Johanna Hurwitz?

1) Yard sales, ice-skating, and surprise parties are just a few of the things that make fourth grade fun. But Julio and his friends know it's time to get serious when the class begins preparing for the big statewide test at the end of the year. Just thinking about it is enough to give anybody a stomachache! Julio and his best friend, Lucas, are going to try every superstition in the book to make sure they pass. They'll wear their underwear inside out, use brand-new pencils, and even—gulp—study. But when test day comes, Julio finds out there are some surprises no one can prepare for!

Your title _____

2) At the animal shelter, Curtis falls in love with Sammy, a friendly puppy with curly black fur, floppy ears, a wagging tail, and perfect white teeth. He's the best dog in the whole world. At home things are different—Sammy steals food and chews sneakers and toys—but Curtis loves him anyway. Then Sammy bites Curtis's mom, and Curtis has to face the fact that Sammy's not perfect after all. Will Curtis have to give Sammy up? Or will he do whatever it takes to keep his dog?

Your title _____

3) Eight-year-old David Bernstein discovers life is much more exciting when he calls himself Ali Baba Bernstein. Only Ali Baba would have dared to grab the class snail and escape to the boys' room for his own magic experiment. David would never have invited every David Bernstein in the phone book to his birthday party—or found himself hailed as a great detective—or discovered adventures and misadventures everywhere he went.

Your title _____

4) The fifth-grade class election is shaping up as a close contest between class clown Lucas Cott and one time teacher's pet Cricket Kaufman. It's just possible that the student with the greatest leadership ability is Julio Sanchez, but Julio's too busy running Lucas's campaign to notice. Or is he? And how can Julio throw his hat into the ring without betraying his best friend?

Your title _____

See the author's titles on page __113__.
Which titles can you find in your library?

JOHANNA HURWITZ:
CIRCLE THE HIDDEN TITLES

Meet the girl who has really tough luck. Karen has a brother, Ozzie. On his own he is always getting into trouble. With his friends, Peewee and Plush, he gets in more trouble. According to Peewee's tale, Ozzie just doesn't use good sense. As if that isn't bad enough, there is also a llama in the family. Can you imagine cleaning up after a llama?

Not only did Karen have a down and up fall, but she had cold and hot winter and an up and down spring. Karen wanted to run for class president, but Russell and the teacher's pet, Elisa, wanted the same job. Russell made a campaign poster that read: "Russell sprouts are good for you." Elisa's poster read "Ever Clever Elisa." Karen couldn't think of anything to put on a poster. Even Stephen, her friend, had no ideas. Then DeDe takes charge. She brings Karen a big poster that says "Karen Is Caring!" What a fourth-grade fuss that caused!

Karen thought sure she would win, but she forgot to make room for Elisa, who brought candy bars for everyone. Monty put up more posters than anyone, saying "Amazing Monty" and "Mighty Monty" for president. Elisa won, and Russell came in second, because rip-roaring Russell was the class clown.

When baseball fever took over in the spring, Karen struck out at bat every time.

Everyone said, "Tough luck, Karen."

But Karen was a caring person. When Aldo made a home run, she made much ado about Aldo and bought Aldo ice cream. She did the same when Ali Baba made a homer, shouting, "Hurray for Ali Baba Bernstein!" When Silvia's folks bought new shoes for Silvia, Karen was the first to admire them.

Karen's tough luck changed after spring break, She was voted the student with the best school spirit. School's out now so maybe this is the beginning of good luck for Karen.

JOHANNA HURWITZ:
KEYS

Answers for Circle the Hidden Titles

Meet the girl who has really **tough luck**. **Karen** has a brother, **Ozzie**. **On his own** he is always getting into trouble. With his friends, **Pee Wee and Plush**, he gets in more trouble. According to **Pee Wee's tale**, Ozzie just doesn't use good sense. As if that isn't bad enough, there is also **a llama in the family**. Can you imagine cleaning up after a llama?

Not only did Karen have a **down and up fall**, but she had **cold and hot winter** and an **up and down spring**. Karen wanted to run for **class president**, but Russell and the **teacher's pet**, Elisa, wanted the same job. Russell made a campaign poster that read: "**Russell sprouts** are good for you." Elisa's poster read "**Ever Clever Elisa**." Karen couldn't think of anything to put on a poster. **Even Stephen**, her friend, had no ideas. Then **DeDe takes charge**. She brings Karen a big poster that says "Karen Is Caring!" What a **fourth grade fuss** that caused!

Karen thought sure she would win, but she forgot to **make room for Elisa**, who brought candy bars for everyone. Monty put up more posters than anyone, saying "**Amazing Monty**" and "**Mighty Monty**" for president. Elisa won, and Russell came in second, because **rip-roaring Russell** was the **class clown**.

When baseball fever took over in the spring, Karen struck out at bat every time.

Everyone said, "**Tough luck, Karen**."

But Karen was a caring person. When Aldo made a home run, she made **much ado about Aldo** and bought **Aldo ice cream**. She did the same when Ali Baba made a homer, shouting, "**Hurray for Ali Baba Bernstein!**" When Silvia's folks bought **new shoes for Silvia**, Karen was the first to admire them.

Karen's tough luck changed after spring break. She was voted the student with the best **school spirit**. **School's out** now so maybe this is the beginning of good luck for Karen.

Answers for Mystery Titles

1. Ice Cream
2. Baseball
3. Clown
4. Llama
5. Shoes
6. *The Down and Up Fall* (B)
7. *Baseball Fever* (E)
8. *School's Out* (F)
9. *Teacher's Pet* (G)
10. *Class Clown* (I)

Answers for Name That Book!

1. *Fourth Grade Fuss*
2. *One Small Dog*
3. *The Adventures of Ali Baba Bernstein*
4. *Class President*

PEG KEHRET (1936–):
THE I HAVE/WHO HAS GAME

Cut the cards apart. Each player gets one card. The player who has the card with the asterisks (****) on it reads the "Who has" question. The player who has the answer card reads the answer and then the next question.

I HAVE: Peg Kehret's books have won the Student Choice Awards in 9 states. **** **WHO HAS:** When did Peg Kehret begin writing for publication?	**I HAVE:** Peg's parents were told she would never walk. **WHO HAS:** How did Peg fool the doctors?
I HAVE: Peg Kehret published her own newspaper at the age of 10, called the *Dog Newspaper.* **WHO HAS:** Why was her newspaper not successful?	**I HAVE:** Peg learned to walk, wrote plays and newspaper articles, attended the University of Minnesota, and married Karl Kehret. **WHO HAS:** When did Peg begin writing for publication as an adult?
I HAVE: In her newspaper Peg wrote too much about her own dog, and her friends got tired of reading about her pet. **WHO HAS:** What happened to Peg in the seventh grade?	**I HAVE:** Peg wrote magazine pieces and a book of monologues for student actors. **WHO HAS:** What inspired Peg to write mysteries for children?
I HAVE: Peg came down with polio in the seventh grade and spent 9 months in hospitals. **WHO HAS:** What were Peg's parents told about her medical condition?	**I HAVE:** Her book of monologues was so successful that she knew she had finally found her voice as a children's writer. **WHO HAS:** What awards have Peg Kehret's books received?

PEG KEHRET:
MYSTERY TITLES

Some words in these titles of books by Peg Kehret have been replaced with Dewey Decimal numbers. Go to the shelf with the Dewey number. Find the subject of the book(s) with that number. Fill in the missing word in each title. The first person to finish all the titles correctly is the winner!

1. 551.22 _____ _____ _____ _____ _____ _____ _____ _____ _____ _____ Terror

2. 551.48 _____ _____ _____ _____ _____ Disaster

3. Nightmare 551.4 _____ _____ _____ _____ _____ _____ _____ _____

4. 327.12 _____ _____ _____ Cat

5. 551.21 _____ _____ _____ _____ _____ _____ _____ Disaster

Some words in these titles of books by Peg Kehret have been replaced with synonyms. Put the letter of the actual title after each synonymous title.

6. Snatched Away _____

7. Unknown Person Adjacent to an Aperture _____

8. Escaped Duplicate _____

9. Undercover Feline _____

10. Tiny Movement of the Feet _____

ACTUAL TITLES
A. *Ghost Dog Secrets*
B. *Abduction*
C. *The Stranger Next Door*
D. *Don't Tell Anyone*
E. *Runaway Twin*
F. *Flood Disaster*
G. *Spy Cat*
H. *Small Steps*
I. *Nightmare Mountain*

Which titles are available in your library?

The key to Mystery Titles is on page __119__.

From *Gateway to Reading: 250+ Author Games and Booktalks to Motivate Middle Readers* by Nancy J. Polette. Santa Barbara, CA: Libraries Unlimited. Copyright © 2013.

PEG KEHRET:
NAME THAT BOOK!

What title would YOU give to each of these books by Peg Kehret?

1) Amy learned a lot in her babysitting course, but not what to do if two thugs show up, intent on kidnapping. Armed with misinformation and a weapon, the men take Amy and little Kendra to a remote cabin in the woods. There they make videos of the girls and mail them to Kendra's wealthy parents in an effort to get ransom money. After several of her escape attempts fail, Amy is forced to make one last, desperate move.

Your title _____

2) A unique story of separated twins and the unexpected consequences of their reunion. Sunny Skyland longs to be reunited with her twin sister, Starr. With only an old photograph—taken a few days before the girls were separated at age 3—to guide her, Sunny begins the cross-country journey that she has dreamed of during her 10 years in various foster homes. Sunny manages to locate her twin, only to be faced with a whole new challenge.

Your title _____

3) As soon as Molly arrives at her aunt and uncle's ranch in rural Washington, things start to go very wrong. Her cousin hates her on sight. Her aunt falls into a mysterious coma. Then, left alone on the huge property, Molly and her cousin discover an intruder lurking in the barn! Armed and desperate, he drags them to the top of a nearby mountain and triggers an avalanche with a gunshot. Can they make it down the mountain alive?

Your title _____

4) Life has been tough for Spencer since his dad left. His mom complains constantly, they never seem to have enough money, and they're always having to move. He knows his father works for the Giants baseball team and lives somewhere in San Francisco—and Spencer's sure that if he can somehow get there, his dad will take him in. But California is a long, dangerous way from Seattle if you only have $24, you're 12, and you're alone.

Your title _____

See the author's titles on page ___119___.
Which titles are in your library?

PEG KEHRET:
CIRCLE THE HIDDEN TITLES

Did you ever wonder what it would be like to fly over a volcano? Disaster can strike anywhere. When a volcano erupts, it can be a nightmare. Mountain lava explodes and burns everything in its path. It is nature's abduction of the land, and there is no place for even a runaway twin to hide.

While the heat of a volcano is dangerous, don't ever get caught in a blizzard. Disaster vehicles are everywhere digging people out of snowdrifts. People should know that small steps are best in a snow storm. A dog trapped in the snow becomes a ghost dog. Secrets are revealed when the snow melts.

Then there was the time of the terrible earthquake. Terror was felt by everyone as homes for both the poorest and the richest kids in town collapsed. The rescue workers are still searching for Candlestick Park, which disappeared when the earth opened up. Along the coast people had trouble escaping the giant wave caused by the earthquake.

Finally, you don't want to get caught in a flood. Disaster boats may never find you. You may think I am an expert on disasters, but I'm not who you think I am.

I really wanted to be a fiction writer. I wrote great stories like the *Ghost's Grave, Spy Cat, Saving Lilly*, and *The Stranger Next Door*, but no one would buy them. Now I am just a nonfiction writer trying to make a living. Don't tell anyone, but my brother made me do it.

From *Gateway to Reading: 250+ Author Games and Booktalks to Motivate Middle Readers* by Nancy J. Polette. Santa Barbara, CA: Libraries Unlimited. Copyright © 2013.

PEG KEHRET:
KEYS

Answers to Circle the Hidden Titles

Did you ever wonder what it would be like to fly over a **volcano**? **Disaster** can strike anywhere. When a volcano erupts, it can be a **nightmare**. **Mountain** lava explodes and burns everything in its path. It is nature's **abduction** of the land, and there is no place for even a **runaway twin** to hide.

While the heat of a volcano is dangerous, don't ever get caught in a **blizzard**. **Disaster** vehicles are everywhere digging people out of snowdrifts. People should know that **small steps** are best in a snow storm. A dog **trapped** in the snow becomes a **ghost dog**. **Secrets** are revealed when the snow melts.

Then there was the time of the terrible **earthquake**. **Terror** was felt by everyone as homes for both the poorest and **the richest kids in town** collapsed. The rescue workers are still **searching for Candlestick Park**, which disappeared when the earth opened up. Along the coast people had trouble **escaping the giant wave** caused by the earthquake.

Finally, you don't want to get caught in a **flood**. **Disaster** boats may never find you. You may think I am an expert on disasters, but **I'm not who you think I am**.

I really wanted to be a fiction writer. I wrote great stories like the *Ghost's Grave*, *Spy Cat*, *Saving Lilly*, and *The Stranger Next Door*, but no one would buy them. Now I am just a nonfiction writer trying to make a living. **Don't tell anyone**, but **my brother made me do it**.

Answers to Mystery Titles

1. Earthquake
2. Flood
3. Mountain
4. Spy
5. Volcano
6. *Abduction* (B)
7. *The Stranger Next Door* (C)
8. *Runaway Twin* (E)
9. *Spy Cat* (G)
10. *Small Steps* (H)

Answers to Name That Book!

1. *Stolen Children*
2. *Runaway Twin*
3. *Nightmare Mountain*
4. *Searching for Candlestick Park*

KATHRYN LASKY (1944–):
THE I HAVE/WHO HAS GAME

Cut the cards apart. Each player gets one card. The player who has the card with the asterisks (****) on it reads the "Who has" question. The player who has the answer card reads the answer and then the next question.

I HAVE:	Among the many honors received for Kathryn Lasky's books are the Newbery Honor for *Sugaring Time* and the Boston-Globe Horn Book Award for *The Weaver's Gift*. ****	**I HAVE:**	Kathryn's husband, a photographer and filmmaker, illustrated several of her books.
WHO HAS:	What inspiration did Kathryn have for writing stories as a child?	**WHO HAS:**	What does Kathryn like about being a writer?
I HAVE:	Kathryn had no inspiration for writing stories as a child. She attended an all-girls' school where only report writing was taught.	**I HAVE:**	Kathryn likes a writer's life because she can set her own working time and be her own boss.
WHO HAS:	How did Kathryn react to this overdose of report writing she got at school?	**WHO HAS:**	Do any of Kathryn's stories reflect her own life?
I HAVE:	As a child Kathryn considered herself to be a fine storyteller and wrote stories when she was not in school.	**I HAVE:**	Kathryn helped her son, Max, write a book about the arrival of his baby sister.
WHO HAS:	With whom did Kathryn share her original stories?	**WHO HAS:**	Does Kathryn write only for children?
I HAVE:	Kathryn did not share her stories with anyone, not her parents and later not her husband.	**I HAVE:**	Kathryn writes for both children and adults. For her adult books she uses the name Kathryn Lasky Knight.
WHO HAS:	When did Kathryn's husband get involved with her books?	**WHO HAS:**	What honors have Kathryn Lasky's books received?

KATHRYN LASKY:
MYSTERY TITLES

Some words in these titles of books by Kathryn Lasky have been replaced with Dewey Decimal numbers. Go to the shelf with the Dewey number. Find the subject of the book(s) with that number. Fill in the missing word in each title. The first person to finish all the titles correctly is the winner!

1. Daughters of the 551.26 _____ _____ _____

2. 135 _____ _____ _____ _____ _____ _____ in the Golden Country

3. Mary, Queen of 941.1 _____ _____ _____ _____ _____

4. Shadow 599.77 _____ _____ _____ _____

5. Shadows in the 551.48 _____ _____ _____ _____ _____

Some words in these titles of books by Kathryn Lasky have been replaced with synonyms. Put the letter of the actual title after each synonymous title.

6. Apprehend _____

7. Heat Remainder _____

8. U.S. March 21st _____

9. Final Arrival at One's Abode _____

10. Trip After Dark _____

ACTUAL TITLES
A. *The Burning*
B. *Vision of Beauty*
C. *The Capture*
D. *Journey to the New World*
E. *Ashes*
F. *American Spring*
G. *The Outcast*
H. *Home at Last*
I. *True North*
J. *The Night Journey*

Which titles are available in your library?

The key to Mystery Titles is on page ___125___.

From *Gateway to Reading: 250+ Author Games and Booktalks to Motivate Middle Readers*
by Nancy J. Polette. Santa Barbara, CA: Libraries Unlimited. Copyright © 2013.

KATHRYN LASKY:
NAME THAT BOOK!

What title would YOU give to each of these books by Kathryn Lasky?

1) Born with a twisted paw, Faolan was abandoned as a wolf pup and left to die. But not only did he survive and make it back to the wolf clan, he proved himself to be one of the most worthy wolves of all. But just as Faolan is about to take his place as one of the revered Wolves of the Watch, a fellow watch wolf goes missing. Faolan is sent to track her down and makes a horrifying discovery: she has been kidnapped by bears. A war is coming between the wolves and the bears, and only Faolan can stop it.

Your title _____

2) When Sofia and her family arrive at Ellis Island after a long and difficult journey from Italy, a cruel twist of fate separates Sofia from her parents and sends her into "quarantine." There, in a state-run hospital, she and her new friend Maureen must learn to overcome the twin hardships of immigration and alienation, while they maintain the hope that they will be reunited with their families.

Your title _____

3) Nyroc has exiled himself from the Pure Ones. He flies alone, feared and despised by those who know him as Kludd's son, hunted by those whose despotism he has rejected, and haunted by ghostly creatures conjured by Nyra to lure him back to the Pure Ones. He yearns for a place he only half believes in—the great tree—and an uncle—the near-mythic Soren—who might be a true father to him. Yet he cannot approach the tree while the rumor of evil clings to him. To prove his worth, Nyroc will fly to The Beyond, seeking the legendary Relic, and bring it a talisman of his own.

Your title _____

4) Soren and his band are sent to the mysterious Northern Kingdoms to gather allies and learn the art of war in preparation for the coming cataclysmic battle against the sinister Pure Ones. Meanwhile, in the Southern Kingdoms, St. Aggies has fallen to the Pure Ones, and they are using its resources to plan a final invasion of The Great Ga'Hoole Tree. With the future of all Owldom in the balance, the parliament of Ga'Hoole must decide whether or not to join forces with the brutal Skench and Sporn and the scattered remnants of St. Aggies who remain faithful to them. A great battle is on the way.

Your title _____

See the author's titles on page __125__.
Which titles are available in your library?

KATHRYN LASKY:
CIRCLE THE HIDDEN TITLES

Everyone wanted to read the journal of Augustus Pelletier. But an even more interesting account of history was told in the diary of Patience Whipple. She was a young girl who wrote about the daughters of the sea and their journey to the New World in the 1600s. One daughter was called Hawksmaid and the other Georgia. Every morning Georgia rises earlier than anyone else.

Patience was a dreamer. Before her long journey watching stars and chasing Orion across the sky, she would dream her dreams. In the golden country of France she might be Marie Antoinette wearing furs and jewels. Or she might become Elizabeth I, Red Rose of the House of Tudor or perhaps Mary, Queen of Scots. She dreamed at night about watching stars chasing Orion across the sky.

Little did Patience know that as an outcast from England it was a time for courage, as she would be taking an ocean voyage to the new world. The trip to the wharves where the ship waited was a night journey to escape the authorities. Patience felt fear at the shadows in the water that looked like a shadow wolf, but felt better as the ship headed true north and then west.

The ocean journey was filled with danger. The waves laid siege against the ship, shattering parts of the hull. Had the ship gone down, there was little hope of rescue. Capture by pirates, plundering and burning the ship, was also a danger.

When the ship reached the New World, the travelers saw a vision of beauty as they beheld an American spring along the wooded shore. They knew they were home at last and when winter came would have Christmas after all in the New World, when cousin Felix takes the stage to wish everyone good fortune.

KATHRYN LASKY:
KEYS

Answers to Circle the Hidden Titles

Everyone wanted to read the **journal of Augustus Pelletier**. But an even more interesting account of history was told in the diary of Patience Whipple. She was a young girl who wrote about the daughters of the sea and their **journey to the New World** in the 1600s. One daughter was called **Hawksmaid** and the other Georgia. Every morning **Georgia rises** earlier than anyone else.

Patience was a dreamer. Before her long **journey** watching stars and **chasing Orion** across the sky, she would dream her **dreams**. **In the golden country** of France she might be **Marie Antoinette** wearing furs and jewels. Or she might become **Elizabeth I, Red Rose of the House of Tudor** or perhaps **Mary, Queen of Scots**. She dreamed at night about watching stars **chasing Orion** across the sky.

Little did Patience know that as an **outcast** from England it was a **time for courage**, as she would be taking an ocean voyage to the new world. The trip to the wharves where the ship waited was a **night journey** to escape the authorities. Patience felt fear at the **shadows in the water** that looked like **a shadow wolf**, but felt better as the ship headed **true north** and then west.

The ocean journey was filled with danger. The waves laid **siege** against the ship, shattering parts of the hull. Had the ship gone down, there was little hope of **rescue**. **Capture** by pirates, plundering and **burning** the ship, was also a danger.

When the ship reached the New World, the travelers saw a **vision of beauty** as they beheld an **American spring** along the wooded shore. They knew they were **home at last** and when winter came would have **Christmas after all** in the New World, when cousin **Felix takes the stage** to wish everyone good fortune.

Answers to Mystery Titles

1. Sea
2. Dreams
3. Scots
4. Wolf
5. Water
6. *The Capture* (C)
7. *Ashes* (E)
8. *American Spring* (F)
9. *Home at Last* (H)
10. *The Night Journey* (J)

Answers to Name That Book!

1. *Watch Wolf*
2. *Hope in My Heart*
3. *The Outcast*
4. *The Burning*

LOIS LOWRY (1937–):
THE I HAVE/WHO HAS GAME

Cut the cards apart. Each player gets one card. The player who has the card with the asterisks (****) on it reads the "Who has" question. The player who has the answer card reads the answer and then the next question.

I HAVE: *The Giver* and *Number the Stars*, both by Lois Lowry, won the prestigious Newbery Medal. **** **WHO HAS:** Why is Lois Lowry able to write about so many different and varied places?	**I HAVE:** When her family settled in Maine, Lois was able to complete her college degree and devote her time to writing. **WHO HAS:** Where does Lois divide her time now?
I HAVE: Lois grew up in a military family and traveled wherever her father was sent. **WHO HAS:** What are some of the places Lois has lived?	**I HAVE:** Lois divides her time between Cambridge, Massachusetts, and an old farmhouse in Maine, where she gardens and reads. **WHO HAS:** What are the themes of Lois Lowry's books?
I HAVE: Lois has lived in Hawaii, Tokyo, and many states from California to Maine. **WHO HAS:** Why was Lois happy to be a middle child?	**I HAVE:** Themes in Lois Lowry's books deal with getting along with each other and caring for the planet we all share. **WHO HAS:** Which of Lois's books should be read as a trilogy?
I HAVE: Being a middle child meant she had more time to herself to daydream and write. **WHO HAS:** When did Lois begin to write professionally?	**I HAVE:** Lowry's trilogy that deals with interdependence includes *The Giver*, *Gathering Blue*, and *Messenger*. **WHO HAS:** What honors have Lois Lowry's books received?

LOIS LOWRY:
MYSTERY TITLES

Some words in these titles of books by Lois Lowry have been replaced with Dewey Decimal numbers. Go to the shelf with the Dewey number. Find the subject of the book(s) with that number. Fill in the missing word in each title. The first person to finish all the titles correctly is the winner!

1. Bless This 599.35 _____ _____ _____ _____ _____

2. Like the Willow 582.16 _____ _____ _____ _____

3. Number the 523.8 _____ _____ _____ _____ _____

4. A Summer to 155.9 _____ _____ _____

5. 590.73 _____ _____ _____ man Sam

Some words in these titles of books by Lois Lowry have been replaced with synonyms. Put the letter of the actual title after each synonymous title.

6. Fall Thoroughfare _____

7. Collecting Azure _____

8. Courier _____

9. Quiet Young Male _____

10. Seeing in Reverse _____

ACTUAL TITLES
A. *Bless This Mouse*
B. *Autumn Street*
C. *Gathering Blue*
D. *The Giver*
E. *Messenger*
F. *Silent Boy*
G. *Looking Back*
H. *Like the Willow Tree*
I. *Number the Stars*
J. *Attaboy, Sam!*

Which titles are available in your library?

The key to Mystery Titles is on page ___131___.

From *Gateway to Reading: 250+ Author Games and Booktalks to Motivate Middle Readers* by Nancy J. Polette. Santa Barbara, CA: Libraries Unlimited. Copyright © 2013.

LOIS LOWRY:
NAME THAT BOOK!

What title would YOU give to each of these books by Lois Lowry?

1) Jonas lives in a seemingly ideal world: a world without conflict, poverty, unemployment, divorce, injustice, or inequality. It is a time in which family values are paramount, teenage rebellion is unheard of, and even good manners are a way of life. December is the time of the annual Ceremony at which each 12-year-old receives a life assignment determined by the Elders. Jonas watches his friend Fiona named Caretaker of the Old and his cheerful pal Asher labeled the Assistant Director of Recreation. But Jonas has been chosen for something special. When his selection leads him to an unnamed man—the man called only the Giver—he begins to sense the dark secrets that underlie the fragile perfection of his world.

Your title _____

2) Open the diary of 11-year-old Lydia Amelia Pierce of Portland, Maine. Orphaned by the devastating 1918 epidemic of Spanish influenza, Lydia and her older brother Daniel are taken to be raised by the Shakers in their small community at Sabbathday Lake, Maine. Mourning the loss of her parents and sister and desperately worried by her brother's sullen anger, Lydia struggles to make sense of her changed life. As the seasons change, she gradually learns to know and love the devout Shaker sisters who become her new family.

Your title _____

3) "I have a plan," Mr. Willoughby said, putting his paper down. He stroked one eyebrow in a satisfied way. "It's thoroughly despicable."

"Lovely," said his wife. "A plan for what?"

"To rid us of the children."

Little do Mr. and Mrs. Willoughby know that while they are trying to rid themselves of their children, the children—four of them—are trying to rid themselves of their terrible parents. Of course no one is recommending that real children do away with their parents. (Unless, of course—heh heh—their parents are as outrageously awful as Mr. and Mrs. Willoughby!)

Your title _____

4) The summer Enid Crowley is 14, she doesn't like much of anything about herself, particularly the name Enid, which reminds her of a lot of awful adjectives: horrid, putrid, sordid, acrid, viscid, squalid. She definitely needs a change. And after meeting a black saxophonist, the local bag lady, a 4-year-old heir to a fortune, and some other very interesting characters, Enid discovers that change sometimes involves more than you bargain for.

Your title _____

See the author's titles on page ___131___.
Which titles are in your library?

LOIS LOWRY:
CIRCLE THE HIDDEN TITLES

Anastasia Krupnik was making a special present for Caroline. It was a book listing 100 good things about her best friend. She has thought of 99 things, but she cannot come up with the one-hundredth thing about Caroline.

Anastasia tried to switch around some of the pages, but that didn't help. She tried looking back at things they had done, but that didn't help.

Zooman Sam, Anastasia's brother, was no help. He was painting a sign for his pet that said, "Bless this mouse."

"Attaboy, Sam," said his friend, Rabble Starkey. "That sign is a good idea. "See you around, Sam," he called. "Stay!" Sam yelled, but Rabble had disappeared.

Anastasia remembered the summer that Caroline's kitten died. Anastasia and Caroline spent time gathering blue violets for the grave. But a summer to die wasn't a good thing to put in the book.

J.P., another friend, came by. He remembered when Caroline had tried to number the stars and what a good chess player she was. "Your move, J.P." she was always telling him. During the school play Caroline did a good job as the giver of glad tidings. She also had to pretend she was a tree like the willow tree.

"I've got it!" Anastasia yelled. At her house on Autumn Street Caroline spends time taking care of terrific tulips in her yard. It makes her house the prettiest on the block.

J.P. answered, "Maybe Caroline will be so pleased with the book about her that she will come over and plant tulips here. Can I be the messenger to deliver your present to Caroline?"

"Be silent, boy," Anastasia answered. "I'll do it myself."

From *Gateway to Reading: 250+ Author Games and Booktalks to Motivate Middle Readers* by Nancy J. Polette. Santa Barbara, CA: Libraries Unlimited. Copyright © 2013.

LOIS LOWRY:
KEYS

Answers to Circle the Hidden Titles

Anastasia Krupnik was making a special present for Caroline. It was a book listing 100 good things about her best friend. She has thought of 99 things, but she cannot come up with the **one hundredth thing about Caroline**.

Anastasia tried to **switcharound** some of the pages, but that didn't help. She tried **looking back** at things they had done, but that didn't help.

Zooman Sam, Anastasia's brother, was no help. He was painting a sign for his pet that said, "**Bless this mouse.**"

"**Attaboy, Sam**," said his friend, **Rabble Starkey**. "That sign is a good idea. "**See you around, Sam**," he called. "**Stay!**" Sam yelled, but Rabble had disappeared.

Anastasia remembered the summer that Caroline's kitten died. Anastasia and Caroline spent time **gathering blue** violets for the grave. But **a summer to die** wasn't a good thing to put in the book.

J.P., another friend, came by. He remembered when Caroline had tried to **number the stars** and what a good chess player she was. "**Your move, J.P.**" she was always telling him. During the school play Caroline did a good job as **the giver** of glad tidings. She also had to pretend she was a tree **like the willow tree.**

"I've got it!" Anastasia yelled. At her house on **Autumn Street** Caroline spends time **taking care of terrific** tulips in her yard. It makes her house the prettiest on the block.

J.P. answered, "Maybe Caroline will be so pleased with the book about her that she will come over and plant tulips here. Can I be the **messenger** to deliver your present to Caroline?"

"Be **silent, boy**," Anastasia answered. "I'll do it myself."

Answers to Mystery Titles

1. Mouse
2. Tree
3. Stars
4. Die
5. Zoo
6. *Autumn Street* (B)
7. *Gathering Blue* (C)
8. *Messenger* (E)
9. *Silent Boy* (F)
10. *Looking Back* (G)

Answers to Name That Book!

1. *The Giver*
2. *Like The Willow Tree*
3. *The Willoughbys*
4. *Taking Care of Terrific*

PATRICIA MACLACHLAN (1938–):
THE I HAVE/WHO HAS GAME

Cut the cards apart. Each player gets one card. The player who has the card with the asterisks (****) on it reads the "Who has" question. The player who has the answer card reads the answer and then the next question.

I HAVE:	Patricia won the Newbery Medal for *Sarah Plain and Tall* as well as the Scott O'Dell Award, The Christopher Award, and the Golden Kite Award. ****	**I HAVE:**	Patricia cares deeply about families and children and writes about what makes a successful family.
WHO HAS:	When did Patricia MacLachlan fall in love with books?	**WHO HAS:**	How did Patricia prepare to become a children's writer?
I HAVE:	Patricia's parents introduced her to the world of books by reading and acting out the stories.	**I HAVE:**	Before writing her first children's book, Patricia read 30–40 children's books a week.
WHO HAS:	What did Patricia's family do when it snowed on cold Wyoming evenings?	**WHO HAS:**	Does Patricia use real people as characters in her books?
I HAVE:	There was no TV, so the family read individually and to each other, sharing exciting tales of wonderful characters.	**I HAVE:**	Patricia says that Cassie Binegar is modeled after herself, and some of the adults are modeled after her mother and father.
WHO HAS:	When did Patricia start her writing career?	**WHO HAS:**	Has Patricia done work other than as a mother and a writer?
I HAVE:	Patricia began writing at the age of 35 after her 3 children were in school.	**I HAVE:**	Patricia has taught children's literature at Smith College.
WHO HAS:	What things that most interest Patricia are found in her books?	**WHO HAS:**	What are some of the awards Patricia has won?

PATRICIA MACLACHLAN:
MYSTERY TITLES

Some words in these titles of books by Patricia MacLachlan have been replaced with Dewey Decimal numbers. Go to the shelf with the Dewey number. Find the subject of the book(s) with that number. Fill in the missing word in each title. The first person to finish all the titles correctly is the winner!

1. Edward's 617.7 _____ _____ _____ _____

2. 649.22 _____ _____ _____ _____

3. More Perfect Than the 523.3 _____ _____ _____ _____

4. 616 _____ _____ _____ _____ Day

5. After 428.1 _____ _____ _____ _____

Some words in these titles of books by Patricia MacLachlan have been replaced with synonyms. Put the letter of the actual title after each synonymous title.

6. Two Day Old Infant _____

7. More Impeccable Than the Evening Satellite _____

8. 24 Hour Illness _____

9. Monikers in Triplicate _____

10. Ones' Initial Knowledge _____

ACTUAL TITLES
A. *All the Places to Live*
B. *Baby*
C. *Seven Kisses in a Row*
D. *More Perfect Than the Moon*
E. *Through Grandpa's Eyes*
F. *Skylark*
G. *Sick Day*
H. *Three Names*
I. *The True Gift*
J. *What You Know First*

Which titles are available in your library?

The key to Mystery Titles is on page ___137___.

From *Gateway to Reading: 250+ Author Games and Booktalks to Motivate Middle Readers* by Nancy J. Polette. Santa Barbara, CA: Libraries Unlimited. Copyright © 2013.

PATRICIA MACLACHLAN:
NAME THAT BOOK!

What title would YOU give to each of these books by Patricia MacLachlan?

1) Their mother died the day after Caleb was born. Their house on the prairie is quiet now, and Papa doesn't sing anymore. Then Papa puts an ad in the paper, asking for a wife, and he receives a letter from one Sarah Elisabeth Wheaton, of Maine. Papa, Anna, and Caleb write back. Caleb asks if she sings. Sarah decides to come for a month. She writes Papa: I will come by train. I will wear a yellow bonnet. I am plain and tall, and tell them I sing. Anna and Caleb wait and wonder. Will Sarah be nice? Will she like them? Will she stay?

Your title _____

2) Minna wishes for many things. She wishes she understood the quote taped above her mother's typewriter: "Fact and fiction are different truths." She wishes her mother would stop writing long enough to really listen to her. She wishes her house were peaceful and orderly like her friend Lucas's. Most of all, she wishes she could find a vibrato on her cello and play Mozart the way he deserves to be played. Minna soon discovers that some things can't be found; they just have to happen. And as she waits for her vibrato to happen, Minna begins to understand some facts and fictions about herself.

Your title _____

3) Anna has done something terrible. She has given me her journal to fill. In Anna's journal the words walk across the page like bird prints in the mud. But it is hard for me. It is hard for me to find things to write about.
   "It's your job now," Anna says as she hands Caleb her journals, asking him to continue writing the family story. But Sarah, Jacob, Anna, Caleb, and their new little sister, Cassie, have already formed a family, and Caleb fears there will be nothing left to write about. But that is before Cassie discovers a mysterious old man in the barn, and everything changes. Everyone is excited about the arrival of a new family member except for Jacob, who holds a bitter grudge.

Your title _____

4) Cassie spends her days watching Grandfather and Caleb in the barn, looking out at Papa working the fields, spying on her mother, Sarah, feeding the goslings. She's an observer, a writer, a storyteller. Everything is as it should be. But change is inevitable, even on the prairie. Something new is expected, and Sarah says it will be the perfect gift. Cassie isn't so sure. But just as life changes, people change too. And Cassie learns that unexpected surprises can bring great joy.

Your title _____

See the author's titles on page ___137___.
Which of these titles are in your library?

PATRICIA MACLACHLAN:
CIRCLE THE HIDDEN TITLES

Cassie Binegar thought that of all the places to live, the valley was her favorite and deserved seven kisses in a row. It was more perfect than the moon. When she was little she could hike through the woods with her friend, Arthur. For the very first time, along with Edward, they saw signs of the changing seasons through Edward's eyes.

The folks on the neighboring farm wanted everyone to think of three names for their new baby. It was said that Cassie's grandpa could tell the future. Cassie tried to look at the new baby through grandpa's eyes. She thought of the name Sarah. Plain and tall girls had plain names, and the baby looked pretty plain to Cassie. Once when the baby's mother had a sick day, Cassie went to help. When she took the baby outside, the infant just kept staring at the sky and making sounds like a bird. They should call her Skylark, Cassie thought. Such a beautiful name would be the true gift Cassie could give the baby.

When Cassie got home, two of the valley's best storytellers had dropped by to visit. First she heard Caleb's story and then listened to the facts and fictions of Minna Pratt, and finally a scary tale of Edward's eyes about a boy who had the true gift of second sight. Cassie never knew for sure whether Minna's stories were true. Minna once told her, "Listen for what you know first that is true, then figure the rest is made up. That's what makes a good storyteller."

From *Gateway to Reading: 250+ Author Games and Booktalks to Motivate Middle Readers*
by Nancy J. Polette. Santa Barbara, CA: Libraries Unlimited. Copyright © 2013.

PATRICIA MACLACHLAN:
KEYS

Answers to Circle the Hidden Titles

Cassie Binegar thought that of **all the places to live**, the valley was her favorite and deserved **seven kisses in a row**. It was **more perfect than the moon**. When she was little she could hike through the woods with her friend, **Arthur**. **For the very first time**, along with Edward, they saw signs of the changing seasons through **Edward's eyes**.

The folks on the neighboring farm wanted everyone to think of **three names** for their new baby. It was said that Cassie's grandpa could tell the future. Cassie tried to look at the new baby **through grandpa's eyes**. She thought of the name **Sarah**. **Plain and tall** girls had plain names, and the **baby** looked pretty plain to Cassie. Once when the baby's mother had a **sick day**, Cassie went to help. When she took the baby outside, the infant just kept staring at the sky and making sounds like a bird. They should call her **Skylark**, Cassie thought. Such a beautiful name would be **the true gift** Cassie could give the **baby**.

When Cassie got home, two of the valley's best storytellers had dropped by to visit. First she heard **Caleb's story** and then listened to the **facts and fictions of Minna Pratt**, and finally a scary tale of **Edward's eyes** about a boy who had **the true gift** of second sight. Cassie never knew for sure whether Minna's stories were true. Minna once told her, "Listen for **what you know first** that is true, then figure the rest is made up. That's what makes a good storyteller."

Answers to Mystery Titles

1. Eyes
2. Baby
3. Moon
4. Sick
5. Word
6. *Baby* (B)
7. *More Perfect Than the Moon* (D)
8. *Sick Day* (G)
9. *Three Names* (H)
10. *What You Know First* (J)

Answers to Name That Book!

1. *Sarah Plain and Tall*
2. *Facts and Fictions of Minna Pratt*
3. *Caleb's Story*
4. *More Perfect Than the Moon*

PHYLLIS REYNOLDS NAYLOR (1933–):
THE I HAVE/WHO HAS GAME

Cut the cards apart. Each player gets one card. The player who has the card with the asterisks (****) on it reads the "Who has" question. The player who has the answer card reads the answer and then the next question.

I HAVE:	Phyllis likes to read, take part in water sports, and visit her two sons and their families. ****	I HAVE:	The fan mail she receives indicates that her readers like the Boys and Girls, Besseldorf, and Alice series.
WHO HAS:	When did Phyllis Reynolds Naylor begin writing?	WHO HAS:	How many books does Phyllis write each year?
I HAVE:	By age 10 Phyllis was bitten by the writing bug. She spent her spare time writing small books for her own pleasure.	I HAVE:	She writes 3 books a year and has a total of more than 100 published books.
WHO HAS:	What was Phyllis's first published piece?	WHO HAS:	Where does she get ideas for her books?
I HAVE:	Her first published piece was a short story written for a church school paper.	I HAVE:	Ideas come from everyday things that happen around her, like the starving dog that followed her home and became the inspiration for *Shiloh*.
WHO HAS:	How many short stories has Phyllis written?	WHO HAS:	Where does Phyllis do a lot of her writing?
I HAVE:	Her first short story was followed by 2,000 more short stories.	I HAVE:	She writes a lot on trains as she travels to make school visits.
WHO HAS:	What are Phyllis Reynolds Naylor's most popular series books?	WHO HAS:	What does Phyllis do when she is not writing or visiting schools?

PHYLLIS REYNOLDS NAYLOR:
MYSTERY TITLES

Some words in these titles of books by Phyllis Reynolds Naylor have been replaced with Dewey Decimal numbers. Go to the shelf with the Dewey number. Find the subject of the book(s) with that number. Fill in the missing word in each title. The first person to finish all the titles correctly is the winner!

1. Anyone Can Eat 594.58 _____ ____ _____ _____ _____

2. 595.76 _____ _____ _____ _____ _____ _____ _____ Lightly Toasted

3. 551.55 _____ _____ _____ _____ _____ _____ _____ _____ Wake

4. Boys 552.5 _____ _____ _____ _____

5. Danny's Desert 599.352 _____ _____ _____ _____

Some words in these titles of books by Phyllis Reynolds Naylor have been replaced with synonyms. Put the letter of the actual title after each synonymous title.

6. Snowstorm's Aftermath _____

7. Young Males Dominate _____

8. Drakes Vanishing _____

9. Frightful Location _____

10. Mole Among Females _____

ACTUAL TITLES
A. *Blizzard's Wake*
B. *Anyone Can Eat Squid*
C. *Eating Enchiladas*
D. *Boys in Control*
E. *The Boys Return*
F. *Ducks Disappearing*
G. *Patches and Scratches*
H. *Fear Place*
I. *A Spy Among the Girls*
J. *Sweet Strawberries*

Which titles are available in your library?

The key to Mystery Titles is on page __143__.

PHYLLIS REYNOLDS NAYLOR:
NAME THAT BOOK!

What title would YOU give to each of these books by Phyllis Reynolds Naylor?

1) Get ready to start your own incredible, amazing life . . . right? Alice McKinley is standing on the edge of something new—and half afraid she might fall off. Graduation is a big deal—that gauntlet of growing up that requires everyone she's known since forever to make huge decisions that will fling them here and there and far from home. But what if Alice wants to be that little dandelion seed that doesn't scatter? What if she doesn't have the heart to fly off into the horizon on the next big breeze? And what if that starts to make her feel like staying close to home means she's a little less incredible than her friends—and her boyfriend Patrick? Sometimes the bravest thing you can do is be honest with yourself—and sometimes the most incredible thing you can do is sneak a little fun into all this soul-searching.

Your title _____

2) Kenny Sykes is on a mission. He's determined to make his mark somehow in his new town and his new school. In the meantime, he has appointed himself the secret savior of the hundreds of crickets who seem bound to commit suicide by jumping into Kenny's pool. Why he wants to save them, he's not entirely sure. But once school starts again, Cricket Man finds that there are more important things that need saving. Namely, Jodie Poindexter: beautiful junior, across-the-street neighbor, and, underneath her composed façade, the most troubled and secretive girl in school.

Your title _____

3) Lord Thistlebottom's *Book of Pitfalls and How to Survive Them* has taught Roxie Warbler how to handle all sorts of situations. If Roxie's ever lost in the desert, or buried in an avalanche, or caught in a dust storm, she knows just what to do. But Lord Thistlebottom has no advice to help Roxie deal with Helvetia's Hooligans, the meanest band of bullies in school. Then Roxie finds herself stranded on a deserted island with not only the Hooligans but also a pair of crooks on the lam, and her survival skills may just save the day—and turn the Hooligans into surprising allies.

Your title _____

4) "One of the most feared of a witch's powers is that of the evil eye." After throwing Mrs. Tuggle's evil glass eye into the creek, Lynn and her best friend, Mouse, anticipate a soothing summer. But when Lynn notices some strange-looking purple plants growing down by the creek, she begins to worry. Is she imagining it, or are the plants sprouting right near where she threw the eye? What's worse is that some girls from school may be starting their own coven of witches—and Mouse might be getting sucked in! Does Mrs. Tuggle have unfinished business with them? And if so, can Lynn fight her evil again?

Your title _____

See the author's titles on page __143__.
Which of these titles are in your library?

From Gateway to Reading: 250+ Author Games and Booktalks to Motivate Middle Readers
by Nancy J. Polette. Santa Barbara, CA: Libraries Unlimited. Copyright © 2013.

In the blizzard's wake the town of Shiloh was a mess. There was an unexploded bomb in the Besseldorf bus depot, a body with a strange face in the Besseldorf funeral parlor, and patches and scratches that created peril in the Besseldorf parachute factory. At Walker's Crossing there was a great chicken debacle. The chickens made a grand escape but refused to cross the road. It was time to call the boys in control, better known as Danny's Desert Rats. To join you had to eat beetles lightly toasted. "Anyone can eat squid," they said. Eating beetles takes more courage.

Their clubhouse where boys rock was named Fear Place, and no girls were allowed. Danny's Desert Rats moved the chickens across the road, all but one. A traitor among the boys took one home for dinner. However, a spy among the girls signaled when the clubhouse was empty and at the boys return they saw the girls take over with a new plan for saving Shiloh. It seems that all the trouble was caused by wild bears searching for enchiladas and sweet strawberries. Emily had just won the lottery so Emily's fortune was used to buy enchiladas and strawberries for the bears. Faith, Hope, and Ivy June put them on the edge of town with a sign that said please do feed the bears. The happy bears, busy eating enchiladas and strawberries never bothered the town again.

PHYLLIS REYNOLDS NAYLOR:
KEYS

Answers to Circle the Hidden Titles

In the **blizzard's wake** the town of **Shiloh** was a mess. There was an unexploded **bomb in the Besseldorf bus depot**, a body with a strange **face in the Besseldorf funeral parlor**, and **patches and scratches** that created **peril in the Besseldorf parachute factory**. At **Walker's Crossing** there was a **great chicken debacle**. The chickens made a **grand escape** but refused to cross the road. It was time to call the **boys in control**, better known as **Danny's Desert Rats**. To join you had to eat **beetles lightly toasted**. "**Anyone can eat squid**," they said. Eating beetles takes more courage.

Their clubhouse where **boys rock** was named **Fear Place**, and no girls were allowed. **Danny's Desert Rats** moved the chickens across the road, all but one. A **traitor among the boys** took one home for dinner. However, **a spy among the girls** signaled when the clubhouse was empty and at **the boys return** they saw the **girls take over** with a new plan for **saving Shiloh**. It seems that all the trouble was caused by wild bears searching for enchiladas and **sweet strawberries**. Emily had just won the lottery so **Emily's fortune** was used to buy enchiladas and strawberries for the bears. **Faith, Hope, and Ivy June** put them on the edge of town with a sign that said **please do feed the bears**. The happy bears, busy **eating enchiladas** and strawberries never bothered the town again.

Answers to Mystery Titles

1. Squid
2. Beetles
3. Blizzard
4. Rock
5. Rats
6. *Blizzard's Wake* (A)
7. *Boys in Control* (D)
8. *Ducks Disappearing* (F)
9. *Fear Place* (H)
10. *A Spy Among the Girls* (I)

Answers to Name That Book!

1. *Incredibly Alice*
2. *Cricket Man*
3. *Roxie and the Hooligans*
4. *Witch Weed*

From *Gateway to Reading: 250+ Author Games and Booktalks to Motivate Middle Readers* by Nancy J. Polette. Santa Barbara, CA: Libraries Unlimited. Copyright © 2013.

SCOTT O'DELL (1898–1989):
THE I HAVE/WHO HAS GAME

Cut the cards apart. Each player gets one card. The player who has the card with the asterisks (****) on it reads the "Who has" question. The player who has the answer card reads the answer and then the next question.

I HAVE:	Among his many awards are the Newbery Medal for *Island of the Blue Dolphins* and the Hans Christian Anderson Award for Lifetime Achievement. ****	I HAVE:	Before he became a famous writer, Scott O'Dell worked as a rancher, a movie cameraman, and a book editor.
WHO HAS:	Why does the ocean play an important part in many of Scott O'Dell's books?	WHO HAS:	What kinds of books did Scott O'Dell write before the age of 60?
I HAVE:	Scott O'Dell spent most of his childhood living near the ocean in California. One of his homes was built on stilts to avoid the waves that came crashing in.	I HAVE:	Before the age of 60 Scott O'Dell wrote adult fiction and nonfiction.
WHO HAS:	How many universities did Scott O'Dell attend?	WHO HAS:	Where did he get the idea for *Island of the Blue Dolphins*?
I HAVE:	He attended 4 universities, taking only those courses that would help him in his writing.	I HAVE:	In researching information for an adult novel, Scott O'Dell read about a young girl who spent 18 years alone on an island.
WHO HAS:	How did Scott O'Dell serve his country in 2 wars?	WHO HAS:	How did *Island of the Blue Dolphins* become published as a children's book?
I HAVE:	Scott O'Dell joined the army in World War I and enlisted in the Air Force in World War II even though he was more than 40 years old.	I HAVE:	Maud Lovelace, an author friend, read the manuscript and encouraged Scott to submit it to a children's publisher.
WHO HAS:	What other jobs did Scott O'Dell have as an adult?	WHO HAS:	What awards have Scott O'Dell's books won?

SCOTT O'DELL: MYSTERY TITLES

Some words in these titles of books by Scott O'Dell have been replaced with Dewey Decimal numbers. Go to the shelf with the Dewey number. Find the subject of the book(s) with that number. Fill in the missing word in each title. The first person to finish all the titles correctly is the winner!

1. The 597.962 _____ _____ _____ _____ _____ _____ _____ Never Sleeps

2. Black 745.5942 _____ _____ _____ _____ _____

3. Island of the Blue 599.53 _____ _____ _____ _____ _____ _____ _____ _____

4. Sing Down the 523.3 _____ _____ _____ _____

5. Streams to the 508.326 _____ _____ _____ _____ _____

Some words in these titles of books by Scott O'Dell have been replaced with synonyms. Put the letter of the actual title after each synonymous title.

6. Stygian Hue Margarite _____

7. Reptile Missing Somnolence _____

8. Warble Below the Earth's Satellite _____

9. Young Person with Conflagration _____

10. Stygian Hue Pentagram _____

ACTUAL TITLES
A. *The Black Pearl*
B. *Black Star, Bright Dawn*
C. *Island of the Blue Dolphins*
D. *My Name Is Not Angelica*
E. *Child of Fire*
F. *The Serpent Never Sleeps*
G. *Sing Down the Moon*
H. *Streams to the River, River to the Sea*
I. *Thunder Rolling in the Mountains*
J. *Zia*

Which titles are available in your library?

The key to Mystery Titles is on page __149__.

SCOTT O'DELL:
NAME THAT BOOK!

What title would YOU give to each of these books by Scott O'Dell?

1) What could make a young boy jump into a ring and challenge a fighting bull? How could a boy no more than 16 stand there calmly and face death? Manuel, the "child of fire," is a boy whose whole world prompts him to take risks, time and time again. He lives just north of the Mexican border and is the leader of a teenage Chicano gang that vies with another gang for power. The book is filled with friendly competitions and bitter struggles. It is also filled with robust, hearty living and some dying. As the rival gangs go their different ways, parole officer Delaney watches and helps where he can.

Your title _____

2) The young seminarian, Julian Escobar, finds himself trapped in the role of the legendary Mayan god Kukulcan, a captive of his own power and of his duties as lord of a great city. His only ally, the sly dwarf Cantu, cares only for the gold that can be plundered from the Mayan temples. Even amid the barbaric splendor of his own court, Julian fears the treachery of the high priest. Julian's travels take him to the palace of Aztec emperor Montezuma, and before long he is caught up in the tragic encounter of Montezuma and Hernán Cortés.

Your title _____

3) The promise of a rich harvest was shattered in the Canyon de Chelly when the Spanish slavers came and later when the white soldiers burned the crops, destroyed the orchards, and forced the Navahos from their homes. Through the eyes of Bright Morning, a young Navaho girl, we see what happens to human beings who are uprooted from the life they know. She is first captured by slavers, then forced with her people on the "Long Walk," which covered more than 200 miles, ending at Bosque Redondo, a reservation that was little more than a prison camp. This is also the story of proud and able Tall Boy, who is maimed not only by a physical wound but by a spiritual wound as well.

Your title _____

4) Julian Escobar, a young Jesuit seminarian who travels to the New World, is the only human survivor when a hurricane sinks a ship laden with gold. He struggles ashore, where he meets a Mayan girl. She teaches him about Kukulcan, the Feathered Serpent, a fair-skinned Mayan god, who sailed away centuries before. When Julian blows up a Mayan idol, he meets a Spanish dwarf who survived an earlier shipwreck. Cantu, the dwarf, persuades Julian to impersonate Kukulcan. Accepted as the returned god, Julian finds himself presiding over a human sacrifice.

Your title _____

See the author's titles on page __149__ .
Which titles can you find in your library?

From Gateway to Reading: 250+ Author Games and Booktalks to Motivate Middle Readers
by Nancy J. Polette. Santa Barbara, CA: Libraries Unlimited. Copyright © 2013.

SCOTT O'DELL:
CIRCLE THE HIDDEN TITLES

Two hundred years ago a young girl named Sarah Bishop wanted to know what the future held for her. She knew that if she followed the streams to the river, she would find the cabin of Pearl, the fortune teller. The folks in the village said that when they heard thunder rolling in the mountains, Pearl could sing down the moon and make the sky black. Pearl had a daughter, Zia, who was said to have these same powers.

Sarah set out at night on the long trip to Pearl's cabin. She rode her horse, Black Star. Bright dawn showed over the horizon before she arrived. A large snake curled up on the step eyed Sarah.

"He won't hurt you, Angelica," Pearl told the girl. "The serpent never sleeps, but he won't bite, either."

"My name is not Angelica," Sarah replied. "It is Sarah. Can you tell what the future holds for me?"

Pearl looked deep into Sarah's eyes. She examined the girl's hands. "A great future is in store," she said. "It will be far away from here, but a girl brave enough to ride through the dark night will be brave enough to face the future. I see a warm tropical island, blue waters, and dolphins playing. You will spend much time on the island of the blue dolphins and will help to make it a place where many will live in happiness."

Sarah knew that the old woman had said all that she would. She paid Pearl with a warm quilt she had made and began her ride home, dreaming of the happy future that was to come.

From *Gateway to Reading: 250+ Author Games and Booktalks to Motivate Middle Readers* by Nancy J. Polette. Santa Barbara, CA: Libraries Unlimited. Copyright © 2013.

SCOTT O'DELL:
KEYS

Answers to Circle the Hidden Titles

Two hundred years ago a young girl named **Sarah Bishop** wanted to know what the future held for her. She knew that if she followed the **streams to the river**, she would find the cabin of Pearl, the fortune teller. The folks in the village said that when they heard **thunder rolling in the mountains**, Pearl could **sing down the moon** and make the sky **black**. **Pearl** had a daughter, **Zia**, who was said to have these same powers.

Sarah set out at night on the long trip to Pearl's cabin. She rode her horse, **Black Star**. **Bright dawn** showed over the horizon before she arrived. A large snake curled up on the step eyed Sarah.

"He won't hurt you, Angelica," Pearl told the girl. "**The serpent never sleeps**, but he won't bite, either."

"**My name is not Angelica**," Sarah replied. "It is Sarah. Can you tell what the future holds for me?"

Pearl looked deep into Sarah's eyes. She examined the girl's hands. "A great future is in store," she said. "It will be far away from here, but a girl brave enough to ride through the dark night will be brave enough to face the future. I see a warm tropical island, blue waters, and dolphins playing. You will spend much time on the **island of the blue dolphins** and will help to make it a place where many will live in happiness."

Sarah knew that the old woman had said all that she would. She paid Pearl with a warm quilt she had made and began her ride home, dreaming of the happy future that was to come.

Answers to Mystery Titles

1. Serpent
2. Pearl
3. Dolphins
4. Moon
5. River
6. *The Black Pearl* (A)
7. *The Serpent Never Sleeps* (F)
8. *Sing Down the Moon* (G)
9. *Child of Fire* (E)
10. *Black Star, Bright Dawn* (B)

Answers to Name That Book!

1. *Child of Fire*
2. *Feathered Serpent*
3. *Sing Down the Moon*
4. *The Captive*

MARY POPE OSBORNE (1949–):
THE I HAVE/WHO HAS GAME

Cut the cards apart. Each player gets one card. The player who has the card with the asterisks (****) on it reads the "Who has" question. The player who has the answer card reads the answer and then the next question.

I HAVE:	Mary's books have won many Children's Choice Awards as well as Notable Books in the Social Studies. ****	I HAVE:	Mary fell in love with the theater. She married an actor and traveled with him during theatrical productions.
WHO HAS:	Why does Mary Pope Osborne always welcome moving to new places?	WHO HAS:	When did Mary start writing for children?
I HAVE:	Mary's father was in the army and moved his family many times when Mary was a child. She enjoyed each new move.	I HAVE:	Mary was 33 when her first book, *Run, Run as Fast as You Can* was published.
WHO HAS:	How did Mary continue moving as a young adult?	WHO HAS:	What kind of books is Mary most noted for?
I HAVE:	As a young adult Mary traveled with a group through 16 Asian countries. Her travels came to a stop when she became ill with blood poisoning.	I HAVE:	Mary is noted for her exciting non-fiction for children, including books about Columbus, Ben Franklin, and George Washington.
WHO HAS:	What did Mary do while recovering from her illness?	WHO HAS:	When did Mary begin the Magic Tree House series?
I HAVE:	During her illness Mary read all of the books of J.R.R. Tolkien.	I HAVE:	The first Magic Tree House book, *Dinosaurs Before Dark*, was published in 1992.
WHO HAS:	What interests does Mary have in addition to reading, writing, and traveling?	WHO HAS:	What awards have Mary's books won?

MARY POPE OSBORNE: MYSTERY TITLES

Some words in these titles of books by Mary Pope Osborne have been replaced with Dewey Decimal numbers. Go to the shelf with the Dewey number. Find the subject of the book(s) with that number. Fill in the missing word in each title. The first person to finish all the titles correctly is the winner!

1. Crazy Days with 597.964 _____ _____ _____ _____ _____ _____

2. 599.53 _____ _____ _____ _____ _____ _____ _____ _____ at Daybreak

3. 551.22 _____ _____ _____ _____ _____ _____ _____ _____ _____ _____ in the Early Morning

4. Good Morning 599.884 _____ _____ _____ _____ _____ _____ _____ _____

5. High Tide in 919.69 _____ _____ _____ _____ _____ _____

Some words in these titles of books by Mary Pope Osborne have been replaced with synonyms. Put the letter of the actual title after each synonymous title.

6. Bison Preceding a Morning Meal _____

7. Australian Dogs at Supper _____

8. Tremors at 5:00 AM _____

9. Last Combat _____

10. Terra Firm of the Deceased _____

ACTUAL TITLES
A. *Afternoon on the Amazon*
B. *The Gray-Eyed Goddess*
C. *Dolphins at Daybreak*
D. *Buffalo Before Breakfast*
E. *The Land of the Dead*
F. *Good Morning, Gorillas*
G. *Dingoes at Dinnertime*
H. *Knight at Dawn*
I. *The Final Battle*
J. *Earthquake in the Early Morning*

Which titles are available in your library?

The key to Mystery Titles is on page __155__.

 From *Gateway to Reading: 250+ Author Games and Booktalks to Motivate Middle Readers* by Nancy J. Polette. Santa Barbara, CA: Libraries Unlimited. Copyright © 2013.

MARY POPE OSBORNE:
NAME THAT BOOK!

What title would YOU give to each of these books by Mary Pope Osborne?

1) Vampire bats and killer ants? That's what Jack and Annie are about to run into when the Magic Tree House whisks them away to the Amazon River. It's not long before they get hopelessly lost. Will they be able to find their way back to the tree house? Or are Jack and Annie stuck forever in the rain forest?

Your title _____

2) Is this town HAUNTED? Jack and Annie wonder when the Magic Tree House whisks them to the Wild West. But before they can say "Boo!" they rush headlong into an adventure filled with horse thieves, a lost colt, rattlesnakes, and a cowboy named Slim. Will Jack and Annie have time to solve the next Tree House Riddle? The answer may depend on a ghost.

Your title _____

3) Merlin's beloved penguin, Penny, has been put under a spell! Jack and Annie must find 4 things to break the spell. The first is a rare and precious emerald. When the magic tree house whisks them back to India over 400 years ago to search for the jewel, they discover an amazing and exotic world filled with great danger. Will Jack and Annie find what they're looking for? Will they avoid the wrath of the all-powerful Great Mogul, survive a crazy ride on a wild elephant, escape an attack by king cobras—and make it back to the Magic Tree House alive?

Your title _____

4) Jack and Annie continue their quest for the secrets of happiness—secrets they need if they're going to save Merlin. But when the Magic Tree House leads them to a tiny deserted island in the middle of the ocean, they're not sure who needs help more: Merlin or themselves! The brother and sister team are soon rescued by a ship of explorers and scientists. But the crew isn't looking for the secrets of happiness. The crew is looking for . . . a sea monster!

Your title _____

See the author's titles on page ___155___.
Which titles can you find in your library?

MARY POPE OSBORNE:
CIRCLE THE HIDDEN TITLES

Come play the craziest computer game ever! Travel the world all in one day.

Visit the land of the dead, where you will meet a gray-eyed goddess and a one-eyed giant. When it's high tide in Hawaii, watch dolphins at daybreak, then continue your trip by sailing on Viking ships. At sunrise visit ancient England and become a knight. At dawn travel back in time to the Great Plains and take a ride on a buffalo. Before breakfast click on ancient Egypt and find yourself looking at mummies. In the morning click again and go to Africa to say, "Good morning, gorillas" and to hunt lions. At lunchtime climb aboard a ship with pirates. Past noon take a brief rest, then spend an afternoon on the Amazon River, but watch out for piranhas!

Click again and find yourself in a ghost town at sundown and watch the final battle at the OK Corral. Listen for the moans of prospector ghosts who did not strike it rich. Then it is time to head to India to see the tigers. At twilight you click again and find yourself in Australia. If it is the season of the sandstorms, you can chase dingoes. At dinnertime you time travel to prehistoric times and see real dinosaurs. Before dark, click again. You are in the Arctic watching polar bears. Past bedtime you are tired from your day's journey. You skip the hour of the Olympics and when it is midnight on the moon you are ready for bed. It is the night of the ninjas, and no time to be out walking around. So you click once more and buy a ticket for a cruise. Tonight on the *Titanic*, after a day of traveling the world you find everyone sleeping. Bobby, your best friend, is the only one awake.

"Let's play the travel game again," he says.

MARY POPE OSBORNE:
KEYS

Answers to Circle the Hidden Titles

Come play the craziest computer game ever! Travel the world all in one day.

Visit **the land of the dead**, where you will meet a **gray-eyed goddess** and a **one-eyed giant**. When it's **high tide in Hawaii**, watch **dolphins at daybreak**, then continue your trip by sailing on **Viking ships**. **At sunrise** visit ancient England and become a **knight**. **At dawn** travel back in time to the Great Plains and take a ride on a **buffalo**. **Before breakfast** click on ancient Egypt and find yourself looking at **mummies**. **In the morning** click again and go to Africa to say, "**Good morning, gorillas**" and to hunt **lions**. **At lunchtime** climb aboard a ship with **pirates**. **Past noon** take a brief rest, then spend an **afternoon on the Amazon** River, but watch out for piranhas!

Click again and find yourself in a **ghost town at sundown** and watch **the final battle** at the OK Corral. Listen for the moans of prospector ghosts who did not strike it rich. Then it is time to head to India to see the **tigers**. **At twilight** you click again and find yourself in Australia. If it is the **season of the sandstorms**, you can chase **dingoes**. **At dinnertime** you time travel to prehistoric times and see real **dinosaurs**. **Before dark**, click again. You are in the Arctic watching **polar bears**. **Past bedtime** you are tired from your day's journey. You skip the **hour of the Olympics** and when it is **midnight on the moon** you are ready for bed. It is the **night of the ninjas**, and no time to be out walking around. So you click once more and buy a ticket for a cruise. **Tonight on the *Titanic***, after a day of traveling the world you find everyone **sleeping**. **Bobby**, your best friend, is the only one awake.

"Let's play the travel game again," he says.

Answers to Mystery Titles

1. Cobras
2. Dolphins
3. Earthquake
4. Gorillas
5. Hawaii
6. *Buffalo Before Breakfast* (D)
7. *Dingoes at Dinnertime* (G)
8. *Earthquake in the Early Morning* (J)
9. *The Final Battle* (I)
10. *The Land of the Dead* (E)

Answers to Name That Book!

1. *Afternoon on the Amazon*
2. *Ghost Town at Sundown*
3. *A Crazy Day with Cobras*
4. *Dark Day in the Deep Sea*

KATHERINE PATERSON (1932–):
THE I HAVE/WHO HAS GAME

Cut the cards apart. Each player gets one card. The player with the **** card reads the "Who has" question. The player with the answer card reads the answer followed by the question.

I HAVE:	Katherine Paterson's books have appeared on many Notable Book and Children's Choice lists. She won the Newbery Medal for *Bridge to Terabithia*. ****	**I HAVE:**	After 2 years' study of Christian education, Katherine went to Japan as a missionary.
WHO HAS:	Why did Katherine Paterson move 18 times in 18 years?	**WHO HAS:**	How did Katherine's life change in 1962?
I HAVE:	Katherine's parents were missionaries in China and were forced to move when wars broke out.	**I HAVE:**	Katherine was married in 1962 and began her writing career while becoming mother to 4 children.
WHO HAS:	What were Katherine's ambitions as a child?	**WHO HAS:**	What was Katherine's first professional writing?
I HAVE:	As a child Katherine dreamed of becoming either a movie star or a missionary.	**I HAVE:**	Her first professional writing was church curriculum materials, which helped her to decide she wanted to write fiction rather than nonfiction.
WHO HAS:	What was one of her first jobs after college?	**WHO HAS:**	What helped Katherine to develop and sell her first novel?
I HAVE:	After college Katherine taught in rural Virginia schools for one year.	**I HAVE:**	Her first novel was written during an adult creative writing class.
WHO HAS:	Why did Katherine spend 4 years in Japan?	**WHO HAS:**	What awards have Katherine Paterson's books won?

KATHERINE PATERSON:
MYSTERY TITLES

Some words in these titles of books by Katherine Paterson have been replaced with Dewey Decimal numbers. Go to the shelf with the Dewey number. Find the subject of the book(s) with that number. Fill in the missing word in each title. The first person to finish all the titles correctly is the winner!

1. Come 783.042 _____ _____ _____ _____, Jimmy Jo

2. Day of the 598.43 _____ _____ _____ _____ _____ _____ _____

3. Field of the 636.7 _____ _____ _____ _____

4. Marvin's Best 232.92 _____ _____ _____ _____ _____ _____ _____ _____ _____

5. Same Stuff as 523.8 _____ _____ _____ _____ _____

Some words in these titles of books by Katherine Paterson have been replaced with synonyms. Put the letter of the actual title after each synonymous title.

6. Monarch's Match _____

7. Clearing of Canines _____

8. Topsy-turvy Female _____

9. Minister's Male Child _____

10. Pentagram Duplicate _____

ACTUAL TITLES
A. *Bridge to Terabithia*
B. *Come Sing, Jimmy Jo*
C. *Field of the Dogs*
D. *Flip-Flop Girl*
E. *The Great Gilly Hopkins*
F. *Jacob Have I Loved*
G. *Jip, His Story*
H. *The King's Equal*
I. *Marvin One Too Many*
J. *Preacher's Boy*
K. *The Same Stuff as Stars*

Which titles are available in your library?

The key to Mystery Titles is on page __161__.

From *Gateway to Reading: 250+ Author Games and Booktalks to Motivate Middle Readers* by Nancy J. Polette. Santa Barbara, CA: Libraries Unlimited. Copyright © 2013.

KATHERINE PATERSON:
NAME THAT BOOK!

What title would YOU give to each of these books by Katherine Paterson?

1) Jess Aaron's greatest ambition is to be the fastest runner in the fifth grade, until a new girl shows up and outruns everyone. That's not a very promising beginning for a friendship, but Jess and Leslie Burke become inseparable. It doesn't matter to Jess that Leslie dresses funny, or that her family has a lot of money but no TV. Leslie has imagination. Together, she and Jess create Terabithia, a magical kingdom in the woods where the two of them reign as king and queen, and their imaginations set the only limits. Then one morning a terrible tragedy occurs. Only when Jess is able to come to grips with this tragedy does he finally understand the strength and courage Leslie has given him.

Your title _____

2) Eleven-year-old Gilly has been stuck in more foster families than she can remember, and she has disliked them all. She has a county-wide reputation for being brash, brilliant, and completely unmanageable. So when she is sent to live with the Trotters—by far the strangest family yet—Gilly decides to put her sharp mind to work. Before long she has devised an elaborate scheme to get her real mother to come rescue her. But the rescue doesn't work out, and the great Gilly Hopkins is left thinking that maybe life with the Trotters wasn't so bad.

Your title _____

3) Sara Louise Bradshaw is sick and tired of her beautiful twin Caroline. Ever since they were born, Caroline has been the pretty one, the talented one, the better sister. Even now, Caroline seems to take everything: Louise's friends, their parents' love, her dreams for the future. For once in her life, Louise wants to be the special one. But in order to do that, she must first figure out who she is . . . and find a way to make a place for herself outside her sister's shadow.

Your title _____

4) Who is the man called Sabura, the mysterious bandit who robs the rich and helps the poor? And what is his connection with Yosida, the harsh and ill-tempered master of feudal Japan's most famous puppet theater? Young Jiro, an apprentice to Yosida, is determined to find out, even at the risk of his own life. Meanwhile, Jiro devotes himself to learning puppetry. Kinshi, the puppet master's son, tutors him. When his sheltered life at the theater is shattered by mobs of hungry, rioting peasants, Jiro becomes aware of responsibilities greater than his craft. As he schemes to help his friend Kinshi and to find his own parent, Jiro stumbles onto a dangerous and powerful secret.

Your title _____

See the author's titles on page __161__.
Which of these books are in your library?

From Gateway to Reading: 250+ Author Games and Booktalks to Motivate Middle Readers
by Nancy J. Polette. Santa Barbara, CA: Libraries Unlimited. Copyright © 2013.

KATHERINE PATERSON:
CIRCLE THE HIDDEN TITLES

Marvin's family didn't have much money, but he hoped to get the Christmas present he wanted most. His old dog, named Flip-Flop Girl, had passed away during the summer. His friend Lyddie had arranged a beautiful funeral for the dog. She asked Jimmy Jo to come over. "Come sing, Jimmy Jo," she said, and he did. It was a beautiful service. Marvin adopted a pelican for a pet and kept a journal recording each day of the pelican, but a pelican wasn't a dog. That is why Marvin's best Christmas ever would be the gift of a new puppy.

"Sorry, Marvin, one too many mouths to feed is something we can't afford," his father told him. "As a preacher's boy you know we have a hard time making ends meet."

Marvin asked his brother, Jacob, "Have I loved one dog too much? I know I could earn the money to feed a puppy. Maybe I could share one of the puppies from the litter at the king's. Equal time there and here means it would only cost half as much to feed it."

No matter how many ideas Marvin had, none of them seemed to get him closer to having a puppy. Then on Christmas Eve he was walking home crossing the bridge to Terabithia, where he lived. There he met Jip. His story was an exciting one. "Did you see the field of the dogs?" Jip asked.

"Where?" Marvin answered. "A field of dogs! Great!"

"Gilly Hopkins is the new vet and is raising dogs. She has a whole field of them and is looking for help to take care of them."

Marvin was so happy at the idea of taking care of a lot of dogs that he had the same stuff as stars in his eyes. What a great new year it would be!

From *Gateway to Reading: 250+ Author Games and Booktalks to Motivate Middle Readers* by Nancy J. Polette. Santa Barbara, CA: Libraries Unlimited. Copyright © 2013.

KATHERINE PATERSON:
KEYS

Answers to Circle the Hidden Titles

Marvin's family didn't have much money, but he hoped to get the Christmas present he wanted most. His old dog, named **Flip-Flop Girl**, had passed away during the summer. His friend **Lyddie** had arranged a beautiful funeral for the dog. She asked Jimmy Jo to come over. "**Come sing, Jimmy Jo**," she said, and he did. It was a beautiful service. Marvin adopted a pelican for a pet and kept a journal recording each **day of the pelican**, but a pelican wasn't a dog. That is why **Marvin's best Christmas ever** would be the gift of a new puppy.

"Sorry, **Marvin, one too many** mouths to feed is something we can't afford," his father told him. "As a **preacher's boy** you know we have a hard time making ends meet."

Marvin asked his brother, **Jacob, "Have I loved** one dog too much? I know I could earn the money to feed a puppy. Maybe I could share one of the puppies from the litter at **the king's. Equal** time there and here means it would only cost half as much to feed it."

No matter how many ideas Marvin had, none of them seemed to get him closer to having a puppy. Then on Christmas Eve he was walking home crossing the **bridge to Terabithia**, where he lived. There he met Jip. His story was an exciting one. "Did you see the **field of the dogs**?" Jip asked.

"Where?" Marvin answered. "A field of dogs! **Great**!"

"**Gilly Hopkins** is the new vet and is raising dogs. She has a whole field of them and is looking for help to take care of them."

Marvin was so happy at the idea of taking care of a lot of dogs that he had the **same stuff as stars** in his eyes. What a great new year it would be!

Answers to Mystery Titles

1. Sing
2. Pelican
3. Dogs
4. Christmas
5. Stars
6. *The King's Equal* (H)
7. *Field of the Dogs* (C)
8. *Flip-Flop Girl* (D)
9. *Preacher's Boy* (J)
10. *The Same Stuff as Stars* (K)

Answers to Name That Book!

1. *Bridge to Terabithia*
2. *The Great Gilly Hopkins*
3. *Jacob Have I Loved*
4. *The Master Puppeteer*

GARY PAULSEN (1939–):
THE I HAVE/WHO HAS GAME

Cut the cards apart. Each player gets one card. The player who has the card with the asterisks (****) on it reads the "Who has" question. The player who has the answer card reads the answer and then the next question.

I HAVE:	*Dogsong* and *Hatchet* were Newbery Honor books as well as ALA Notable Books. Many other titles have made several "best books" lists. ********	**I HAVE:**	Gary once survived a storm at sea in a small boat and uses this experience in *The Voyage of the Frog*.
WHO HAS:	In what ways is Gary's childhood in Minnesota reflected in his books?	**WHO HAS:**	Does Gary have a family?
I HAVE:	Gary made a hobby of raising sled dogs, which adapted well to the cold Minnesota winters. He tells about the dogs in *Dogsong*.	**I HAVE:**	Gary is married to Ruth Paulsen, an artist, who has illustrated several of his books. He has one son.
WHO HAS:	How much education did Gary have before becoming an award-winning author?	**WHO HAS:**	What causes does Gary feel strongly about?
I HAVE:	Gary had two years at Bemidji College and spent a brief time at the University of Colorado.	**I HAVE:**	Gary feels strongly about and works for nuclear disarmament.
WHO HAS:	What jobs has Gary held as an adult?	**WHO HAS:**	What real-life experience of Gary's is told about in *Dogsong*?
I HAVE:	After 4 years in the army Gary worked as a teacher, an engineer, an actor, a director, a rancher, and a singer.	**I HAVE:**	Gary and his dogs ran the Alaskan Iditarod Race twice, almost losing his life on the second run.
WHO HAS:	How did Gary's sailboat experience become the basis for *The Voyage of the Frog*?	**WHO HAS:**	What awards have Gary Paulsen's books won?

GARY PAULSEN:
MYSTERY TITLES

Some words in these titles of books by Gary Paulsen have been replaced with Dewey Decimal numbers. Go to the shelf with the Dewey number. Find the subject of the book(s) with that number. Fill in the missing word in each title. The first person to finish all the titles correctly is the winner!

1. Alicia's 783.042 _____ _____ _____ _____

2. Brian's 508.2 _____ _____ _____ _____ _____ _____

3. 629.22 _____ _____ _____

4. 636.7 _____ _____ _____ Song

5. 551.42 _____ _____ _____ _____ _____ _____

Some words in these titles of books by Gary Paulsen have been replaced with synonyms. Put the letter of the actual title after each synonymous title.

6. Tool for Chopping _____

7. Canine Ditties _____

8. Land Surrounded by Water _____

9. Tributary _____

10. Champions of Calamity _____

ACTUAL TITLES
A. *The Car*
B. *A Christmas Sonata*
C. *The Cookcamp*
D. *Dogsong*
E. *The Glass Cafe*
F. *Hatchet*
G. *The Island*
H. *Lawn Boy*
I. *Masters of Disaster*
J. *The Quilt*
K. *The Rifle*
L. *The River*
M. *Soldier's Heart*

Which titles are available in your library?

The key to Mystery Titles is on page __167__.

From *Gateway to Reading: 250+ Author Games and Booktalks to Motivate Middle Readers* by Nancy J. Polette. Santa Barbara, CA: Libraries Unlimited. Copyright © 2013.

GARY PAULSEN:
NAME THAT BOOK!

What title would YOU give to each of these books by Gary Paulsen?

1) Coyote Runs, an Apache boy, takes part in his first raid. But he is to be a man for only a short time. More than a hundred years later, while camping near Dog Canyon, 15-year-old Brennan Cole becomes obsessed with a skull that he finds, pierced by a bullet. He learns that it is the skull of an Apache boy executed by soldiers in 1864. A mystical link joins Brennan and Coyote Runs, and Brennan knows that neither boy will find peace until Coyote Runs' skull is carried back to an ancient sacred place.

Your title _____

2) On his way to visit his recently divorced father in the Canadian mountains, 13-year-old Brian Robeson is the only survivor when the single-engine plane crashes. His body battered, his clothes in shreds, Brian must now stay alive in the boundless Canadian wilderness. When all is stripped down to the barest essentials, Brian discovers some stark and simple truths: self-pity doesn't work; despair doesn't work. And if Brian is to survive physically as well as mentally, he must discover courage.

Your title _____

3) Lost your shoe? Can't find your homework? Ask Mudshark. At least, until the Psychic Parrot takes up residence in the school library. The word in school is that the parrot can outthink Mudshark. And right now the school needs someone who's good at solving problems. There's an escaped gerbil running the halls, a near-nuclear emergency in the faculty restroom, and an unexplained phenomenon involving disappearing erasers. Once Mudshark solves the mystery of the erasers, he plans to investigate the Psychic Parrot.

Your title _____

4) A wonderful grandmother reaches out to a boy of 14, offering him a haven from his harsh and painful family life. She arranges a summer job for him on the farm where she is a cook for Gunnar and Olaf, elderly brothers. Farm life offers the camaraderie and routine of hard work, good food, peaceful evenings spent making music together, and even learning to dance. Life with Alicia gives the boy strength and faith in himself, drawing him away from the edge and into the center of life.

Your title _____

See the author's titles on page __167__.
Which titles can you find in your library?

From *Gateway to Reading: 250+ Author Games and Booktalks to Motivate Middle Readers* by Nancy J. Polette. Santa Barbara, CA: Libraries Unlimited. Copyright © 2013.

GARY PAULSEN:
CIRCLE THE HIDDEN TITLES

Harris and me, a couple of time hackers, always looked forward to visiting Tucket's home. The old man was full of tales worth hearing. If you mentioned riding a horse, Tucket's ride was a tale of adventure. If you talked about prospecting, Tucket's gold strike was the biggest ever. All Mr. Tucket needed for an adventure was a hatchet, a rifle, a tent, and a river and the guts to tackle them all. His tales always featured masters of disaster.

He told a tale about Brian's return to the wilderness after he'd almost died there a year earlier, and Brian's hunt for the white fox. Mr. Tucket was head of a cookcamp on an island, and this tale would stop a soldier's heart. The first sign of danger was the white fox. Chronicles could be written about terrible things that happen when a white fox appears. At the sound of an eerie howl, one man ran for his car. Another man, Nightjohn, said it was a dogsong, but there were no dogs around. Still another thought it might be a Christmas sonata sung by coyotes.

"Call me Francis Tucket," Mr. Tucket exclaimed. "That's Alicia's song!" There was fear around the campfire. Alicia was a ghost who had entertained in the glass cafe. As the music got louder, the men looked up to see Alicia floating above the trees that formed a winter room for her. There was a quilt around her shoulders.

"Beware of the voyage of the frog," she moaned and then faded away.

"What does that mean?" Brian asked.

"I don't know," Mr. Tucket answered. "But I wouldn't go near any frogs if I were you. I'd stay away from a mudshark too."

And for the rest of Brian's winter he took great care to avoid frogs and mudsharks.

From *Gateway to Reading: 250+ Author Games and Booktalks to Motivate Middle Readers* by Nancy J. Polette. Santa Barbara, CA: Libraries Unlimited. Copyright © 2013.

GARY PAULSEN:
KEYS

Answers to Circle the Hidden Titles

Harris and me, a couple of **time hackers**, always looked forward to visiting **Tucket's home**. The old man was full of tales worth hearing. If you mentioned riding a horse, **Tucket's ride** was a tale of adventure. If you talked about prospecting, **Tucket's gold** strike was the biggest ever. All **Mr. Tucket** needed for an adventure was a **hatchet**, a **rifle**, a **tent**, and a **river** and the **guts** to tackle them all. His tales always featured **masters of disaster**.

He told a tale about **Brian's return** to the wilderness after he'd almost died there a year earlier, and **Brian's hunt** for the white fox. **Mr. Tucket** was head of a **cookcamp** on an **island**, and this tale would stop a **soldier's heart**. The first sign of danger was **the white fox**. **Chronicles** could be written about terrible things that happen when a white fox appears. At the sound of an eerie howl, one man ran for his car. Another man, **Nightjohn**, said it was a **dogsong**, but there were no dogs around. Still another thought it might be a **Christmas sonata** sung by coyotes.

"**Call me Francis Tucket**," Mr. Tucket exclaimed. "That's **Alicia's song**!" There was fear around the campfire. Alicia was a ghost who had entertained in the **glass cafe**. As the music got louder, the men looked up to see Alicia floating above the trees that formed a **winter room** for her. There was a **quilt** around her shoulders.

"Beware of **the voyage of the frog**," she moaned and then faded away.

"What does that mean?" Brian asked.

"I don't know," **Mr. Tucket** answered. "But I wouldn't go near any frogs if I were you. I'd stay away from a **mudshark** too."

And for the rest of **Brian's winter** he took great care to avoid frogs and mudsharks.

Answers to Mystery Titles

1. Song
2. Winter
3. Car
4. Dog
5. Island
6. *Hatchet* (F)
7. *Dogsong* (D)
8. *The Island* (G)
9. *The River* (L)
10. *Masters of Disaster* (I)

Answers to Name That Book!

1. *Canyons*
2. *Hatchet*
3. *Mudshark*
4. *Alicia's Song*

WILLO DAVIS ROBERTS (1928–2004):
THE I HAVE/WHO HAS GAME

Cut the cards apart. Each player gets one card. The player who has the card with the asterisks (****) on it reads the "Who has" question. The player who has the answer card reads the answer and then the next question.

I HAVE:	Three of her mysteries have won the Edgar Allan Poe Award. Many of her titles have won state children's choice awards. ****	**I HAVE:**	Her first published work was an adult mystery titled *Murder at Grand Bay*.
WHO HAS:	What memories does Willo Davis Roberts have of her childhood?	**WHO HAS:**	Why was finding time to write difficult for Willo Davis Roberts?
I HAVE:	She remembers having a hard time making friends because she was shy and her family moved a lot.	**I HAVE:**	To bring in money she worked full time in a hospital to help provide for her 4 children. For a time she wrote adult nurse novels.
WHO HAS:	Why did Willo Davis Roberts have trouble learning her multiplication tables?	**WHO HAS:**	What was her first children's book?
I HAVE:	In her fourth-grade year her family moved six times.	**I HAVE:**	Her first children's book was *The View from the Cherry Tree*, which she wrote as an adult novel, and she was upset when her editor said it was a children's book.
WHO HAS:	What happened to Willo Davis Roberts after graduating from high school?	**WHO HAS:**	What are some of the issues Willo Davis Roberts writes about?
I HAVE:	Willo Davis Roberts married, and she and her husband tried dairy farming, which ran them into debt.	**I HAVE:**	Willo Davis Roberts writes about sibling relationships, abduction, loss and grieving, shifting family dynamics, physical abuse, and more.
WHO HAS:	What was her first published work?	**WHO HAS:**	What awards have books by Willo Davis Roberts won?

WILLO DAVIS ROBERTS:
MYSTERY TITLES

Some words in these titles of books by Willo Davis Roberts have been replaced with Dewey Decimal numbers. Go to the shelf with the Dewey number. Find the subject of the book(s) with that number. Fill in the missing word in each title. The first person to finish all the titles correctly is the winner!

1. Blood on His 612.11 _____ _____ _____ _____ _____

2. Jo and the 364.16 _____ _____ _____ _____ _____ _____

3. Secrets at Hidden 551.442 _____ _____ _____ _____ _____ _____

4. Twisted 508.2 _____ _____ _____ _____ _____ _____

5. View from the Cherry 582.16 _____ _____ _____ _____

Some words in these titles of books by Willo Davis Roberts have been replaced with synonyms. Put the letter of the actual title after each synonymous title.

6. Male Arm Appendages with Hemoglobin _____

7. Captured _____

8. Corkscrew June to August _____

9. Captive _____

10. Insurrectionist _____

ACTUAL TITLES
A. *The Absolutely True Story*
B. *Blood on His Hands*
C. *Caught*
D. *Hostage*
E. *The Kidnappers*
F. *The One Left Behind*
G. *Rebel*
H. *Twisted Summer*
I. *The View from the Cherry Tree*

Which titles are available in your library

The key to Mystery Titles is on page __173__.

WILLO DAVIS ROBERTS:
NAME THAT BOOK!

What title would YOU give to each of these books by Willo Davis Roberts?

1) Katie Welker would rather read a book than deal with other people. Other people don't have silver eyes. Other people can't make things happen just by thinking about them! But these special powers make Katie unusual, and it's hard to make friends. Katie knows that she's different, but she has never done anything to hurt anyone, so why is everyone afraid of her? Maybe there are other kids out there who have the same silver eyes . . . and the same talents . . . and maybe they'll be willing to help her.

Your title _____

2) Through a series of miscommunications, Mandy's family has left her by herself in their big house on Lake Michigan. But it's the absence of her twin sister, Angel, that she feels the most. One year ago Angel died, and Mandy clings to the pain of her loss. At first Mandy is almost relieved to have the time to herself. But quickly the loneliness consumes her, until she stumbles upon two boys, one her age, the other not yet two, who are also on their own. Running away from men who wish to do them harm, the boys turn to Mandy for help. But what can she do for these boys when she can barely take care of herself?

Your title _____

3) First Pa's truck was robbed, then Pa ran off, leaving Rick, Kenny, and Ma to fend for themselves, and now Ma has disappeared too. Rick just knows Ma would never leave them on purpose, but then, where is she? Waiting in Uncle Henry's trailer park doesn't seem like the best way to find out. Instead, the brothers, along with their new friends Connie and Julie, decide to search the abandoned Wonderland Amusement Park next door for answers. But what they find inside sends them on the most terrifying roller-coaster ride of their lives. Could whoever took Ma be after them too?

Your title _____

4) All Buddy wants is a normal family. But with her mother dead, her father missing, and her brother on the road searching for him, Buddy has a hard time believing it will ever happen. Instead she's living with relatives she hardly knows, who resent her for reasons she can't figure out. They think everything about her is strange, especially her name. Buddy can't give up hope that her father is out there, somewhere, and that her brother will find him so they can be a family again. But until then can Buddy find some way to accept her new life? Or will she always feel different?

Your title _____

See the author's titles on page ___173___.
Which titles can you find in your library?

WILLO DAVIS ROBERTS:
CIRCLE THE HIDDEN TITLES

This is an absolutely true story about me and my cousin Jo. Jo wanted everyone to call her Buddy, but I think Buddy is a stupid name for a girl. The summer began peacefully enough, but if you are wondering what could go wrong, let me tell you! Jo and I were pawns in a scheme by kidnappers to get money from the wealthy Prufrock family. The Prufrock mansion was at the edge of town in a place called Hidden Valley. They had acres of land, and and my favorite hiding place on the grounds was a cherry tree. My view from the cherry tree let me in on all the secrets at Hidden Valley.

On this particular summer day, being the one left behind when the gang went swimming, I was watching from my tree when I saw Jo come out the back door of the mansion. I was unaware of the undercurrents of danger that surrounded the farm. She was going to the kennels to feed the dogs. Mr. Prufrock raised Irish setters, and was he ever proud of those dogs! Suddenly a masked bandit jumped into the yard and grabbed Jo. Jo and the bandit struggled, but the bandit was bigger, and when he pulled out his gun, Jo froze. She was scared stiff.

"Let her go," I shouted, which was a dumb thing to do because the bandit pointed the gun at me and told me to come down out of the tree. We were caught! He took both of us hostage.

The bandit put us in the back of a van. He told us he was holding us hostage for one million dollars. He thought the Prufrocks were our parents. The bandit had things all twisted. Summer jobs were hard to get, and Jo and I were happy to get jobs at the Prufrocks taking care of the dogs. Jo fed them and I exercised them.

Then an announcement came over the radio in the van. Two children (that was us) had disappeared, and the police were searching for them everywhere. When the bandit heard our names, he knew he had made a mistake. Not wanting our blood on his hands, he stopped the van and let us out. Jo, who was always a bit of a rebel, shook her fist at him.

It was a long walk home, but we didn't mind. It was better than being kidnapped!

WILLO DAVIS ROBERTS:
KEYS

Answers to Circle the Hidden Titles

This is an **absolutely true story** about me and my cousin Jo. Jo wanted everyone to call her Buddy, but I think **Buddy is a stupid name for a girl**. The summer began peacefully enough, but if you are wondering **what could go wrong**, let me tell you! Jo and I were **pawns** in a scheme by **kidnappers** to get money from the wealthy Prufrock family. The Prufrock mansion was at the edge of town in a place called Hidden Valley. They had acres of land, and and my favorite hiding place on the grounds was a cherry tree. My **view from the cherry tree** let me in on all the **secrets at Hidden Valley**.

On this particular summer day, being **the one left behind** when the gang went swimming, I was watching from my tree when I saw Jo come out the back door of the mansion. I was unaware of the **undercurrents** of danger that surrounded the farm. She was going to the kennels to feed the dogs. Mr. Prufrock raised Irish setters, and was he ever proud of those dogs! Suddenly a masked bandit jumped into the yard and grabbed Jo. **Jo and the bandit** struggled, but the bandit was bigger, and when he pulled out his gun, Jo froze. She was **scared stiff**.

"Let her go," I shouted, which was a dumb thing to do because the bandit pointed the gun at me and told me to come down out of the tree. We were **caught**! He took both of us **hostage**.

The bandit put us in the back of a van. He told us he was holding us **hostage** for one million dollars. He thought the Prufrocks were our parents. The bandit had things all **twisted**. **Summer** jobs were hard to get, and Jo and I were happy to get jobs at the Prufrocks taking care of the dogs. Jo fed them and I exercised them.

Then an announcement came over the radio in the van. Two children (that was us) had disappeared, and the police were searching for them everywhere. When the bandit heard our names, he knew he had made a mistake. Not wanting our **blood on his hands,** he stopped the van and let us out. Jo, who was always a bit of a **rebel**, shook her fist at him.

It was a long walk home, but we didn't mind. It was better than being kidnapped!

Answers to Mystery Titles

1. Blood
2. Bandit
3. Valley
4. Summer
5. Tree
6. *Blood on His Hands* (B)
7. *Caught* (C)
8. *Twisted Summer* (H)
9. *Hostage* (D)
10. *Rebel* (G)

Answers to Name That Book!

1. *The Girl with the Silver Eyes*
2. *The One Left Behind*
3. *Scared Stiff*
4. *Buddy Is a Stupid Name for a Girl*

RON ROY (1940–):
THE I HAVE/WHO HAS GAME

Cut the cards apart. Each player gets one card. The player who has the card with the asterisks (****) on it reads the "Who has" question. The player who has the answer card reads the answer and then the next question.

I HAVE:	Ron Roy's A–Z Mysteries are popular because they challenge young readers to solve a mystery while reading about characters like themselves. ****	**I HAVE:**	In his early years as teacher he decided he wanted to write and spent evenings and weekends writing.
WHO HAS:	Why does Ron Roy say he had a perfect childhood?	**WHO HAS:**	How successful were the first manuscripts Ron sent to publishers?
I HAVE:	Ron describes his perfect childhood as having two loving parents, a woods to explore behind his house, and a library across the street.	**I HAVE:**	Ron's manuscripts sent to publishers were rejected for the first 4 years that he sent them out.
WHO HAS:	What did Ron Roy enjoy doing as a child?	**WHO HAS:**	What was Ron's first published book?
HAVE:	As a child Ron caught small creatures and studied them before letting them go. He also loved reading adventure tales.	**I HAVE:**	Ron's first published book was *A Thousand Pails of Water*, about a boy who saves a stranded whale by keeping it wet.
WHO HAS:	What job did Ron have after college?	**WHO HAS:**	How many books for children has Ron Roy written?
I HAVE:	After college Ron became a teacher of children in grades two through five.	**I HAVE:**	Ron Roy has written more than 50 books for children.
WHO HAS:	When did Ron decide to write for children?	**WHO HAS:**	What are Ron's most popular books?

RON ROY:
MYSTERY TITLES

Some words in these titles of books by Ron Roy have been replaced with Dewey Decimal numbers. Go to the shelf with the Dewey number. Find the subject of the book(s) with that number. Fill in the missing word in each title. The first person to finish all the titles correctly is the winner!

1. Bald 364.15 _____ _____ _____ _____ _____ _____

2. 363.25 _____ _____ _____ _____ _____ _____ _____ _____ _____ Camp

3. Falcon 598.097 _____ _____ _____ _____ _____ _____ _____ _____

4. 599.75 _____ _____ _____ _____ _____ _____ _____ Jewel

5. White 599.77 _____ _____ _____ _____

Some words in these titles of books by Ron Roy have been replaced with synonyms. Put the letter of the actual title after each synonymous title.

6. Ghost Filled Stopping Place _____

7. Unfilled Casing _____

8. Snatched Monarch _____

9. Hairless Robber _____

10. Missing Writer _____

ACTUAL TITLES
A. *The Absent Author*
B. *The Bald Bandit*
C. *The Canary Caper*
D. *The Empty Envelope*
E. *The Haunted Hotel*
F. *The Kidnapped King*
G. *The Missing Mummy*
H. *The Runaway Racehorse*
I. *The School Skeleton*
J. *The Talking T. Rex*

Which titles are available in your library?

The key to Mystery Titles is on page __179__.

 From *Gateway to Reading: 250+ Author Games and Booktalks to Motivate Middle Readers*
by Nancy J. Polette. Santa Barbara, CA: Libraries Unlimited. Copyright © 2013.

RON ROY:
NAME THAT BOOK!

What title would YOU give to each of these books by Ron Roy?

1) Dink writes to his favorite author, mystery writer Wallis Wallace, and invites him to visit Green Lawn. To Dink's amazement, Wallace says he'll come! But when the big day arrives, Wallace is nowhere to be found. The police think he just missed his plane, but Dink suspects foul play. It's up to Dink and his two best friends, Josh and Ruth Rose, to find the famous writer—before it's too late!

Your title _____

2) The Green Lawn Savings Bank has been robbed! When a private detective comes to Dink's door looking for the kid who videotaped the crime, Dink and his friends volunteer to find him. After all, there's a reward! But tracking down one red-headed kid isn't so easy, especially if he doesn't want to be found. Can the trio find that kid—and his tape—before the bandit does?

Your title _____

3) Dink, Josh, and Ruth Rose get an urgent call from Mrs. Davis. Her canary is missing! The little bird has vanished without a trace, and he's not the only one. Two other pets are missing. The kids suspect a pet-napper, and now that Ruth Rose's cat, Tiger, has turned up missing too, it's become personal!

Your title _____

4) The presidential election is less than a week away, but KC and Marshall have more important things on their minds—their Halloween party at the White House! The morning after the costume party, though, KC and Marshall wake up to a trick, not a treat. Someone has posted damaging photos of the president on the Internet, photos that were digitally doctored! Will they ruin President Thornton's chances for a second term? Or can KC and Marshall rescue the election?

Your title _____

5) Marshall and his friend are watching fourth of July fireworks with the president of the United States when they see smoke and sparks in the distance. It's more fireworks, but they are not part of the holiday plan. They're coming from the FBI building! Is it just a prank? Or are these fireworks masking a bigger mystery . . . and a capital crime?

Your title _____

See the author's titles on page ___179___ .
Which titles can you find in your library?

RON ROY:
CIRCLE THE HIDDEN TITLES

Detective Pip Ramsey had been called from his Detective Camp by Miss Mayflower to start a Mayflower treasure hunt to find the missing jaguar's jewel, the ninth nugget of King Tut, which was kidnapped 2,000 years ago from the casket of a missing mummy.

Recently the jewel turned up in a nest of falcon's feathers. Miss Mayflower, a birdwatcher who found it, thought she had won the lucky lottery or a bet on a runaway racehorse. Whether it was a case of finders keepers was a quicksand question. If the jewel was found, an unwilling umpire had to decide if it belonged to Miss Mayflower or the government.

The suspects were all staying at the haunted hotel located on Invisible Island. The haunted hotel was a real zombie zone, a great place for a vampire's vacation or a howling white wolf. Pip looked for clues. One guest, an author, was missing from the hotel. The absent author might have taken the jewel. Pip found an empty envelope with strange markings on it. He also found a half-finished panda puzzle. He started down the dark steps to explore the hotel's deadly dungeon, when he froze. A school skeleton hung at the top of the stairs!

Pip looked down, expecting to see a talking T. Rex. A small canary was hopping about on the bottom step. Pip followed the canary, which led him to an overturned toy yellow yacht. The door to the yacht was open. Pip looked inside. There was the missing jewel. The bald bandit canary had taken it! Knowing they wouldn't be called on to help solve the mystery, there was a celebration with fireworks at the FBI.

Detective Pip had done it again. He returned the jewel to Miss Mayflower, collected his fee, and filed the case away under the heading "The Canary Caper."

From *Gateway to Reading: 250+ Author Games and Booktalks to Motivate Middle Readers* by Nancy J. Polette. Santa Barbara, CA: Libraries Unlimited. Copyright © 2013.

RON ROY:
KEYS

Answers to Circle the Hidden Titles

Detective Pip Ramsey had been called from his **Detective Camp** by Miss Mayflower to start a **Mayflower treasure hunt** to find the missing **jaguar's jewel**, the **ninth nugget** of King Tut, which was **kidnapped** 2,000 years ago from the casket of a **missing mummy**.

Recently the jewel turned up in a nest of **falcon's feathers**. Miss Mayflower, a birdwatcher who found it, thought she had won the **lucky lottery** or a bet on a **runaway racehorse**. Whether it was a case of finders keepers was a **quicksand question**. If the jewel was found, an **unwilling umpire** had to decide if it belonged to Miss Mayflower or the government.

The suspects were all staying at the **haunted hotel** located on **Invisible Island**. The **haunted hotel** was a real **zombie zone**, a great place for a **vampire's vacation** or a howling **white wolf**. Pip looked for clues. One guest, an author, was missing from the hotel. **The absent author** might have taken the jewel. Pip found an **empty envelope** with strange markings on it. He also found a half-finished **panda puzzle**. He started down the dark steps to explore the hotel's **deadly dungeon**, when he froze. **A school skeleton** hung at the top of the stairs!

Pip looked down, expecting to see a **talking T. Rex**. A small canary was hopping about on the bottom step. Pip followed the canary, which led him to an overturned toy **yellow yacht**. The door to the yacht was open. Pip looked inside. There was the missing jewel. The **bald bandit** canary had taken it! Knowing they wouldn't be called on to help solve the mystery, there was a celebration with **fireworks at the FBI**.

Detective Pip had done it again. He returned the jewel to Miss Mayflower, collected his fee, and filed the case away under the heading "**The Canary Caper**."

Answers to Mystery Titles

1. Bandit
2. Detective
3. Feathers
4. Jaguar's
5. Wolf
6. *The Haunted Hotel* (E)
7. *The Empty Envelope* (D)
8. *The Kidnapped King* (F)
9. *The Bald Bandit* (B)
10. *The Absent Author* (A)

Answers to Name That Book!

1. *The Absent Author*
2. *The Bald Bandit*
3. *The Canary Caper*
4. *The Election Day Disaster*
5. *Fireworks at the FBI*

JON SCIESZKA (1954–):
THE I HAVE/WHO HAS GAME

Cut the cards apart. Each player gets one card. The player who has the card with the asterisks (****) on it reads the "Who has" question. The player who has the answer card reads the answer and then the next question.

I HAVE:	*The Stinky Cheese Man* won a Caldecott Honor Medal. *The True Story of the 3 Little Pigs* is among the most popular children's books of all time. ****	**I HAVE:**	Jon Scieszka says his ideas come from everywhere: kids, animals, books, movies, or just staring out the window,
WHO HAS:	What book started Jon Scieszka on his writing career?	**WHO HAS:**	What does Jon Scieszka say is the hardest part of writing.
I HAVE:	When, as a child, Jon Scieszka read *Green Eggs and Ham* by Dr. Seuss, he discovered books could be silly. He credits that book as the inspiration for his writing *The Stinky Cheese Man*.	**I HAVE:**	Jon Scieszka says the hardest part of writing is rewriting to make a story as good as it can be.
WHO HAS:	What jobs did Jon Scieszka have before he became a full-time writer?	**WHO HAS:**	What honor did Jon Scieszka receive in 2008?
I HAVE:	Jon Scieszka was a teacher of first through eighth grades.	**I HAVE:**	Jon Scieszka was appointed the first National Ambassador for Young People's Literature in 2008 by the Library of Congress.
WHO HAS:	What did Jon Scieszka learn about children during his years as a teacher?	**WHO HAS:**	What does Jon Scieszka do as the National Ambassador for Young People's Literature?
I HAVE:	Jon learned that children of all ages can be both silly and smart.	**I HAVE:**	He tells people about the importance of children's literature in developing lifelong literacy and education.
WHO HAS:	Where does Jon Scieszka get his ideas for his books?	**WHO HAS:**	What honors or awards have Jon Scieszka's books received?

JON SCIESZKA:
MYSTERY TITLES

Some words in these titles of books by Jon Scieszka have been replaced with Dewey Decimal numbers. Go to the shelf with the Dewey number. Find the subject of the book(s) with that number. Fill in the missing word in each title. The first person to finish all the titles correctly is the winner!

1. Hey, Kid, Want to Buy a 624.2 _____ _____ _____ _____ _____ _____ ?

2. It's All 489.382 _____ _____ _____ _____ _____ to Me

3. 940.1 _____ _____ _____ _____ _____ _____ _____ of the Kitchen Table

4. Seen 702.8 _____ _____ _____ ?

5. 948.022 _____ _____ _____ _____ _____ _____ It and Liking It

Some words in these titles of books by Jon Scieszka have been replaced with synonyms. Put the letter of the actual title after each synonymous title.

6. The Fine, the Awful and the Silly _____

7. Ho! Young Person, Desire a Span over Water? _____

8. Champions of the Scullery's Four-Legged Slab _____

9. Gazed upon an Illustration? _____

10. Perusing a Tome in June through August Is Murder _____

ACTUAL TITLES
A. *The Good, the Bad, and the Goofy*
B. *Hey Kid, Want to Buy a Bridge?*
C. *It's All Greek to Me*
D. *Knights of the Kitchen Table*
E. *Me Oh Maya*
F. *The Not-So-Jolly Roger*
G. *Seen Art?*
H. *See You Later, Gladiator*
I. *Tut, Tut*
J. *Your Mother Was a Neanderthal*
K *Viking It and Liking It*
L. *Spaceheadz*
M. *Summer Reading Is Killing Me!*

Which titles are available in your library?

The key to Mystery Titles is on page __185__.

JON SCIESZKA:
NAME THAT BOOK!

What title would YOU give to each of these books by Jon Scieszka?

1) The dynamic trio, Joe, Sam, and Fred, are at it once again in this new segment of The Time Warp Trio series. The boys are about to start rehearsing their school play about ancient Greece when the script gets knocked into *The Book*, a magical time-warping tome reminiscent of *The Never Ending Story*. Suddenly they find themselves in Hades, and so begins their quest to get back to the future. The celestial crew on Mount Olympus are a bunch of wise-cracking smart alecks, sounding a lot like certain American 11-year-old boys, many of whom might find the insulting tone very funny.

Your title _____

2) What would happen if 3 regular kids from Brooklyn got a mysterious blue book with silver designs that could transport them anywhere in time or space? What if these three guys met up with King Arthur, the knights of the Round Table, Merlin the magician, one burping and gas-leaking giant, and a fire-breathing dragon? The Time Warp Trio series would happen.

Your title _____

3) Joe, Sam, and Fred accidentally warp back to the 1700s and run into Edward Teach (better known as Blackbeard the pirate). Mr. Teach lights fuses in his beard, drinks gunpowder mixed in his rum, shoots and stabs his own men, and sings very poorly. He also makes it very difficult for the Time Warp Trio to find *The Book* so they can warp safely back home.

Your title _____

4) The good news about the Stone Age is that there are no homework assignments or tests. The bad news is that there are hungry saber-toothed tigers, rampaging woolly mammoths, a tribe of cavemen who love rotten meat, and a tribe of cave women who look like they are getting ready to sacrifice the Time Warp Trio. If this book costs $14.99 in hardcover, $4.99 in paperback, and there are 3 members in a trio, would you do your math homework if you were a woolly mammoth?

Your title _____

See the author's titles on page __185__.
Which titles can you find in your library?

From *Gateway to Reading: 250+ Author Games and Booktalks to Motivate Middle Readers* by Nancy J. Polette. Santa Barbara, CA: Libraries Unlimited. Copyright © 2013.

JON SCIESZKA:
CIRCLE THE HIDDEN TITLES

Miss Beowulf, our English teacher, has assigned summer reading. My parents think this is a great idea, but Me oh Maya, summer reading is killing me. The books are all about dead people who lived a long time ago. Oh say, I can't see how this prepares me for the future. By 2095 there probably won't be any books to be seen. Art and images will take over in a technological world. Reading about King Tut, the Vikings, and ancient Greece isn't my idea of summer fun. My label for these books is the good, the bad, and the goofy. It's all Greek to me. Our teacher says, however, that we should spend the summer "Viking it and liking it."

One good thing has happened, however. I have found some neat new lines to use on my family and friends. When my little brother gets into my stuff I can say, "Tut, Tut, Charlie, or Hey kid, want to buy a bridge?" instead of, "Get out of here you little creep."

When the spaceheadz bully down the street starts making nasty cracks, I can come back with, "Your mother was a Neanderthal!" He probably won't even know what it means.

Instead of being the "Hole-Up Gang," my buddies and I can become the Knights of the Kitchen Table. When Roger cracks one of his dumb jokes, I can come back with, "Not-so-jolly, Roger."

Yes, summer reading may be boring, but it sure has increased my vocabulary. Maybe that's what Miss Beowulf had in mind!

JON SCIESZKA:
KEYS

Answers to Circle the Hidden titles

Miss Beowulf, our English teacher, has assigned summer reading. My parents think this is a great idea, but **Me oh Maya, summer reading is killing me**. The books are all about dead people who lived a long time ago. **Oh say, I can't see** how this prepares me for the future. By **2095** there probably won't be any books to be **seen**. **Art** and images will take over in a technological world. Reading about King Tut, the Vikings, and ancient Greece isn't my idea of summer fun. My label for these books is **the good, the bad, and the goofy**. **It's all Greek to me**. Our teacher says, however, that we should spend the summer "**Viking it and liking it**."

One good thing has happened, however. I have found some neat new lines to use on my family and friends. When my little brother gets into my stuff I can say, "**Tut, Tut**, Charlie, or **Hey kid, want to buy a bridge?**" instead of, "Get out of here you little creep."

When the **spaceheadz** bully down the street starts making nasty cracks, I can come back with, "**Your mother was a Neanderthal**!" He probably won't even know what it means.

Instead of being the "Hole-Up Gang," my buddies and I can become the **Knights of the Kitchen Table**. When Roger cracks one of his dumb jokes, I can come back with, "**Not-so-jolly, Roger**."

Yes, summer reading may be boring, but it sure has increased my vocabulary. Maybe that's what Miss Beowulf had in mind!

Answers to Mystery Titles

1. Bridge
2. Greek
3. Knights
4. Art
5. Viking
6. *The Good, the Bad, and the Goofy* (A)
7. *Hey Kid, Want to Buy a Bridge?* (B)
8. *Knights of the Kitchen Table* (D)
9. *Seen Art?* (G)
10. *Summer Reading Is Killing Me!* (M)

Answers to Name That Book!

1. *It's All Greek to Me*
2. *Knights of the Kitchen Table*
3. *The Not-So-Jolly Roger*
4. *Your Mother Was a Neanderthal*

GLORIA SKURZYNSKI (1930–):
THE I HAVE/WHO HAS GAME

Cut the cards apart. Each player gets one card. The player who has the card with the asterisks (****) on it reads the "Who has" question. The player who has the answer card reads the answer and then the next question.

I HAVE:	*Wolf Stalker* was the first novel ever published by the National Geographic Society in its 109-year history. ****	I HAVE:	Gloria submitted 58 manuscripts to publishers before having one accepted.
WHO HAS:	Why does Gloria believe that growing up in a Pennsylvania steel town was important?	WHO HAS:	What does Gloria write about?
I HAVE:	Having lived in the time of the steel mills, which are now gone, Gloria can re-create that time for young readers who will never experience it.	I HAVE:	Gloria writes about the steel mill days of long ago and of the worlds that may exist in the future.
WHO HAS:	What were Gloria's favorite childhood activities?	WHO HAS:	Does Gloria have a family?
I HAVE:	Going to the library and to movies gave her a desire to become a writer.	I HAVE:	Gloria and her space engineer husband have 5 daughters. One, Alane Ferguson, is an author.
WHO HAS:	How did fan mail exchanges with author Phyllis McGinley inspire Gloria to write?	WHO HAS:	What is important about Gloria's National Geographic mysteries?
I HAVE:	Phyllis McGinley's letters convinced Gloria to become a full-time writer.	I HAVE:	Gloria weaves environmental information into exciting mysteries set in the nation's national parks.
WHO HAS:	How many manuscripts did Gloria submit to publishers before one was accepted for publication?	WHO HAS:	What was unusual about *Wolf Stalker*?

GLORIA SKURZYNSKI:
MYSTERY TITLES

Some words in these titles of books by Gloria Skurzynski have been replaced with Dewey Decimal numbers. Go to the shelf with the Dewey number. Find the subject of the book(s) with that number. Fill in the missing word in each title. The first person to finish all the titles correctly is the winner!

1. Deadly 551.48 _____ _____ _____ _____ _____ _____

2. Ghost 636.1 _____ _____ _____ _____ _____ _____

3. Minstrel in the 720.43 _____ _____ _____ _____ _____

4. Rage of 369.43 _____ _____ _____ _____

5. 595.44 _____ _____ _____ _____ _____ _____ _____ Voice

Some words in these titles of books by Gloria Skurzynski have been replaced with synonyms. Put the letter of the actual title after each synonymous title.

6. Precipice Dangler _____

7. Revolution _____

8. Conscious below Ground _____

9. Extreme Anger of Conflagration _____

10. Spirit Equines _____

ACTUAL TITLES
A. *Buried Alive*
B. *Cliff-Hanger*
C. *Deadly Waters*
D. *Ghost Horses*
E. *The Hunted*
F. *Out of the Deep*
G. *Over the Edge*
H. *Rage of Fire*
I. *The Revolt*
J. *Running Scared*

Which titles are available in your library?

The key to Mystery Titles is on page ___191___.

From *Gateway to Reading: 250+ Author Games and Booktalks to Motivate Middle Readers* by Nancy J. Polette. Santa Barbara, CA: Libraries Unlimited. Copyright © 2013.

GLORIA SKURZYNSKI:
NAME THAT BOOK!

What title would YOU give to each of these books by Gloria Skurzynski?

1) Something very strange is going on in Great Smoky Mountains National Park. A teenage girl is the latest victim in a growing number of bear attacks. Officials must figure out what's causing the bizarre bear behavior or close the park. Can the Landons help? Soon Jack and Ashley are searching for answers with their new friends Yonah Firekiller, a 16-year-old Cherokee boy, and 14-year-old Merle Chapman, whose family once lived on park land. But a heated argument over ancestral land rights puts the Landon kids in the middle of a clash of cultures. Tensions mount when Merle is caught in a lie—a lie that leads straight to the heart-pounding solution.

Your title _____

2) The Landon family is southbound—headed for Florida to investigate a mysterious illness plaguing endangered manatees in Everglades National Park. Jack, Ashley, and their friend Bridger soon find themselves in deadly waters with a 7-foot shark, an injured manatee—and a mystery to solve. Who was the stranger in the speedboat who snatched Jack's camera? And what does he have to do with the manatees? Join the heart-stopping chase through a maze of mangrove islands to find out!

Your title _____

3) Grizzly cubs are missing from Montana's Glacier National Park, and the Landon family is there to help figure out why. But for 12-year-old Jack, the real mystery is his sister Ashley's strange behavior. What was she doing in the woods alone so early in the morning? And why did she lie to their parents? Challenging Ashley, Jack discovers she has been sneaking food to a 10-year-old runaway from Mexico. After listening to Miguel's story, Jack decides to help too. The compelling plot builds to a spine-chilling climax as the kids run for their lives, desperately trying to escape an enraged mother grizzly who holds the key to the park's present mystery.

Your title _____

4) When his mother, a wildlife veterinarian, is asked to investigate a cougar attack in Mesa Verde National Park, 12-year-old Jack Landon looks forward to exploring the park's ancient cliff dwellings. But his life becomes unexpectedly complicated when he helps an abandoned girl named Lucky. In a midnight showdown at the park's Spruce Tree House, Jack realizes there is more to fear than a killer cat.

Your title _____

See the author's titles on page ___191___.
Which titles can you find in your library?

GLORIA SKURZYNSKI:
CIRCLE THE HIDDEN TITLES

Movie Review

Four thumbs up for *Rage of Fire*! Don't miss this cliff-hanger. You will know thrills. You will feel chills. If you think of yourself as a brave person, you won't escape from fear! You will be running scared from the theater. Nothing like this has ever before been seen.

Billy Radish, popular action star, faces an evil minstrel in the tower of London who is out to destroy the world. The wizened minstrel sings with a raspy spider's voice, summoning all of the poisonous insects of the world to keep mankind buried alive in a virtual war. In their revolt against mankind, they come from out of the deep, crawling over the edge of the world to create a valley of death.

Billy Radish will thrill you as he fights the giant insects. As the insects attack by the thousands and we think it is time to tell the hero goodbye, Billy Radish shows what he is made of. As he gathers all of his strength, the insects become the hunted enemy. He leads them through deadly waters and fights them with raging fire. See a horrible screaming ghost, horses in a gigantic stampede, and an attack by the most deadly insects ever brought to the screen.

This film is not for the faint-hearted. In each theater trained medical personnel will be standing by in case of heart attacks.

GLORIA SKURZYNSKI:
KEYS

Answers to Circle the Hidden titles

Movie Review

Four thumbs up for *Rage of Fire*! Don't miss this **cliff-hanger**. You will know thrills. You will feel chills. If you think of yourself as a brave person, you won't **escape from fear**! You will be **running scared** from the theater. Nothing like this has ever before been seen.

Billy Radish, popular action star, faces an evil **minstrel in the tower** of London who is out to destroy the world. The wizened minstrel sings with a raspy **spider's voice**, summoning all of the poisonous insects of the world to keep mankind **buried alive** in a **virtual war**. In their **revolt** against mankind, they come from **out of the deep**, crawling **over the edge** of the world to create a **valley of death**.

Billy Radish will thrill you as he fights the giant insects. As the insects attack by the thousands and we think it is time to tell the hero **goodbye, Billy Radish** shows what he is made of. As he gathers all of his strength, the insects become **the hunted** enemy. He leads them through **deadly waters** and fights them with raging fire. See a horrible screaming **ghost, horses** in a gigantic stampede, and an attack by the most deadly insects ever brought to the screen.

This film is not for the faint-hearted. In each theater trained medical personnel will be standing by in case of heart attacks.

Answers to Mystery Titles

1. Waters
2. Horses
3. Tower
4. Fire
5. Spider's
6. *Cliff-Hanger* (B)
7. *The Revolt* (I)
8. *Buried Alive* (A)
9. *Rage of Fire* (H)
10. *Ghost Horses* (D)

Answers to Name That Book!

1. *Night of the Black Bear*
2. *Deadly Waters*
3. *The Hunted*
4. *Cliff-Hanger*

ZILPHA KEATLEY SNYDER (1927–):
THE I HAVE/WHO HAS GAME

Cut the cards apart. Each player gets one card. The player who has the card with the asterisks (****) on it reads the "Who has" question. The player who has the answer card reads the answer and then the next question.

I HAVE:	Zilpha Keatley Snyder won the Newbery Medal for *The Egypt Game*. Many of her books have been state Children's Choice Award winners. **** 	**I HAVE:**	Zilpha was 8 years old when she decided to become a writer.
WHO HAS:	Where did Zilpha live as a child?	**WHO HAS:**	What kind of student was Zilpha during her first 5 years of school?
I HAVE:	Zilpha lived in various places in California, where there were always many animals.	**I HAVE:**	Zilpha was a good student, particularly in reading and writing. She did not do as well in math or sports.
WHO HAS:	When did she learn to read?	**WHO HAS:**	What happened to Zilpha in seventh grade?
I HAVE:	Zilpha taught herself to read at a very early age by listening to lessons her mother gave her older sister.	**I HAVE:**	In seventh grade Zilpha felt she was a misfit. Having no friends, she spent her time with books and daydreams.
WHO HAS:	How did Zilpha's parents influence her becoming a writer?	**WHO HAS:**	When did she begin writing for children?
I HAVE:	Both Zilpha's parents were storytellers, relating true accounts of past events.	**I HAVE:**	After teaching all day Zilpha wrote at night in the early 1960s, when *Season of Ponies* was published.
WHO HAS:	When did Zilpha decide that she would become a writer?	**WHO HAS:**	What awards have Zilpha Keatley Snyder's books won?

ZILPHA KEATLEY SNYDER: MYSTERY TITLES

Some words in these titles of books by Zilpha Keatley Snyder have been replaced with Dewey Decimal numbers. Go to the shelf with the Dewey number. Find the subject of the book(s) with that number. Fill in the missing word in each title. The first person to finish all the titles correctly is the winner!

1. 636.8 _____ _____ _____ Running

2. 932 _____ _____ _____ _____ _____ Game

3. 949.049 _____ _____ _____ _____ ____ Game

4. Gib and the Gray 133.1 _____ _____ _____ _____ _____

5. 133.43 _____ _____ _____ _____ _____ _____ _____ of Worm

Some words in these titles of books by Zilpha Keatley Snyder have been replaced with synonyms. Put the letter of the actual title after each synonymous title.

6. Romany Pastime _____

7. Encroachers _____

8. Truants _____

9. God of Love Missing Top Appendage _____

10. Feline Moving Rapidly _____

ACTUAL TITLES
A. *Cat Running*
B. *The Egypt Game*
C. *The Gypsy Game*
D. *Season of Ponies*
E. *The Headless Cupid*
F. *The Runaways*
G. *Spyhole Secrets*
H. *The Trespassers*
I. *The Witches of Worm*

Which titles are available in your library?

The key to Mystery Titles is on page __197__.

From *Gateway to Reading: 250+ Author Games and Booktalks to Motivate Middle Readers* by Nancy J. Polette. Santa Barbara, CA: Libraries Unlimited. Copyright © 2013.

ZILPHA KEATLEY SNYDER: NAME THAT BOOK!

What title would YOU give to each of these books by Zilpha Keatley Snyder?

1) Hallie Meredith is angry at God and feeling sorry for herself. Her beloved father died in a car accident, and her whole life has been turned upside down. Her mother has had to find a job, and they have moved to a cramped apartment in an old mansion, away from Hallie's old friends and her school. Hallie discovers the old mansion's mysterious attic and a secret window where she can spy straight into another family's life. At first it's a game, sneaking up to the attic, watching the strange doings of this odd family. But as the mystery of what is going on on the other side of the window deepens, Hallie becomes increasingly involved in the intimate lives of people she really doesn't know, and the game turns into a kind of addiction. When she sees signs of danger, Hallie tries to help, and that may be the best way she can help herself as well.

Your title _____

2) Cats. Jessica has never liked them. Especially not a skinny, ugly kitten that looks like a worm. Jessica wishes she had never brought Worm home with her, because now he's making her do terrible things. She is sure she isn't imagining the evil voice coming from the cat, telling her to play mean tricks on people. But how can she explain what's happening?

   Witches. Jessica has read enough books to know that Worm must be a witch's cat. He has cast a spell on her, but to whom can she turn? After all, no one will believe that Worm has bewitched her . . . or worse.

Your title _____

3) Abby O'Malley is a girl who likes things to make sense, but her flighty mother never makes sense. Abby's mom seems to think that she and Abby are descended from a line of witches, and that they have special powers. The problem is, Abby knows that she can do certain things that other people can't. Sometimes when she holds an object in her hand, she is overpowered by sounds and pictures that show where the owner is and what he or she is doing. Abby thinks of this as her "magic nation," because that is what her kindergarten teacher told her it was called. Now age 11, Abby has an inkling that her teacher may have been saying it was her "imagination," which unfortunately she knows it is not. Now some things are happening in her mother's detective agency, cases in which Abby's magic nation thing might come in handy. But does Abby want to admit that such a sensible girl could have such an unsensible power?

Your title _____

See the author's titles on page ___197___.
Which titles can you find in your library?

ZILPHA KEATLEY SNYDER:
CIRCLE THE HIDDEN TITLES

This is a sad love story. Gib Stone and Libby Rock were a modern Romeo and Juliet. They loved each other, but their families had been feuding for years. Various members of the families would play mean jokes and call them a game. Unseen, one of Libby's brothers wrote graffiti all over the Stones' barn. It looked like hieroglyphics. When finally caught, he said he was playing the Egypt game.

One of Gib's brothers wrote bad fortunes all over the Rocks' barn and called it the gypsy game. He was always peeking through holes and had plenty of spyhole secrets.

Late one foggy night, Gib rode his horse to meet Libby. Libby thought it looked like Gib and the gray ghost instead of Gib and his horse. As Gib approached, a black cat running for its life crossed the road. Gib's horse reared and threw him. "It sure is a night for the witches of worm to be about," Libby thought.

Gib approached Libby and reached in his pocket. "I brought you one of the treasures of Weatherby manor to remember me by," he said. "Libby, on Wednesday I'm leaving here for good." Gib handed Libby a small cupid, but its head was broken off. "It must have broke when I fell off the horse," Gib said. "I didn't mean to bring you a headless cupid."

Then Gib told Libby they would both be runaways. They would use their bronze pen to leave a note and would travel only at night so they wouldn't be caught as trespassers.

Even though she loved him, Libby refused. "We must wait until we are older," she said. "Maybe our families will stop feuding by then."

Sadly, Gib rode home alone. He never saw Libby again until 100 years later, when they met as ghosts. Even today people say you can see the young lovers as the ghosts of Rathburn Park.

From *Gateway to Reading: 250+ Author Games and Booktalks to Motivate Middle Readers* by Nancy J. Polette. Santa Barbara, CA: Libraries Unlimited. Copyright © 2013.

ZILPHA KEATLEY SNYDER:
KEYS

Answers to Circle the Hidden Titles

This is a sad love story. Gib Stone and Libby Rock were a modern Romeo and Juliet. They loved each other, but their families had been feuding for years. Various members of the families would play mean jokes and call them a game. **Unseen**, one of Libby's brothers wrote graffiti all over the Stones' barn. It looked like hieroglyphics. When finally caught, he said he was playing **the Egypt game**.

One of Gib's brothers wrote bad fortunes all over the Rocks' barn and called it **the gypsy game**. He was always peeking through holes and had plenty of **spyhole secrets**.

Late one foggy night, Gib rode his horse to meet Libby. Libby thought it looked like **Gib and the gray ghost** instead of Gib and his horse. As Gib approached, a black **cat running** for its life crossed the road. Gib's horse reared and threw him. "It sure is a night for **the witches of worm** to be about," Libby thought.

Gib approached Libby and reached in his pocket. "I brought you one of **the treasures of Weatherby manor** to remember me by," he said. "**Libby, on Wednesday** I'm leaving here for good." Gib handed Libby a small cupid, but its head was broken off. "It must have broke when I fell off the horse," Gib said. "I didn't mean to bring you a **headless cupid**."

Then Gib told Libby they would both be **runaways**. They would use their **bronze pen** to leave a note and would travel only at night so they wouldn't be caught as **trespassers**.

Even though she loved him, Libby refused. "We must wait until we are older," she said. "Maybe our families will stop feuding by then."

Sadly, **Gib rides home** alone. He never saw Libby again until 100 years later, when they met as ghosts. Even today people say you can see the young lovers as **the ghosts of Rathburn Park**.

Answers to Mystery Titles

1. Cat
2. Egypt
3. Gypsy
4. Ghost
5. Witches
6. *The Gypsy Game* (C)
7. *The Trespassers* (H)
8. *The Runaways* (F)
9. *The Headless Cupid* (E)
10. *Cat Running* (A)

Answers to Name That Book!

1. *Spyhole Secrets*
2. *The Witches of Worm*
3. *The Magic Nation Thing*

JERRY SPINELLI (1941–):
THE I HAVE/WHO HAS GAME

Cut the cards apart. Each player gets one card. The player who has the card with the asterisks (****) on it reads the "Who has" question. The player who has the answer card reads the answer and then the next question.

I HAVE: Jerry Spinelli was awarded the Newbery Medal by the American Library Association for his novel *Maniac Magee*. **** **WHO HAS:** Where did Jerry Spinelli grow up?	**I HAVE:** Jerry's first novels written for adults were rejected by every publisher who saw them. **WHO HAS:** How did Jerry acquire a ready-made family?
I HAVE: Jerry Spinelli grew up in Norristown, Pennsylvania, where he had a happy childhood doing the everyday things that growing boys do, like bike riding and playing baseball. **WHO HAS:** What was Jerry's first published work?	**I HAVE:** In his thirties Jerry married Eileen Spinelli, an author who had six children. **WHO HAS:** When did Jerry begin writing for children?
I HAVE: A poem Jerry wrote about a win by his high school football team was published in the town newspaper. **WHO HAS:** What effect did the publication of his poem have on Jerry?	**I HAVE:** Jerry wrote poetry about his new family and realized that he had the beginning of a children's novel, *Space Station Seventh Grade*. **WHO HAS:** Where do the ideas for Jerry's books come from?
I HAVE: When Jerry saw his published poem in the paper, he knew that he wanted to become a writer. **WHO HAS:** What happened to Jerry's first novels written for adults?	**I HAVE:** Ideas for Jerry's books come from his own childhood memories and from the children around him. **WHO HAS:** What major award has one of Jerry's books won?

JERRY SPINELLI:
MYSTERY TITLES

Some words in these titles of books by Jerry Spinelli have been replaced with Dewey Decimal numbers. Go to the shelf with the Dewey number. Find the subject of the book(s) with that number. Fill in the missing word in each title. The first person to finish all the titles correctly is the winner!

1. 591.468 _____ _____ _____ _____

2. Fourth Grade 599.352 _____ _____ _____ _____

3 Bath 551.48 _____ _____ _____ _____ _____

4. 027 _____ _____ _____ _____ _____ _____ _____ Card

5. 523.8 _____ _____ _____ _____girl

Some words in these titles of books by Jerry Spinelli have been replaced with synonyms. Put the letter of the actual title after each synonymous title.

6. Ovum _____

7. Largest Marine Mammal

   Sunset to Sunrise _____

8. Collapse and Shatter _____

9. Pulsar Female _____

10. Azure Streamer Dejection _____

ACTUAL TITLES
A. *The Bathwater Gang*
B. *Blue Ribbon Blues*
C. *Crash*
D. *Eggs*
E. *Knots in My Yo-yo String*
F. *Milkweed*
G. *Stargirl*
H. *Night of the Whale*
I. *Dump Days*

Which titles are available in your library?

The key to Mystery Titles is on page __203__.

JERRY SPINELLI:
NAME THAT BOOK!

What title would YOU give to each of these books by Jerry Spinelli?

1) For as long as he can remember, Palmer LaRue has dreaded the day he turns 10: the day he'll be a wringer. But Palmer doesn't want to be a wringer. It's one of the first things he learned about himself, and it's one of the biggest things he has to hide. In Palmer's town being a wringer is an honor, a tradition passed down from father to son. Palmer can't stop himself from being a wringer, just like he can't stop himself from growing one year older, just like he can't stand up to a whole town—right?

Your title _____

2) He's a boy called Jew. Gypsy. Stop thief. Filthy son of Abraham. He's a boy who lives in the streets of Warsaw and steals food for himself and the other orphans. He believes in bread and mothers and angels. He's a boy who wants to be a Nazi, with tall shiny jackboots of his own—until the day that suddenly makes him change his mind. And when the trains come to empty the Jews from the ghetto of the damned, he's a boy who realizes it's safest of all to be nobody. Here is a tale of heartbreak, hope, and survival through the bright eyes of a young Holocaust orphan.

Your title _____

3) He wasn't born with the name Maniac Magee. He came into this world named Jeffrey Lionel Magee, but when his parents died and his life changed, so did his name. And Maniac Magee became a legend. Even today kids talk about how fast he could run; about how he hit an inside-the-park "frog" homer; how no knot, no matter how snarled, would stay that way once he began to untie it. But the thing Maniac Magee is best known for is what he did for the kids from the East Side and those from the West Side.

Your title _____

4) Ever since her family moved to Aunt Sally's farm, Tooter has known that farm life is definitely not for her. There's no pizzeria for miles, her nearest neighbor is a dumb boy, and even her own pet chicken hates her! So Tooter decides to show everyone what she's made of by winning the blue ribbon at the County Fair's goat show. Now all she has to do is keep her little brother—and his paintbrush—away from her prize goat!

Your title _____

See the author's titles on page <u> 203 </u>.
Which titles can you find in your library?

JERRY SPINELLI:
CIRCLE THE HIDDEN TITLES

Maniac Magee has the blue ribbon blues. He is the craziest kid in our fourth grade. He thought for sure he would win the school contest for the best idea on how to welcome new students to the school. Unfortunately he was a loser. The blue ribbon went to Tooter Pepperday, who suggested we give each new student a guide to show him or her around.

I thought Maniac's ideas were better. He wanted to give the new kids a library card that would let them check out as many books as they wanted. "Then," he said, "I'll hang my giant yo-yo in the gym and put a knot in the string for each new student. When we count the knots in my yo-yo string, we'll know how many there are."

Maniac had more ideas. Boys could be invited to join either the Bathwater Gang (kids who never had to take a bath) or the Fourth Grade Rats (kids who stuffed as much in their lockers as the lockers would hold). New girls could join the Stargirl Gang, who met every day to talk about their favorite movie stars.

Maniac also thought new girls should be allowed to join the wrestling team. What guy wouldn't like to say, "There's a girl in my hammerlock"?

Ideas came out of Maniac's head like eggs from a chicken or clothes from a wringer. But as I said, he didn't win the blue ribbon.

My name is Milkweed. Just read on the bulletin board about a creative thinking contest. In 50 words or less, tell what you would do if a plane crash-landed on the playground. I just know when I tell him about it that Maniac will win this one!

From *Gateway to Reading: 250+ Author Games and Booktalks to Motivate Middle Readers* by Nancy J. Polette. Santa Barbara, CA: Libraries Unlimited. Copyright © 2013.

JERRY SPINELLI:
KEYS

Answers to Circle the Hidden Titles

Maniac Magee has the **blue ribbon blues**. He is the craziest kid in our fourth grade. He thought for sure he would win the school contest for the best idea on how to welcome new students to the school. Unfortunately he was a **loser**. The blue ribbon went to **Tooter Pepperday**, who suggested we give each new student a guide to show him or her around.

I thought Maniac's ideas were better. He wanted to give the new kids a **library card** that would let them check out as many books as they wanted. "Then," he said, "I'll hang my giant yo-yo in the gym and put a knot in the string for each new student. When we count the **knots in my yo-yo string**, we'll know how many there are."

Maniac had more ideas. Boys could be invited to join either **the Bathwater Gang** (kids who never had to take a bath) or the **Fourth Grade Rats** (kids who stuffed as much in their lockers as the lockers would hold). New girls could join the **Stargirl** Gang, who met every day to talk about their favorite movie stars.

Maniac also thought new girls should be allowed to join the wrestling team. What guy wouldn't like to say, **"There's a girl in my hammerlock"**?

Ideas came out of Maniac's head like **eggs** from a chicken or clothes from a **wringer**. But as I said, he didn't win the blue ribbon.

My name is **Milkweed**. Just read on the bulletin board about a creative thinking contest. In 50 words or less, tell what you would do if a plane **crash**-landed on the playground. I just know when I tell him about it that Maniac will win this one!

Answers to Mystery Titles

1. Eggs
2. Rats
3. Water
4. Library
5. Star
6. *Eggs* (D)
7. *Night of the Whale* (H)
8. *Crash* (C)
9. *Stargirl* (G)
10. *Blue Ribbon Blues* (B)

Answers to Name That Book!

1. *Wringer*
2. *Milkweed*
3. *Maniac Magee*
4. *Blue Ribbon Blues*

MILDRED D. TAYLOR (1943–):
THE I HAVE/WHO HAS GAME

Cut the cards apart. Each player gets one card. The player who has the card with the asterisks (****) on it reads the "Who has" question. The player who has the answer card reads the answer and then the next question.

I HAVE:	*Roll of Thunder, Hear My Cry* won the Newbery Award. Other awards are The Jason, Jane Adams, Boston Globe Horn Book, Coretta Scott King, and Christopher. ****	I HAVE:	Her father's storytelling was responsible for Mildred D. Taylor's decision to become a writer.
WHO HAS:	Since she did not grow up in the South how was Mildred Taylor able to write so well about it?	WHO HAS:	What did Mildred D. Taylor do after graduating from college?
I HAVE:	Mildred learned about the South from visits she made and stories her father told.	I HAVE:	After graduating from college Mildred Taylor joined the Peace Corps and taught history in Ethiopia.
WHO HAS:	What surprised Mildred on her first day of school in Toledo, Ohio?	WHO HAS:	What was Mildred D. Taylor's first big break as a writer?
I HAVE:	Mildred was surprised that she was the only black child in her class.	I HAVE:	Her first big break as a writer was when she won a contest for *Song of the Trees* in 1975, sponsored by the Council on Interracial Books for Children.
WHO HAS:	Why did Mildred's father move his family to Toledo, Ohio?	WHO HAS:	What are the themes of Mildred D. Taylor's books?
I HAVE:	The family moved to Toledo, Ohio, because of outbreaks of violence in Jackson, Mississippi, in the early 1940s.	I HAVE:	Themes in many of Mildred Taylor's books deal with racism and family strength.
WHO HAS:	What or who was responsible for Mildred D. Taylor's decision to become a writer?	WHO HAS:	What awards have Mildred D. Taylor's books won?

MILDRED D. TAYLOR:
MYSTERY TITLES

Some words in these titles of books by Mildred D. Taylor have been replaced with Dewey Decimal numbers. Go to the shelf with the Dewey number. Find the subject of the book(s) with that number. Fill in the missing word in each title. The first person to finish all the titles correctly is the winner!

1. 177.62 _____ _____ _____ _____ _____ _____ _____ _____ _____ _____

2. 333.73 _____ _____ _____ _____

3 976.2 _____ _____ _____ _____ _____ _____ _____ _____ _____ _____ _____ Bridge

4. Road to 917.68 _____ _____ _____ _____ _____ _____ _____

5. Song of the 582 _____ _____ _____ _____ _____

Some words in these titles of books by Mildred D. Taylor have been replaced with synonyms. Put the letter of the actual title after each synonymous title.

6. Excavation for Water _____

7. Span over the 20th State _____

8 Arbor Melody _____

9. Close Companions _____

10. Terra Firma _____

ACTUAL TITLES
A. *The Friendship*
B. *The Gold Cadillac*
C. *The Land*
D. *Let the Circle Be Unbroken*
E. *Mississippi Bridge*
F. *The Road to Memphis*
G. *Roll of Thunder, Hear My Cry*
H. *Song of the Trees*
I. *The Well*

Which titles are available in your library?

The key to Mystery Titles is on page __209__.

From *Gateway to Reading: 250+ Author Games and Booktalks to Motivate Middle Readers* by Nancy J. Polette. Santa Barbara, CA: Libraries Unlimited. Copyright © 2013.

MILDRED D. TAYLOR: NAME THAT BOOK!

What title would YOU give to each of these books by Mildred D. Taylor?

1) Jeremy Simms watches from the porch of the general store as the passengers board the weekly bus from Jackson. When several white passengers arrive late, the driver roughly orders the black passengers off to make room. Then, in the driving rain, disaster strikes, and Jeremy witnesses a shocking end to the day's drama. Set in Mississippi in the 1930s, this is a gripping story of racial injustice.

Your title _____

2) The son of a prosperous landowner and a former slave, Paul-Edward Logan is unlike any other boy he knows. His white father has acknowledged him and raised him openly, something unusual in post–Civil War Georgia. But as he grows into a man he learns that life for someone like him is not easy. Black people distrust him because he looks white. White people discriminate against him when they learn of his black heritage. Even within his own family he faces betrayal and degradation. So at the age of 14, he sets out toward the only dream he has ever had: to find land every bit as good as his father's and make it his own.

Your title _____

3) Set in Mississippi at the height of the Great Depression, this is the story of one family's struggle to maintain their pride and independence. It is a story of physical survival and of the survival of the human spirit. Cassie, Stacey, Little Man, and Christopher-John experience racial antagonism and hard times, but they learn from their parents the pride and self-respect they need to survive. Owning their own land meant much to the Logan family because it gave them freedom. But when Papa used his land to back credit for black families to shop in Vicksburg, that freedom is threatened. Live day by day with the Logan family in the turbulent year they experience in this moving novel.

Your title _____

See the author's titles on page ___209___ .
Which titles can you find in your library?

MILDRED D. TAYLOR:
CIRCLE THE HIDDEN TITLES

The old tree had occupied land on a corner of the crossroads for more than 200 years. In that time it had seen barefoot families, horses and buggies, and even a gold Cadillac go past, all on their way to cross the Mississippi bridge.

Poets who sing the song of the trees wrote about it:

I think that I shall never see

A bigger, stronger friendship tree.

And indeed, the tree was a friend to all. It gave shelter from the hot sun to those on the road to Memphis. When storms lit up the sky, the tree seemed to call to travelers. "At the first roll of thunder, hear my cry, for I will welcome you and protect you." Somehow travelers heard the tree and knew that all would be well.

"From seed, to seedling, to trunk, to branches, to full-grown tree that drops more seeds, let the circle be unbroken," the tree seems to say, "for I or my offspring will always be here to give comfort to the traveler."

From *Gateway to Reading: 250+ Author Games and Booktalks to Motivate Middle Readers*
by Nancy J. Polette. Santa Barbara, CA: Libraries Unlimited. Copyright © 2013.

MILDRED D. TAYLOR:
KEYS

Answers to Circle the Hidden Titles

The old tree had occupied **land** on a corner of the crossroads for more than 200 years. In that time it had seen barefoot families, horses and buggies, and even a **gold Cadillac** go past, all on their way to cross the **Mississippi bridge**.

Poets who sing the **song of the trees** wrote about it:

I think that I shall never see
A bigger, stronger **friendship** tree.

And indeed, the tree was a friend to all. It gave shelter from the hot sun to those on **the road to Memphis**. When storms lit up the sky, the tree seemed to call to travelers. "At the first **roll of thunder, hear my cry**, for I will welcome you and protect you." Somehow travelers heard the tree and knew that all would be **well**.

"From seed, to seedling, to trunk, to branches, to full-grown tree that drops more seeds, **let the circle be unbroken**," the tree seems to say, "for I or my offspring will always be here to give comfort to the traveler."

Answers to Mystery Titles

1. Friendship
2. Land
3. Mississippi
4. Memphis
5. Trees
6. *The Well* (I)
7. *Mississippi Bridge* (E)
8. *Song of the Trees* (H)
9. *The Friendship* (A)
10. *The Land* (C)

Answers to Name That Book!

1. *Mississippi Bridge*
2. *The Land*
3. *Roll of Thunder, Hear My Cry*

THEODORE TAYLOR (1921–2006):
THE I HAVE/WHO HAS GAME

Cut the cards apart. Each player gets one card. The player who has the card with the asterisks (****) on it reads the "Who has" question. The player who has the answer card reads the answer and then the next question.

I HAVE: *The Cay* won the Lewis Carroll Shelf Award and 11 other awards and has passed the 4 million copy mark. **** **WHO HAS:** When did Theodore Taylor begin writing for publication?	**I HAVE:** After the war Theodore became a press agent, editor, and Hollywood producer working with major stars. **WHO HAS:** When did Theodore become a full-time writer?
I HAVE: Theodore Taylor began writing about high school sports for the Portsmouth, Virginia, *Evening Star.* **WHO HAS:** What happened when Theodore was 17?	**I HAVE:** In the late 1950s Theodore became a full time writer. *The Cay* was made into a movie starring James Earl Jones. **WHO HAS:** How are Theodore Taylor's life experiences reflected in his books?
I HAVE: At age 17 Theodore left home to get a job as copy boy at the *Washington, D.C. Daily News.* **WHO HAS:** How did Theodore Taylor serve his country in World War II?	**I HAVE:** *The Maldonado Miracle* and the Teetoncey Trilogy take place in the outer banks of North Carolina, where Theodore grew up. **WHO HAS:** What were the loves of Theodore Taylor's life.
I HAVE: Theodore was a cadet AB Seaman on a gasoline tanker and a naval officer in the Pacific. **WHO HAS:** What jobs did Theodore hold after the war?	**I HAVE:** The loves of Theodore Taylor's life were his wife, Flora; ocean fishing; and world travel. **WHO HAS:** What awards have Theodore Taylor's books won?

THEODORE TAYLOR:
MYSTERY TITLES

Some words in these titles of books by Theodore Taylor have been replaced with Dewey Decimal numbers. Go to the shelf with the Dewey number. Find the subject of the book(s) with that number. Fill in the missing word in each title. The first person to finish all the titles correctly is the winner!

1. 327.17 _____ _____ _____ _____

2. 551.3 _____ _____ _____ Drift

3. Rogue 551.463 _____ _____ _____ _____

4. 359.009 _____ _____ _____ _____ _____ _____ Returns

5. Sweet Friday 551.42 _____ _____ _____ _____ _____ _____

Some words in these titles of books by Theodore Taylor have been replaced with synonyms. Put the letter of the actual title after each synonymous title.

6. Captive _____

7. Mariner Comes Back _____

8. Explosive Device _____

9. Secret Shooter _____

10. Moving Frozen Water _____

ACTUAL TITLES
A. *The Bomb*
B. *The Cay*
C. *Ice Drift*
D. *Rogue Wave*
E. *A Sailor Returns*
F. *Sweet Friday Island*
G. *Sniper*
H. *The Hostage*
I. *Walking Up a Rainbow*

Which titles are available in your library?

The key to Mystery Titles is on page __215__.

THEODORE TAYLOR: NAME THAT BOOK!

What title would YOU give to each of these books by Theodore Taylor?

A) When the freighter on which they are traveling is torpedoed by a German submarine during World War II, an adolescent white boy, blinded by a blow on the head, and an old black man are stranded on a tiny Caribbean island, where the boy acquires a new kind of vision, courage, and love from his old companion as Timothy, the black man, teaches the boy survival skills and eventually loses his life while saving the boy's life in a hurricane.

Your title _____

2) Twelve-year-old Jose Maldonado used to dream of becoming a fine artist. But this son of a poor Mexican farmer now focuses on survival, not art. After Jose's mother died, his father left to work in the United States, leaving Jose on his own in Mexico. When it's time for father and son to reunite, things go terribly wrong. Jose's attempt to cross the border is harrowing, and his stay at a migrant worker camp turns into a nightmare, forcing him to flee for his life. Hiding out in a church seems a wise thing to do—until the blood dripping from his wounded shoulder lands on a statue of Christ. Now everyone thinks the statue itself is bleeding. Jose's accidental "miracle" kick-starts a media frenzy—and threatens the future of an entire town.

Your title _____

3) No one can definitely say when Friar Tuck began to go blind. Young, beautiful, so free-spirited, the dog had a long life ahead. Helen adored Tuck from the first moment he was placed in her arms, a squirming fat sausage of creamy yellow fur. And very soon Tuck returned her love. He faithfully slept on the rug beside her bed, guarded her against strangers, and rejoiced in their long walks together. So when Tuck began to lose his sight, Helen fought to be his eyes. She wouldn't let his blindness end his life or even limit it. Instead, Helen thought up a unique solution to Tuck's trouble, one that would keep Tuck free, proud, and hers forever.

Your title _____

4) In 1868 14-year-old Alika and his younger brother, Sulu, are hunting for seals on an ice floe attached to their island in the Arctic. Suddenly the ice starts to shake, and they hear a loud crack—the terrible sound of the floe breaking free from land. The boys watch with horror as the dark expanse of water between the ice and the shore rapidly widens, and they start drifting south—away from their home, their family, and everything they've ever known. Throughout their 6-month journey down the Greenland Strait, the brothers face bitter cold, starvation, and most frightening of all, vicious polar bears. But they still remain hopeful that one day they'll be rescued.

Your title _____

See the author's titles on page __215__.
Which titles can you find in your library?

From *Gateway to Reading: 250+ Author Games and Booktalks to Motivate Middle Readers* by Nancy J. Polette. Santa Barbara, CA: Libraries Unlimited. Copyright © 2013.

THEODORE TAYLOR:
CIRCLE THE HIDDEN TITLES

During World War II, few people in the United States knew that the enemy was near our shores. The lord of the kill, the German submarine, a modern Billy the Kid, lurked in the waters off the coasts. Timothy of the cay knew. His ship had been blown out from under him. The cay was one of the many tiny islands far off the Florida coast. A rogue wave carried Timothy to shore along with another passenger named Tuck. The trouble with Tuck was that he was lazy and not willing to do the hard work necessary to survive on the cay. Getting Tuck to catch fish or gather wood for the fire was as difficult as walking up a rainbow or finding an ice drift in the Caribbean.

Unknown to Timothy, Teetoncey and Ben O'Neal, sailors, had also been washed up on the island. Teetoncey was also a writer and kept all Ben's stories in his head, for one day he would write the odyssey of Ben O'Neal.

It was several Fridays after the torpedo or bomb sank Timothy's ship that the castaways met. Teetoncey, Ben, and Timothy became friends and were walking about the cay when they came upon a berry bush and watched the birds eating the sweet berries. Timothy tried some. They were delicious. He would call this cay Sweet Friday Island.

Timothy ate so many berries he became sleepy, so he went to sleep under the warm sun and dreamed a cooling ice drift and of his wife, Maria. He was sleeping so soundly that he almost did not hear Tuck's cry. The freighter *Maldonado* was offshore and was sending a small boat to rescue the castaways. It was a *Maldonado* miracle. "No matter what the danger," said Ben, "a sailor returns to his ship to serve his country the best way he can."

While Timothy was glad to be rid of Tuck, he hoped one day to bring Maria back to the beautiful cay and enjoy its wonders together.

From *Gateway to Reading: 250+ Author Games and Booktalks to Motivate Middle Readers* by Nancy J. Polette. Santa Barbara, CA: Libraries Unlimited. Copyright © 2013.

THEODORE TAYLOR:
KEYS

Answers to Circle the Hidden Titles

During World War II, few people in the United States knew that the enemy was near our shores. The **lord of the kill**, the German submarine, a modern **Billy the Kid**, lurked in the waters off the coasts. **Timothy of the cay** knew. His ship had been blown out from under him. **The cay** was one of the many tiny islands far off the Florida coast. A **rogue wave** carried Timothy to shore along with another passenger named Tuck. The **trouble with Tuck** was that he was lazy and not willing to do the hard work necessary to survive on the cay. Getting Tuck to catch fish or gather wood for the fire was as difficult as **walking up a rainbow** or finding an **ice drift** in the Caribbean.

Unknown to Timothy, **Teetoncey and Ben O'Neal**, sailors, had also been washed up on the island. **Teetoncey** was also a writer and kept all Ben's stories in his head, for one day he would write the **odyssey of Ben O'Neal**.

It was several Fridays after the torpedo or **bomb** sank Timothy's ship that the castaways met. Teetoncey, Ben, and Timothy became friends and were walking about **the cay** when they came upon a berry bush and watched the birds eating the sweet berries. Timothy tried some. They were delicious. He would call this cay **Sweet Friday Island**.

Timothy ate so many berries he became sleepy, so he went to sleep under the warm sun and dreamed a cooling **ice drift** and of his wife, **Maria**. He was sleeping so soundly that he almost did not hear Tuck's cry. The freighter *Maldonado* was offshore and was sending a small boat to rescue the castaways. It was a *Maldonado* **miracle**. "No matter what the danger," said Ben, "a **sailor returns** to his ship to serve his country the best way he can."

While Timothy was glad to be rid of Tuck, he hoped one day to bring **Maria** back to the beautiful cay and enjoy its wonders together.

Answers to Mystery Titles

1. Bomb
2. Ice
3. Wave
4. Sailor
5. Island
6. *The Hostage* (H)
7. *A Sailor Returns* (E)
8. *The Bomb* (A)
9. *Sniper* (G)
10. *Ice Drift* (C)

Answers to Name That Book!

1. *The Cay*
2. *The Maldonado Miracle*
3. *The Trouble with Tuck*
4. *Ice Drift*

BARBARA BROOKS WALLACE (1923–):
THE I HAVE/WHO HAS GAME

Cut the cards apart. Each player gets one card. The player who has the card with the asterisks (****) on it reads the "Who has" question. The player who has the answer card reads the answer and then the next question.

I HAVE:	She won the NLAPW Children's Book Award, The William Allen White Award, and two Edgar Allan Poe Awards from the Mystery Writers of America for her Peppermint series. ****	I HAVE:	Barbara and her husband have a cat and a turtle and enjoy visits with their two grandchildren.
WHO HAS:	What was different about Barbara's childhood?	WHO HAS:	Who are Barbara's favorite authors?
I HAVE:	Barbara was born and grew up in China. Her father worked for Standard Oil and her mother was a nurse.	I HAVE:	Barbara's favorite authors are Charles Dickens, Anthony Trollope, and Jane Austen.
WHO HAS:	What was Barbara's first home in San Francisco?	WHO HAS:	How are the works of Barbara's favorite authors reflected in her books.
I HAVE:	Barbara's first home in San Francisco was a shabby, white-pillared mansion, which became Sugar Hill Hall in her Peppermint novels.	I HAVE:	Many of Barbara's novels are set in the Victorian era and feature characters similar to those created by Charles Dickens.
WHO HAS:	What jobs did Barbara have after graduating from college?	WHO HAS:	What is special about her Miss Switch Trilogy?
I HAVE:	After graduating from college, Barbara worked for an advertising agency and for the Red Cross.	I HAVE:	The Miss Switch Trilogy became a television series and an ABC Weekend Special.
WHO HAS:	Does Barbara have any pets?	WHO HAS:	What awards have Barbara Wallace's books won?

BARBARA BROOKS WALLACE:
MYSTERY TITLES

Some words in these titles of books by Barbara Brooks Wallace have been replaced with Dewey Decimal numbers. Go to the shelf with the Dewey number. Find the subject of the book(s) with that number. Fill in the missing word in each title. The first person to finish all the titles correctly is the winner!

1. Barrel in the 643.5 _____ _____ _____ _____ _____ _____ _____ _____

2. Cousins in the 728.81 _____ _____ _____ _____ _____ _____

3 133.1 _____ _____ _____ _____ _____ _____ in the Gallery

4. 598.887 _____ _____ _____ _____ _____ _____ _____ _____ in the Scullery

5. The 649.144 _____ _____ _____ _____ in the Tavern

Some words in these titles of books by Barbara Brooks Wallace have been replaced with synonyms. Put the letter of the actual title after each synonymous title.

6. Sibling's Children in the Citadel _____

7. Notable Occurrence on Impeccable Land _____

8 Duplicate in the Alehouse _____

9. Spirits in the Balcony _____

10. Difficulty with Young Woman's Exchange _____

ACTUAL TITLES
A. *The Barrel in the Basement*
B. *Cousins in the Castle*
C. *Ghosts in the Gallery*
D. *Julia and the Third Bad Thing*
E. *Palmer Patch*
F. *Peppermints in the Parlor*
G. *Sparrows in the Scullery*
H. *The Trouble with Miss Switch*
I. *The Twin in the Tavern*
J. *The Interesting Thing That Happened at Perfect Acres, Inc.*

Which titles are available in your library?

The key to Mystery Titles is on page __221__.

 From *Gateway to Reading: 250+ Author Games and Booktalks to Motivate Middle Readers* by Nancy J. Polette. Santa Barbara, CA: Libraries Unlimited. Copyright © 2013.

BARBARA BROOKS WALLACE:
NAME THAT BOOK!

What title would YOU give to each of these books by Barbara Brooks Wallace?

1) Fifth grade was a year full of flying brooms, spells gone wrong, and general craziness for Rupert P. Brown III. Sixth grade should be a little more normal, right? Wrong! Sixth grade brings a new teacher named Miss Blossom, a principal who is every girl's crush, a bird who's got a thing for math, and a whacked-out computer that leads Rupert to a Web site called computowitch.com—with a password that's also the name of an evil witch from Rupert's past! As clever as he is, Rupert can probably use some help—and who better to assist than his favorite bewitching teacher, Miss Switch?

Your title _____

2) Emily Luccock is looking forward to living at Sugar Hill Hall. She remembers her aunt and uncle's grand old mansion well, with its enormous, elegant parlor and white china cups filled with hot chocolate. But this time things are different. Her aunt's once bright and lively home is now dead with silence. Evil lurks in every corner, and the dark, shadowed walls watch and whisper late at night. And no one ever speaks. Everything's changed at Sugar Hill Hall, and Emily knows something awful is happening there. What has become of Uncle Twice? Why is Aunt Twice a prisoner in her own home? Emily is desperate to uncover the truth. Time is running out, and she must find a way to save the people and home she cares so much about.

Your title _____

3) Emily Luccock has survived the horrors of Sugar Hill Hall and been reunited with her beloved Aunt and Uncle Twice. Now she is devastated to be left at Mrs. Spilking's Select Academy while her aunt and uncle sail for India. But nothing can top Emily's misery once she spies the dreary school, icy Mrs. Spilking, and, once again, a bowl of tantalizing yet forbidden peppermints! Emily tries to keep her spirits up while counting the days until she can rejoin Aunt and Uncle Twice. But she soon realizes her aunt and uncle have all but forgotten her, and worse, Mrs. Spilking's behavior grows increasingly cruel—and suspicious. Can Emily discover what's going on at the dreadful school before her future is destroyed forever?

Your title _____

4) What is the secret? In a grim tenement district of New York City, before the turn of the century, young Robin decides to take his baby brother, Danny, and escape from his brutal stepfather. Surviving on the street is no easy feat, until he discovers a place called St. Something and joins up with the tough but loyal street boys who make St. Something their home. Robin knows he cannot hide forever—but what he does not know is how many untold secrets lie before him, and how the answers are with the most unlikely person.

Your title _____

See the author's titles on page ___221___.
Which titles can you find in your library?

My name is Charlie, and I want to tell you about the interesting thing that happened at Perfect Acres, Inc., named because the old castle was a perfect place for ghosts. One hid in a barrel in the basement. Two ghost cousins in the castle were the same ghosts in the gallery that frightened visitors. Even the sparrows in the scullery are ghost birds.

One day my friends Julia, Palmer Patch, and Miss Switch decided to explore the old castle. I wanted to take along a lunch, so I went to find our cook and said, "Hello, Claudia, can you fix us a picnic lunch?"

"Can do, Missy Charlie," she answered.

"Fine," I said, "but remember the perils of peppermints. Julia is allergic to them. That time she got one whiff of peppermints in the parlor she nearly choked to death. We really have to watch out for Julia. And the third bad thing not to put in the lunch is apples. If Miss Switch comes with us, she can't bite into an apple. The trouble with Miss Switch is that she has false teeth that fall out.

The most interesting thing that happened on our trip was when we stopped at a haunted tavern on the way to Perfect Acres. Guess what? The stable boy was my twin brother. Never in a million years did I expect to find my twin in the tavern.

One day I'll write about the old castle and call it the Secret in St. Something.

Answers to Circle the Hidden Titles

My name is Charlie, and I want to tell you about **the interesting thing that happened at Perfect Acres, Inc.**, named because the old castle was a perfect place for ghosts. One hid in a **barrel in the basement**. Two ghost **cousins in the castle** were the same **ghosts in the gallery** that frightened visitors. Even the **sparrows in the scullery** are ghost birds.

One day my friends Julia, **Palmer Patch**, and Miss Switch decided to explore the old castle. I wanted to take along a lunch, so I went to find our cook and said, "**Hello, Claudia**, can you fix us a picnic lunch?"

"**Can do, Missy Charlie**," she answered.

"Fine," I said, "but remember **the perils of peppermints**. Julia is allergic to them. That time she got one whiff of **peppermints in the parlor** she nearly choked to death. We really have to watch out for **Julia**. **And the third bad thing** not to put in the lunch is apples. If Miss Switch comes with us, she can't bite into an apple. **The trouble with Miss Switch** is that she has false teeth that fall out.

The most interesting thing that happened on our trip was when we stopped at a haunted tavern on the way to Perfect Acres. Guess what? The stable boy was my twin brother. Never in a million years did I expect to find my **twin in the tavern**.

One day I'll write about the old castle and call it the **Secret in St. Something**.

Answers to Mystery Titles

1. Basement
2. Castle
3. Ghosts
4. Sparrows
5. Twin
6. *Cousins in the Castle* (B)
7. *The Interesting Thing That Happened at Perfect Acres, Inc.* (J)
8. *The Twin in the Tavern* (I)
9. *Ghosts in the Gallery* (C)
10. *The Trouble with Miss Switch* (H)

Answers to Name That Book!

1. *Miss Switch Online*
2. *Peppermints in the Parlor*
3. *The Perils of Peppermints*
4. *Secret in St. Something*

BILL WALLACE (1947–2012):
THE I HAVE/WHO HAS GAME

Cut the cards apart. Each player gets one card. The player who has the card with the asterisks (****) on it reads the "Who has" question. The player who has the answer card reads the answer and then the next question.

I HAVE: Bill won the Arrell Gibson Lifetime Achievement Award, the Texas Blue Bonnet Award, and the Oklahoma Children's Book Award for *A Dog Called Kitty*. **** **WHO HAS:** Where did Bill Wallace grow up?	**I HAVE:** To keep his fourth graders quiet after lunch, Bill made up stories to tell them. **WHO HAS:** How did the children react to Bill's stories?
I HAVE: Bill Wallace was born and grew up in Oklahoma. **WHO HAS:** What jobs did Bill Wallace hold after college?	**I HAVE:** The children liked Bill's stories and encouraged him to seek a publisher. **WHO HAS:** What was Bill's first published book?
I HAVE: Bill hauled hay and was a sales clerk, hospital orderly, jackhammer operator, and teacher. **WHO HAS:** What teaching jobs did Bill have?	**I HAVE:** Bill's first published book was *A Dog Called Kitty*. **WHO HAS:** Has Bill had a coauthor on any of his books?
I HAVE: Bill taught kindergarten and fourth grade and was a ninth-grade principal. **WHO HAS:** What inspired Bill to start writing?	**I HAVE:** Bill's wife, Carol, coauthored *The Flying Flea* and three other titles with him. **WHO HAS:** What writing awards has Bill Wallace won?

BILL WALLACE:
MYSTERY TITLES

Some words in these titles of books by Bill Wallace have been replaced with Dewey Decimal numbers. Go to the shelf with the Dewey number. Find the subject of the book(s) with that number. Fill in the missing word in each title. The first person to finish all the titles correctly is the winner!

1. Blackwater 574.973 _____ _____ _____ _____ _____

2. 599.772 _____ _____ _____ _____ _____ _____ Autumn

3. 636.7 _____ _____ _____ Called Kitty

4. Eye of the Great 599.78 _____ _____ _____ _____

5. Trapped in Death 55.4 _____ _____ _____ _____

Some words in these titles of books by Bill Wallace have been replaced with synonyms. Put the letter of the actual title after each synonymous title.

6. Canine Assuming Persona St. Nick _____

7. Choice of Offspring _____

8. Comeliness _____

9. Mucus Mixture _____

10. Canines Forbidden _____

ACTUAL TITLES
A. *Beauty*
B. *Journey into Terror*
D. *The Dog Who Thought He Was Santa*
E. *Never Say Quit*
F. *No Dogs Allowed*
G. *Pick of the Litter*
H. *Red Dog*
I. *Snot Stew*
J. *True Friends*

Which titles are available in your library?

The key to Mystery Titles is on page __227__.

From *Gateway to Reading: 250+ Author Games and Booktalks to Motivate Middle Readers* by Nancy J. Polette. Santa Barbara, CA: Libraries Unlimited. Copyright © 2013.

BILL WALLACE:
NAME THAT BOOK!

What title would YOU give to each of these books by Bill Wallace?

1) When the pup shows up at the farm, small and fuzzy, with a floppy wet tongue and a bushy tail that's always wagging, no one knows where he's from. Motherless and hungry, he needs to be fed or he'll starve to death. Most boys would welcome such a dog into their lives, feed it and train it and raise it to be a good farm pet. But Ricky's different. Ever since he was attacked as a baby by a mad dog, he's been afraid of them. This is an unforgettable adventure story about the trust that grows between a boy and a mongrel.

Your title _____

2) What better occupation for a dog lover than to raise hunting dogs! This is how Tom's grandfather makes his living, but he needs help after heart problems arise. Fifth grader Tom, who has been in trouble at school, goes to help Grandpa, finding that the hours are long and the work is hard. However, Tom develops a special fondness for a beagle pup in a recent litter. He names the pup Tad and uses it as a sounding board for his many questions about life and especially what to do about a girl named Angie he met on a trip with his parents to Six Flags. The problem arises when Grandpa promises the owner of the litter's sire that he can have the pick of the litter. Tom knows that Tad will most likely be the man's choice. How can Tom give up the dog he has come to believe is his best friend?

Your title _____

3) Callie was getting too old to catch mice, so I got the job. I am a cat, but I do not eat birds, only mice. A baby bird who couldn't fly fell out of her nest, and I had to protect her from the monster rats in the barn (that's saying a mouthful!) and Bullsnake under the woodpile. We named her Flea. Callie and I had to teach Flea to fly. After all, how could she stay up north with us when her bird family was flying to Florida? I'm not a Florida kind of cat. It's just too hot for us furry types. I know I'll miss my Flea. But she'll come back, after she's seen the world!

Your title _____

4) It's not easy being a kitten. Don't get me wrong; I love being scratched behind the ears, chasing Butch the dog, and eating Mother's stew. My brother Toby and I learned about "people things" when we were adopted by Sarah and Ben. The only problem with kid-people is the games they like to play, like "Dress the Cat" and "Snot Stew." It's not stew! But what is it? It's making a bully out of Toby and a wreck out of me!

Your title _____

See the author's titles on page ___227___.
Which of these books are in your library?

BILL WALLACE:
CIRCLE THE HIDDEN TITLES

It was a Florida vacation to remember. I had to look after that doggone calf that was always hungry on the farm. One afternoon I took time off from feeding the critter, and my friend Buzz and I decided to go skinny-dipping at Monster Lake. My friend Buzz and I decided to try it, not knowing the lake was part of the blackwater swamp. We soon found out. We started out early in the morning with our dogs. My dog called Kitty, who was the pick of the litter, and Buzz's red dog were in the lead. They ran without a leash, since no signs said No Dogs Allowed. We had been walking for about an hour, enjoying the beauty of the lake, when the dogs set up a howl. They just wouldn't quit. It sounded like a coyote autumn! Coming right at us was an 8-foot alligator.

We felt as if we were looking into the eye of the great bear, except this bear had green scales. True friends don't run away from each other, so I stuck by Buzz, who was frozen to the spot. Besides, running in a swamp is a bad thing to do. There is danger in quicksand. Swamp land is full of it. Fortunately the alligator took off.

The dogs stopped howling, and it was then we saw this bigfoot creature coming right at us. Its smell was totally disgusting. We turned and walked as fast as we could toward a cave we had spotted earlier. My dog, who thought he was Santa, brought me a big stick. We entered the cave but looked up to see Bigfoot blocking the entrance. We were trapped in death cave!

Buzz and I have a motto: "Never say quit!" so we started yelling and throwing rocks at the creature. To our surprise it turned and ran.

Next summer instead of taking a journey into terror, I think I'll stay home and play with my pet ferret in the bedroom and cook up some snot stew!

From *Gateway to Reading: 250+ Author Games and Booktalks to Motivate Middle Readers* by Nancy J. Polette. Santa Barbara, CA: Libraries Unlimited. Copyright © 2013.

BILL WALLACE:
KEYS

Answers to Circle the Hidden Titles

It was a Florida vacation to remember. I had to look after **that doggone calf** that was always hungry on the farm. One afternoon I took time off from feeding the critter, and my friend Buzz and I decided to go **skinny-dipping at Monster Lake**. My friend Buzz and I decided to try it, not knowing the lake was part of the **blackwater swamp**. We soon found out. We started out early in the morning with our dogs. My **dog called Kitty**, who was the **pick of the litter**, and Buzz's **red dog** were in the lead. They ran without a leash, since no signs said **No Dogs Allowed**. We had been walking for about an hour, enjoying the **beauty** of the lake, when the dogs set up a howl. They just wouldn't quit. It sounded like a **coyote autumn**! Coming right at us was an 8-foot alligator.

We felt as if we were looking into the **eye of the great bear**, except this bear had green scales. **True friends** don't run away from each other, so I stuck by Buzz, who was frozen to the spot. Besides, running in a swamp is a bad thing to do. There is **danger in quicksand. Swamp** land is full of it. Fortunately the alligator took off.

The dogs stopped howling, and it was then we saw this bigfoot creature coming right at us. Its smell was **totally disgusting**. We turned and walked as fast as we could toward a cave we had spotted earlier. My **dog, who thought he was Santa**, brought me a big stick. We entered the cave but looked up to see Bigfoot blocking the entrance. We were **trapped in death cave**!

Buzz and I have a motto: "**Never say quit!**" so we started yelling and throwing rocks at the creature. To our surprise it turned and ran.

Next summer instead of taking a **journey into terror**, I think I'll stay home and play with my pet **ferret in the bedroom** and cook up some **snot stew**!

Answers to Mystery Titles

1. Swamp
2. Coyote
3. Dog
4. Bear
5. Cave
6. *The Dog Who Thought He Was Santa* (D)
7. *Pick of the Litter* (G)
8. *Beauty* (A)
9. *Snot Stew* (I)
10. *No Dogs Allowed* (F)

Answers to Name That Book!

1. *A Dog Called Kitty*
2. *Pick of the Litter*
3. *The Flying Flea, Callie, and Me*
4. *Snot Stew*

BETTY REN WRIGHT (1927–　):
THE I HAVE/WHO HAS GAME

Cut the cards apart. Each player gets one card. The player who has the card with the asterisks (****) on it reads the "Who has" question. The player who has the answer card reads the answer and then the next question.

I HAVE:	She has won nine state children's choice awards, including the Texas Bluebonnet Award for *The Dollhouse Murders*. ****	I HAVE:	As a children's book editor Betty wrote the text for several picture books and wrote short fiction for magazines.
WHO HAS:	When did Betty begin writing?	WHO HAS:	When did Betty start writing full time?
I HAVE:	From the age of eight Betty has always kept a notebook in which she writes stories and poems.	I HAVE:	Betty started writing full time after her marriage to George Frederiksen in 1976.
WHO HAS:	Where did Betty grow up?	WHO HAS:	How many children's books has Betty Ren Wright written?
I HAVE:	Betty went to grade school, high school, and college in the Milwaukee, Wisconsin, area.	I HAVE:	Betty Ren Wright has written more than 35 picture books and 25 novels for young readers.
WHO HAS:	What was Betty's job after college?	WHO HAS:	What is the most popular of all her books?
I HAVE:	After graduating from college Betty worked as a children's book editor for Western Publishing.	I HAVE:	*The Dollhouse Murders* has been published in 12 languages and has been popular for more than 20 years.
WHO HAS:	What writing did she do as a children's book editor?	WHO HAS:	What awards have Betty Ren Wright's books earned?

BETTY REN WRIGHT:
MYSTERY TITLES

Some words in these titles of books by Betty Ren Wright have been replaced with Dewey Decimal numbers. Go to the shelf with the Dewey number. Find the subject of the book(s) with that number. Fill in the missing word in each title. The first person to finish all the titles correctly is the winner!

1. Christina's 133.1 _____ _____ _____ _____ _____

2. 688.7221 _____ _____ _____ _____ house Murders

3. 133.1 _____ _____ _____ _____ _____ in the Family

4. Ghost of 641.6 _____ _____ _____ _____ _____ _____ _____ Hill

5. 523.32 _____ _____ _____ _____ light Man

Some words in these titles of books by Betty Ren Wright have been replaced with synonyms. Put the letter of the actual title after each synonymous title.

6. Spirit Among the Clan _____

7. Ascending from Gloom _____

8. Overabundance of Hidden Revelations _____

9. Abode with Spirit Integration _____

10. Male under Luna Illumination _____

ACTUAL TITLES
A. *The Dollhouse Murders*
B. *The Ghost Comes Calling*
C. *A Ghost in the Family*
D. *A Ghost in the House*
E. *Haunted Summer*
F. *Moonlight Man*
G. *Nothing But Trouble*
H. *Out of the Dark*
I. *The Scariest Night*
J. *Too Many Secrets*
K. *The Wish Master*

Which titles are available in your library?

The key to Mystery Titles is on page __233__.

From *Gateway to Reading: 250+ Author Games and Booktalks to Motivate Middle Readers* by Nancy J. Polette. Santa Barbara, CA: Libraries Unlimited. Copyright © 2013.

BETTY REN WRIGHT:
NAME THAT BOOK!

What title would YOU give to each of these books by Betty Ren Wright?

1) Amy is terrified. She hears scratching and scurrying noises coming from the dollhouse, and the dolls she was playing with are not where she left them. Dolls can't move by themselves, she tells herself. But every night when Amy goes into the attic to check on the dollhouse, it is filled with an eerie light, and the dolls have moved again! Are the dolls trying to tell her something? Are their movements connected to the grisly murders of her own great-grandparents?

Your title _____

2) Christina dreads spending the summer with crabby Uncle Ralph in his spooky Victorian mansion. Things change, however, when she sees the ghostly figure of a small, sad boy. Could he be linked to the murders that happened in the house 30 years before? And what evil, chilling presence is lurking in the attic?

Your title _____

3) Charlene's uncle buys the old town mansion to fix it up and turn it into a bed-and-breakfast inn. Charli feels it is haunted. At the same time, 14-year-old Sophia, whose parents died several years ago, comes to live with the Crandalls (Charli's cousins). Her gift of premonition got her into trouble at previous foster homes. Sophia is determined to fit in with the Crandalls and keeps her skill a secret. She instantly gets along with the two four-year-old boys and the baby. Meanwhile, Charli is jealous of Sophia's new role in her cousin's house. Charli witnesses strange signs, like a shadow of a crib rocking without a crib, a baby crying, and a quilt that shows up in different rooms, but no one else believes the house is haunted until Sophia uses her gift to save the baby before the ghost does him harm.

Your title _____

4) Martin and Peter love their family's new cabin up on Popcorn Hill. They like the stray sheepdog that roams around their place even more. But when they hear ghostly laughter in their room at night, they're afraid that things on Popcorn Hill may not be what they seem. Are Martin and Peter brave enough to meet a ghost or two?

Your title _____

See the author's titles on page __233__.
Which of these books are in your library?

BETTY REN WRIGHT:
CIRCLE THE HIDDEN TITLES

No one believed Christina's ghost stories, but they loved to hear her tell them. Christina was an old woman who had bad luck. Every time she moved she swore there was a ghost in the house that came at night. Even when she broke her leg and spent time in the hospital, she insisted there was a ghost in room 11.

When Christina moved to a boarding house named Crandall's Castle on Popcorn Hill in Boston, she said the ghost of Popcorn Hill was a moonlight man who arrived out of the dark at the stroke of midnight and caused nothing but trouble. One morning Christina's daughter found the heads broken off the dolls in her dollhouse. Christina knew the moonlight man was responsible for the dollhouse murders. The way Christina told it, having a ghost in the family was no fun at all. One of the scariest nights you can have is when a ghost comes calling at midnight.

If you want to experience a haunted summer with too many secrets, you can get your wish. Master your fears and head for Mercy Manor, where Christina lives now. You can be sure if Christina is there that the ghosts of Mercy Manor are right there with her, and who knows? You may be able to take one home with you!

BETTY REN WRIGHT:
KEYS

Answers to Circle the Hidden Titles

No one believed **Christina's ghost** stories, but they loved to hear her tell them. Christina was an old woman who had bad luck. Every time she moved she swore there was **a ghost in the house** that came at night. Even when she broke her leg and spent time in the hospital, she insisted there was a **ghost in room 11**.

When Christina moved to a boarding house named **Crandall's Castle** on Popcorn Hill in Boston, she said **the ghost of Popcorn Hill** was a **moonlight man** who arrived **out of the dark** at the stroke of midnight and caused **nothing but trouble**. One morning Christina's daughter found the heads broken off the dolls in her dollhouse. Christina knew the **moonlight man** was responsible for **the dollhouse murders**. The way Christina told it, having **a ghost in the family** was no fun at all. One of the **scariest nights** you can have is when a **ghost comes calling** at midnight.

If you want to experience a **haunted summer** with **too many secrets**, you can get your **wish**. **Master** your fears and head for Mercy Manor, where Christina lives now. You can be sure if Christina is there that the **ghosts of Mercy Manor** are right there with her, and who knows? You may be able to take one home with you!

Answers to Name That Book!

1. *The Dollhouse Murders*
2. *Christina's Ghost*
3. *Crandall's Castle*
4. *The Ghost of Popcorn Hill*

Answers to Mystery Titles

1. Ghost
2. Doll
3. Ghost
4. Popcorn
5. Moon
6. *A Ghost in the Family* (C)
7. *Out of the Dark* (H)
8. *Too Many Secrets* (J)
9. *A Ghost in the House* (D)
10. *Moonlight Man* (F)

LAURENCE YEP (1948–):
THE I HAVE/WHO HAS GAME

Cut the cards apart. Each player gets one card. The player who has the card with the asterisks (****) on it reads the "Who has" question. The player who has the answer card reads the answer and then the next question.

I HAVE: The theme is about outsiders who do not fit into society. **** **WHO HAS:** Where was Laurence Yep born?	**I HAVE:** Laurence wanted to be a chemist. **WHO HAS:** What was his first published work?
I HAVE: Laurence was born in San Francisco's Chinatown. **WHO HAS:** How did his family's store help him?	**I HAVE:** His first published work was a magazine story. **WHO HAS:** Who urged him to write for children?
I HAVE: Working in the store allowed him to meet people from different cultures. **WHO HAS:** Why did Laurence feel he was an outsider in school?	**I HAVE:** Joanne Ryder, an editor at Harper-Collins, urged him to write for children. **WHO HAS:** What was his first book?
I HAVE: Laurence felt like an outsider because he did not speak Chinese in the bilingual school in Chinatown. **WHO HAS:** What did Laurence want to be as an adult?	**I HAVE:** *Sweetwater* was his first book. **WHO HAS:** What is the major theme of Laurence Yep's books?

LAURENCE YEP:
MYSTERY TITLES

Some words in these titles of books by Laurence Yep have been replaced with Dewey Decimal numbers. Go to the shelf with the Dewey number. Find the subject of the book(s) with that number. Fill in the missing word in each title. The first person to finish all the titles correctly is the winner!

1. 599.756 _____ _____ _____ _____ _____ _____ Blood

2. 508.14 _____ _____ _____ _____ _____ _____ _____ _____ Light

3. Curse of the 599.32 _____ _____ _____ _____ _____ _____ _____ _____

4. Thief of 616.12 _____ _____ _____ _____ _____ _____

5. Case of the Goblin 639.41 _____ _____ _____ _____ _____ _____

Some words in these titles of books by Laurence Yep have been replaced with synonyms. Put the letter of the actual title after each synonymous title.

6. The Reptile's Offspring _____

7. The Betrayer _____

8. Ocean Polished Surface _____

9. Dragon Byway _____

10. Celestial Aquatic Animal _____

ACTUAL TITLES
A. *The Rainbow People*
B. *Dragon's Gate*
C. *The Serpent's Children*
D. *Sea Glass*
E. *Tiger's Blood*
F. *Spring Pearl*
G. *The Traitor*
H. *Dragon Road*
I. *Angelfish*

Which titles are available in your library?

The key to Mystery Titles is on page __239__.

LAURENCE YEP:
NAME THAT BOOK!

What title would YOU give to each of these books by Laurence Yep?

1) Tom's Chinese grandmother wants to teach him her powers, but he proves to be a reluctant pupil. Then a monster kills the grandmother, and Tom finds himself in the middle of a wild adventure to find and rescue the phoenix egg. One who owns the egg can control the world. So with the help of Mr. Hu—the appointed guardian of the egg—a dragon, and a monkey, Tom sets off to find the thief and rescue the egg, which has taken the form of a rose. Nonstop action moves across the city and into Goblin Square in search of the evil ones who have stolen the egg and are determined to rule the world.

Your title _____

2) Whoever finds the five lost treasures of Emperor Yu will have the power to control not only the world but the universe. Scirye's sister loses her life while attempting to prevent the theft of one of the treasures, and Scirye knows she must find the treasure and return it to its rightful place. She teams up with Leech, a young boy, and a dragon named Bayang. How can a young girl with no special powers confront the evil forces who have stolen the treasure? Magic helps when a new island in Hawaii grows up from the ocean and Pele, the goddess of volcanoes, befriends Scirye and Leech.

Your title _____

3) When Otter's Uncle Foxfire returns to China with tales of wealth from working on the railroad in the American West, Otter is determined to follow in his uncle's footsteps. However, the real world of the workers is that of cold and hunger, the foreman's whip, and the ever-present danger of avalanches. The boy experiences prejudice everywhere he turns and realizes that far from returning to China as a rich man, it will take all of his courage just to survive.

Your title _____

See the author's titles on page __239__.
Which of these books are in your library?

LAURENCE YEP:
CIRCLE THE HIDDEN TITLES

The serpent's children have been kidnapped, and it is up to you to find the traitor who planned the terrible deed. The girl child is named Angelfish, and her brother is called the child of the owl. Look carefully through your sea glass, and in the distance you will see this thief of hearts dragging the children down Dragon Road to his cave in the mountain. Light from the moon shows the way for you to follow.

Finding the children should be easy because in the past you have solved the case of the goblin pearls and the case of the firecrackers. But wait! You hear a rumbling from the mountain, and the earth begins to tremble. It is a sign that the earth dragon awakes. Mixed with the mountain sounds is the roar of a tiger. Blood on the trail leads you to the cave where the kidnapper has left the children. The kidnapper, who was bitten by the tiger, has fled. The only problem is that after a day in the cave, the children have picked up cockroach cooties and will have to be scrubbed with sweetwater before they can be returned home.

LAURENCE YEP:
KEYS

Answers to Circle the Hidden Titles

The serpent's children have been kidnapped, and it is up to you to find **the traitor** who planned the terrible deed. The girl child is named **Angelfish,** and her brother is called the **child of the owl.** Look carefully through your **sea glass,** and in the distance you will see this **thief of hearts** dragging the children down **Dragon Road** to his cave in the **mountain. Light** from the moon shows the way for you to follow.

Finding the children should be easy because in the past you have solved **the case of the goblin pearls** and **the case of the firecrackers.** But wait! You hear a rumbling from the mountain, and the earth begins to tremble. It is a sign that **the earth dragon awakes.** Mixed with the mountain sounds is the roar of **tigers. Blood** on the trail leads you to the cave where the kidnapper has left the children. The kidnapper, who was bitten by the tiger, has fled. The only problem is that after a day in the cave, the children have picked up **cockroach cooties** and will have to be scrubbed with **sweetwater** before they can be returned home.

Answers to Mystery Titles

1. Tiger's
2. Mountain
3. Squirrel
4. Hearts
5. Pearls
6. *The Serpent's Children* (C)
7. *The Traitor* (G)
8. *Sea Glass* (D)
9. *Dragon Road* (H)
10. *Angelfish* (I)

Answers to Name That Book!

1. *Tiger's Blood*
2. *City of Fire*
3. *Dragon's Gate*

Authors and Titles with Publishing Information

LLOYD ALEXANDER

The Arkadians. Dutton, 1995.

The Beggar Queen. Doubleday, 1984.

Black Cauldron. Holt, 1965.

The Book of Three. Holt, 1964.

The Castle of Llyr. Holt, 1966.

The Drackenberg Adventure. Dutton, 1988.

Dream-of-Jade: The Emperor's Cat. Cricket Books, 2005.

The El Dorado Adventure. Dutton, 1987.

The Fortune-Tellers. Dutton, 1992.

Gawgon and the Boy. Dutton, 2001.

Gypsy Rizka. Dutton, 1999.

The High King. Dutton, 1968.

The House Gobbaleen. Dutton, 1999.

How the Cat Swallowed Thunder. Dutton, 1999.

Iron Ring. Dutton, 1991.

The Philadelphia Adventure. Dutton, 1990.

The Remarkable Journey of Prince Jen. Dutton, 1991.

The Rope Trick. Dutton, 2002.

Taran Wanderer. Holt, 1999.

Time Cat. Holt, 2003.

The Xanadu Adventure. Dutton, 2005.

AVI

Abigail Takes the Wheel. Harper, 1999.

The Barn. Orchard, 1994.

The Book Without Words. Hyperion, 2005.

Crispin: The Cross of Lead. Hyperion, 2002.

Don't You Know There's a War On? Hyperion, 2001.

The End of the Beginning. Harcourt, 2004.

Ereth's Birthday. Harper, 2000.

The Escape from Home. Orchard, 1996.

The Fighting Ground. Harper, 1984.

Finding Providence. HarperCollins, 1997.

The Good Dog. Atheneum, 2001.

Hard Gold. Hyperion, 2008.

Midnight Magic. Scholastic, 1999.

Murder at Midnight. Scholastic, 2009

Nothing But the Truth. Orchard, 1991.

Perloo the Bold. Scholastic, 1998.

Poppy. Orchard, 1995.

Poppy and Rye. Avon, 1998.

Poppy's Return. HarperCollins, 2005.

Prairie School. Harper, 2001.

Ragweed. Harper, 1999.

Romeo and Juliet Together. Orchard, 1987.

Secret School. Harcourt, 2001.

Silent Movie. Atheneum, 2003.

Smuggler's Island. Beech Tree, 1994.

Something Upstairs. Orchard, 1998.

Things That Sometimes Happen. Atheneum, 2002.

The True Confessions of Charlotte Doyle. Orchard Books, 2003.

Who Was That Masked Man Anyway? Orchard, 1992.

Windcatcher. Bradbury, 1991.

Wolf Rider. Simon & Schuster, 1986.

BETSY BYARS

The Animal, the Vegetable, and John D. Jones. Doubleday, 1985.

Ant Plays Bear. Viking, 1997.

The Black Tower. Viking, 2006.

The Burning Questions of Bingo Brown. Viking, 1988.

Cat Diaries. Holt, 2010.

The Computer Nut. Viking, 1986.

Cracker Jackson. Viking, 1986.

Cybil War. Viking, 1990.

Dark Stairs. Viking, 1994.

Dead Letter. Viking, 1996.

Death's Door. Viking, 1997.

Disappearing Acts. Viking, 1998.

Dog Diaries. Holt, 2007.

Golly Sisters Go West. Harper, 1989.

Hooray for the Golly Sisters. Harper, 1992.

Keeper of the Doves. Viking, 2002.

King of Murder. Viking, 2006.

McMummy. Viking, 1993.

Me Tarzan. Harper, 2000.

The Midnight Fox. Viking, 1996.

My Brother, Ant. Viking, 1996.

The Night Swimmers. Delacorte, 1980.

The Pinballs. HarperCollins, 1977.

The Seven Treasure Hunts. HarperCollins, 1991.

Summer of the Swans. Viking, 1970.

Tarot Says Beware. Viking, 1995.

Tornado. Harper, 1996.
Trouble River. Viking, 1989.
Wanted . . . Mud Blossom. Delacorte, 1991.

ANDREW CLEMENTS
Frindle. Simon & Schuster, 1996.
The Jacket. Simon & Schuster, 2002.
Jake Drake, Bully Buster. Simon & Schuster, 2001.
The Janitor's Boy. Simon & Schuster, 2001.
The Landry News. Simon & Schuster, 1999.
The Last Holiday Concert. Simon & Schuster, 2004.
Lunch Money. Simon & Schuster, 2005.
No Talking. Simon & Schuster, 2007.
The Report Card. Simon & Schuster, 2004.
Room One. Simon & Schuster, 2006.
School Story. Simon & Schuster, 2002.
Things Not Seen. Philomel, 2003.
Troublemaker. Simon & Schuster, 2001.
We the Children. Atheneum, 2010.
A Week in the Woods. Simon & Schuster, 2002.

BRUCE COVILLE
Aliens Ate My Homework. Pocket Books, 1993.
Dark Whispers. Scholastic, 2008.
Dragon of Doom. Simon & Schuster, 2005.
Dragonslayers. Pocket Books, 1994.
The Evil Elves. Simon & Schuster, 2004.
Fortune's Journey. Browndeer, 1995.
Goblins in the Castle. Pocket Books, 1992.
I Left My Sneakers in Dimension X. Pocket Books, 1994.
Into the Land of the Unicorns. Scholastic, 1994.
Jennifer Murdley's Toad. Harcourt, 1992.
Jeremy Thatcher, Dragon Hatcher. Harcourt, 1993.
Juliet Dove, Queen of Love. Harcourt, 2003.
The Last Hunt. Scholastic, 2010.
The Monsters of Morley Manor. Harcourt, 2001.
The Monster's Ring. Harcourt, 2002.
My Teacher Glows in the Dark. Pocket Books, 1991.
My Teacher Is an Alien. Pocket Books, 1989.
Oddly Enough. Jane Yolen Books, 1994.
Peanut Butter Lover Boy. Minstrel, 2000.
Planet of the Dips. Pocket Books, 1995.
Sarah's Unicorn. HarperCollins, 1989.
Song of the Wanderer. Scholastic, 2008.
Too Many Aliens. Pocket Books, 2000.
The Weeping Werewolf. Simon & Schuster, 2004.

William Shakespeare's Midsummer Night's Dream. Pocket Books, 1992.
The World's Worst Fairy Godmother. Dial, 1992.

SHARON CREECH
Absolutely Normal Chaos. Harper, 1995.
Bloomability. Harper, 1998.
The Castle Corona. HarperCollins, 2007.
Chasing Redbird. Harper, 1997.
A Fine, Fine School. Harper, 2001.
Fishing in the Air. Harper, 2000.
Granny Torrelli Makes Soup. HarperCollins, 2003.
Heartbeat. HarperCollins, 2004.
Love That Dog. Harper, 2001.
Pleasing the Ghost. Harper, 1996.
Replay. HarperCollins, 2002.
Ruby Holler. Harper, 2002.
The Unfinished Angel. HarperCollins, 2009.
Walk Two Moons. Harper, 1994.
The Wanderer. Harper, 2000.

CHRISTOPHER PAUL CURTIS
Bud, Not Buddy. Delacorte, 2002.
Elijah of Buxton. Scholastic, 2007.
Mr. Chickee's Funny Money. Wendy Lamb, 2006.
Mr. Chickee's Messy Mission. Wendy Lamb, 2007.
The Watsons Go to Birmingham—1963. Delacorte, 1997.

ROALD DAHL
The BFG. Knopf, 2001.
Charlie and the Chocolate Factory. Knopf, 2000.
Charlie and the Great Glass Elevator. Knopf, 2002.
Danny, Champion of the World. Knopf, 1978.
Fantastic Mr. Fox. Viking, 1990.
George's Marvelous Medicine. Knopf, 2002.
James and the Giant Peach. Knopf, 1995.
The Magic Finger. Viking, 1995.
Matilda. Viking, 1988.
The Minipins. Viking, 1993.
More About Boy. Farrar, 2009.
The Twits. Knopf, 2002.
Vile Verses. Viking, 2005.
The Witches. Farrar, 1983.
The Wonderful Story of Henry Sugar. Knopf, 1997.

CYNTHIA DEFELICE
The Apprenticeship of Lucas Whitaker. Dutton, 1995.

Casey in the Bath. Farrar, 1996.
The Dancing Skeleton. Macmillan, 1989.
Devil's Bridge. Macmillan, 1992.
The Ghost of Cutler Creek. Farrar, 2004.
The Ghost of Poplar Point. Farrar, 2007.
The Light on Hogback Hill. Macmillan, 1993.
Lostman's River. Macmillan, 1994.
Missing Manatee. Farrar, 2005.
Mule Eggs. Orchard, 1994.
Signal. Farrar, 2009.
Three Perfect Peaches. Orchard, 1995.
Weasel. Macmillan, 1990.
When Grandpa Kissed His Elbow. Macmillan, 1992.
Willy's Silly Grandma. Orchard, 1997.

KATE DICAMILLO

Because of Winn-Dixie. Candlewick, 2005.
Great Joy. Candlewick, 2007.
The Magician's Elephant. Candlewick, 2009.
Mercy Watson to the Rescue. Candlewick, 2005.
The Miraculous Journey of Edward Tulane. Candlewick, 2006.
The Tale of Despereaux. Candlewick, 2004.
The Tiger Rising. Candlewick, 2004.

SID FLEISCHMAN

The Abracadabra Kid. Greenwillow, 1998.
Bandit's Moon. Greenwillow, 1998.
Bo and Mzzz Mad. Greenwillow, 2001.
By the Great Horn Spoon. Little Brown, 1963.
A Carnival of Animals. Greenwillow, 2000.
Disappearing Act. Greenwillow, 2003.
Dream Stealer. Greenwillow, 2009.
The Ghost on Saturday Night. Greenwillow, 1997.
The Giant Rat of Sumatra. Greenwillow, 2005.
Jim Ugly. Greenwillow, 1992.
Midnight Horse. Greenwillow, 1990.
Mr. Mysterious & Co. Greenwillow, 1997.
The Scarebird. Greenwillow, 1994.
The 13th Floor. Greenwillow, 1995.
The Trouble Begins at 8. Greenwillow, 2008.
The Whipping Boy. Greenwillow, 1986.

PAULA FOX

Amzat and His Brothers. Orchard, 1993.
Blowfish Live in the Sea. Bradbury, 2000.
Eagle Kite. Orchard, 1995.

The Little Swineherd. Dutton, 1995.
Monkey Island. Orchard, 1991.
One-Eyed Cat. Bradbury, 1984.
Portrait of Ivan. Bradbury, 2001.
The Slave Dancer. Bradbury, 1973.
The Stone-Faced Boy. Front Street, 2005.
The Village by the Sea. Orchard, 1988.
Western Wind. Orchard, 1993.

NEIL GAIMAN

Blueberry Girl. HarperCollins, 2008.
Coraline. HarperCollins, 2002.
Crazy Hair. HarperCollins, 2009.
The Dangerous Alphabet. HarperCollins, 2008.
The Graveyard Book. HarperCollins, 2010.
Instructions. HarperCollins, 2010.
M Is for Magic. HarperCollins, 2008.
Odd and the Frost Giants. HarperCollins, 2009.
The Wolves in the Walls. HarperCollins, 2003.

JEAN CRAIGHEAD GEORGE

Acorn Pancakes, Dandelion Salad and 38 Other Wild Recipes. Harper, 1995.
The Cats of Rockville Station. Dutton, 2009.
Charlie's Raven. Dutton, 2004.
Cliff Hanger. HarperCollins, 2002.
Dear Rebecca, Winter Is Here. Harper, 1993.
Fire Storm. HarperCollins, 2003.
The First Thanksgiving. Philomel, 1993.
Frightful's Daughter. Dutton, 2002.
Frightful's Mountain. Dutton, 1999.
Julie. HarperCollins, 1996.
Julie of the Wolves. Harper, 1973.
Look to the North. Harper, 1997.
The Missing Gator of Gumbo Limbo. Harper, 1992.
Morning, Noon, and Night. HarperCollins, 1999.
My Side of the Mountain. Dutton, 1988.
On the Far Side of the Mountain. Dutton, 1990.
One Day in the Woods. Harper, 1988.
The Talking Earth. Harper, 1983.
A Tarantula in My Purse. Harper, 1996.
There's an Owl in the Shower. Harper, 1995.
Tree Castle Island. HarperCollins, 2002.

PATRICIA REILLY GIFF

All About Stacy. Yearling, 1988.
All the Way Home. Delacorte, 2001.

B-E-S-T Friends. Yearling, 1988.
Big Whopper. Wendy Lamb, 2010.
Dance with Rosie. Viking, 1996.
Don't Tell the Girls. Holiday House, 2010.
Eleven. Wendy Lamb, 2008.
Fancy Feet. Yearling, 1988.
Flying Feet. Wendy Lamb, 2011.
Fourth Grade Celebrity. Doubleday, 1989.
House of Tailors. Wendy Lamb, 2004.
Lily's Crossing. Delacorte, 1997.
Maggie's Door. Wendy Lamb, 2003.
Nory Ryan's Song. Delacorte, 2000.
Not-so-perfect Rosie. Viking, 1997.
Number One Kid. Wendy Lamb, 2010.
Pictures of Hollis Woods. Wendy Lamb, 2002.
Watch Out! Man-eating Snake. Yearling, 1988.
Wild Girl. Wendy Lamb, 2009.
Willow Run. Wendy Lamb, 2005.

JAMIE GILSON
Bug in a Rug. Clarion, 1998.
Can't Catch Me, I'm the Gingerbread Man. Beech Tree, 1997.
Chess! I Love It, I Love It, I Love It! Clarion, 2008.
Do Banana's Chew Gum? Lothrop, 1980.
Double Dog Dare. Lothrop, 1988.
4B Goes Wild. Lothrop, 1983.
Gotcha! Clarion, 2006.
Hello, My Name Is Scrambled Eggs. Lothrop, 1985.
Hobie Hanson, Greatest Hero of the Mall. Lothrop, 1989.
Hobie Hanson, You're Weird. Lothrop, 1987.
It Goes Eeeeeeeeeeeee! Clarion, 1994.
Soccer Circus. Lothrop, 1993.
Stink Alley. HarperCollins, 2002.
Thirteen Ways to Sink a Sub. Lothrop, 2009.
Wagon Train 911. Lothrop, 1996.

MARY DOWNING HAHN
All the Lovely Bad Ones. Clarion, 2008.
Anna All Year Round. Clarion, 1999.
Anna on the Farm. Clarion, 2001.
As Ever, Gordy. Clarion, 1998.
Daphne's Book. Clarion, 1983.
Dead Man in Indian Creek. Clarion, 1990.
The Doll in the Garden. Clarion, 1989.
Following My Own Footsteps. Clarion, 1996.

The Gentleman Outlaw and Me, Eli. Clarion, 1996.
The Ghost of Crutchfield Hall. Clarion, 2010.
Look for Me by Moonlight. Clarion, 1995.
The Old Willis Place. Clarion, 2004.
Promises to the Dead. Clarion, 2000.
The Spanish Kidnapping Disaster. Clarion, 1991.
Stepping on the Cracks. Clarion, 1991.
Time for Andrew. Clarion, 1994.
Wait Till Helen Comes. Clarion, 2010.
Witch Catcher. Clarion, 2006.

KAREN HESSE
Aleutian Sparrow. McElderry, 2003.
Lester's Dog. Coward, 1996.
Letters from Rifka. Holt, 1992.
A Light in the Storm. Scholastic, 2011.
The Music of Dolphins. Scholastic, 1996.
Out of the Dust. Scholastic, 1997.
Phoenix Rising. Holt, 1994.
Sable. Holt, 1994.
Stowaway. Simon & Schuster, 2000.
A Time of Angels. Hyperion, 1995.
Wish on a Unicorn. Holt, 1991.
Witness. Scholastic, 2001.

JOHANNA HURWITZ
The Adventures of Ali Baba Bernstein. Morrow, 1985.
Aldo Applesauce. Morrow, 1979.
Aldo Ice Cream. Morrow, 1981.
Amazing Monty. Candlewick, 2010.
Baseball Fever. Morrow, 1991.
Class Clown. Morrow, 2009.
Class President. Morrow, 1990.
Cold and Hot Winter. Morrow, 1988.
DeDe Takes Charge. Morrow, 1984.
The Down and Up Fall. Morrow, 1996.
Even Stephen. Morrow, 1996.
Ever-clever Elisa. Harper Trophy, 2002.
Fourth Grade Fuss. HarperCollins, 2010.
Hurray for Ali Baba Bernstein. Morrow, 1989.
A Llama in the Family. Morrow, 1994.
Make Room for Elisa. Morrow, 1993.
Mighty Monty. Candlewick, 2008.
Much Ado About Aldo. Morrow, 1994.
New Shoes for Silvia. Morrow, 1993.
One Small Dog. HarperCollins, 2000.
Ozzie on His Own. Morrow, 1995.

Pee Wee and Plush. SeaStar, 2002.
Pee Wee's Tale. SeaStar, 2000.
Rip-Roaring Russell. Morrow, 1983.
Russell Sprouts. Morrow, 1987.
School Spirit. Morrow, 1994.
School's Out. Morrow, 1991.
Spring Break. Morrow, 1997.
Teacher's Pet. Morrow, 1988.
Tough Luck Karen. Morrow, 1982.
The Up and Down Spring. Morrow, 1983.

PEG KEHRET
Abduction. Dutton, 2004.
Blizzard Disaster. Minstrel, 1998.
Don't Tell Anyone. Dutton, 2000.
Earthquake Terror. Cobblestone, 1996.
Escaping the Giant Wave. Simon & Schuster, 2003.
Flood Disaster. Minstrel, 1999.
Ghost Dog Secrets. Dutton, 2010.
Ghost's Grave. Dutton, 2005.
I'm Not Who You Think I Am. Dutton, 1999.
My Brother Made Me Do It. Minstrel, 2000.
Nightmare Mountain. Cobblestone, 1989.
The Richest Kids in Town. Cobblestone, 1994.
Runaway Twin. Dutton, 2009.
Saving Lilly. Minstrel, 2001.
Searching for Candlestick Park. Cobblestone, 1997.
Small Steps. Whitman, 1996.
Spy Cat. Dutton, 2003.
Stolen Children. Dutton, 2010.
The Stranger Next Door. Dutton, 2002.
Trapped. Dutton, 2006.
Volcano Disaster. Minstrel, 1998.

KATHRYN LASKY
American Spring. Scholastic, 2004.
Ashes. Viking, 2010.
Burning. Scholastic, 2004.
Capture. Scholastic, 2003.
Chasing Orion. Candlewick, 2010.
Christmas After All. Scholastic, 2001.
Dreams in the Golden Country. Scholastic, 1998.
Elizabeth I: Red Rose of the House of Tudor. Harcourt, 1999.
Felix Takes the Stage. Scholastic, 2010.
Georgia Rises. Farrar, 2009.
Hawksmaid. HarperCollins, 2010.

Home at Last. Scholastic, 2003.
Hope in My Heart. Scholastic, 2003.
The Journal of Augustus Pelletier. Scholastic, 2000.
Journey. Scholastic, 2003.
Journey to the New World. Scholastic, 2010.
Marie Antoinette. Scholastic, 2000.
Mary, Queen of Scots. Scholastic, 2002.
The Night Journey. Warne, 1986.
The Outcast. Scholastic, 2005.
The Rescue. Scholastic, 2004.
Shadow Wolf. Scholastic, 2010.
Shadows in the Water. Harcourt, 2008.
The Siege. Scholastic, 2004.
Sugaring Time. Aladdin, 1983, 1986.
Time for Courage. Scholastic, 2002.
True North. Blue Sky Press, 1996.
Vision of Beauty. Candlewick, 2000.
Watch Wolf. Scholastic, 2011.
The Weaver's Gift. Warne, 1980.

LOIS LOWRY
Anastasia Krupnik. Houghton Mifflin, 1979.
Attaboy, Sam! Houghton Mifflin, 1992.
Autumn Street. Houghton Mifflin, 1980.
Bless This Mouse. Houghton Mifflin, 2011.
Gathering Blue. Houghton Mifflin, 1999.
The Giver. Houghton Mifflin, 1993.
Like the Willow Tree. Scholastic, 2011.
Looking Back. Houghton Mifflin, 1998.
Messenger. Houghton Mifflin, 2004.
Number the Stars. Houghton Mifflin, 1989.
One Hundredth Thing About Caroline. Houghton Mifflin, 1986.
Rabble Starkey. Houghton Mifflin, 1987.
See You Around, Sam. Houghton, 1986.
Silent Boy. Houghton Mifflin, 2003.
Stay! Houghton Mifflin, 1997.
A Summer to Die. Houghton Mifflin, 1977.
Switcharound. Houghton Mifflin, 1985.
Taking Care of Terrific. Houghton Mifflin, 1983.
The Willoughbys. Houghton Mifflin, 2008.
Your Move, J.P. Houghton Mifflin, 1990.
Zooman Sam. Houghton Mifflin, 1999.

PATRICIA MACLACHLAN
All the Places to Love. Harper, 1994.
Arthur, for the Very First Time. Harper, 1989.

Baby. Delacorte, 1995.
Caleb's Story. Harper, 2001.
Cassie Binegar. Harper, 1982.
Edward's Eyes. Atheneum, 2007.
Facts and Fictions of Minna Pratt. Harper, 1988.
More Perfect Than the Moon. HarperCollins, 2004.
Sarah Plain and Tall. Harper, 1985.
Seven Kisses in a Row. Harper, 1983.
Sick Day. Doubleday, 2001.
Skylark. Harper, 1994.
Three Names. Harper, 1991.
Through Grandpa's Eyes. Harper, 1989.
The True Gift. Atheneum, 2009.
What You Know First. Harper, 1995.

PHYLLIS REYNOLDS NAYLOR

Anyone Can Eat Squid. Cavendish, 2005.
Beetles Lightly Toasted. Atheneum, 1992.
Blizzard's Wake. Atheneum, 2002.
Bomb in the Besseldorf Bus Depot. Atheneum, 1996.
Boys in Control. Delacorte, 2003.
The Boys Return. Delacorte, 2001.
Boys Rock! Delacorte, 2005.
Cricket Man. Atheneum, 2008.
Danny's Desert Rats. Atheneum, 1998.
Ducks Disappearing. Atheneum, 1997.
Eating Enchiladas. Cavendish, 2008.
Emily's Fortune. Delacorte, 2010.
Face in the Besseldorf Funeral Parlor. Atheneum, 1993.
Faith, Hope and Ivy June. Delacorte, 2009.
Fear Place. Atheneum, 1994.
Girls Take Over. Delacorte, 2002.
Grand Escape. Atheneum, 1993.
Great Chicken Debacle. Cavendish, 2001.
Incredibly Alice. Atheneum, 2011.
Patches and Scratches. Cavendish, 2007.
Peril in the Besseldorf Parachute Factory. Atheneum, 1999.
Please Do Feed the Bears. Atheneum, 2002.
Roxie and the Hooligans. Atheneum, 2006.
Saving Shiloh. Atheneum, 1997.
Shiloh. Atheneum, 1991.
A Spy Among the Girls. Delacorte, 2000.
Sweet Strawberries. Atheneum, 1999.
Traitor Among the Boys. Delacorte, 1999.
Walker's Crossing. Atheneum, 1999.
Witch Weed. Aladdin, 2004.

SCOTT O'DELL

The Black Pearl. Houghton Mifflin, 1967.
Black Star, Bright Dawn. Houghton Mifflin, 1988.
The Captive. Houghton Mifflin, 1987.
Child of Fire. Houghton Mifflin, 1985.
Feathered Serpent. Houghton Mifflin, 1987.
Island of the Blue Dolphins. Houghton Mifflin, 1960.
My Name Is Not Angelica. Houghton Mifflin, 1989.
Sarah Bishop. Houghton Mifflin, 1980.
The Serpent Never Sleeps. Houghton Mifflin, 1987.
Sing Down the Moon. Houghton Mifflin, 1970.
Streams to the River, River to the Sea. Houghton Mifflin, 1986.
Thunder Rolling in the Mountains. Houghton Mifflin, 1992.
Zia. Houghton Mifflin, 1976.

MARY POPE OSBORNE

Afternoon on the Amazon. Random, 1995.
Buffalo Before Breakfast. Random, 1999.
A Crazy Day with Cobras. Random, 2011.
Dark Day in the Deep Sea. Random, 2008.
Dingoes at Dinnertime. Random, 2000.
Dinosaurs Before Dark. Random, 1992.
Dolphins at Daybreak. Random, 1997.
Earthquake in the Early Morning. Random, 2001.
The Final Battle. Hyperion, 2004.
Ghost Town at Sundown. Random, 1997.
Good Morning Gorillas. Random, 2002.
The Gray-eyed Goddess. Hyperion, 2003.
High Tide in Hawaii. Random, 2003.
Hour of the Olympics. Random, 1998.
Knight at Dawn. Random, 1993.
The Land of the Dead. Hyperion, 2002.
Lions at Lunchtime. Random, 1998.
Midnight on the Moon. Random, 1996.
Mummies in the Morning. Random, 1993.
Night of the Ninjas. Random, 1995.
One-Eyed Giant. Hyperion, 2003.
Pirates Past Noon. Random, 1994.
Polar Bears Past Bedtime. Random, 1998.
Run, Run as Fast as You Can. Dial, 1982.
Season of the Sandstorms. Random, 2005.
Sleeping Bobby. Atheneum, 2005.
Tigers at Twilight. Random, 1999.
Tonight on the Titanic. Random, 1999.
Viking Ships at Sunrise. Random, 1998.

KATHERINE PATERSON

Bridge to Terabithia. Crowell, 1977.
Come Sing, Jimmy Jo. Lodestar, 1995.
The Day of the Pelican. Clarion, 2009.
Field of the Dogs. HarperCollins, 2001.
Flip-Flop Girl. Lodestar, 1996.
The Great Gilly Hopkins. HarperCollins, 1978.
Jacob Have I Loved. HarperCollins, 1980.
Jip, His Story. Lodestar, 1996.
The King's Equal. HarperCollins, 1992.
Lyddie. Lodestar, 1992.
Marvin One Too Many. HarperCollins, 2001.
Marvin's Best Christmas Present Ever. HarperCollins, 1997.
The Master Puppeteer. Crowell, 1975.
Preacher's Boy. Clarion, 1999.
The Same Stuff as Stars. Clarion, 2002.

GARY PAULSEN

Alicia's Song. Delacorte, 1999.
Brian's Hunt. Wendy Lamb, 2003.
Brian's Return. Delacorte, 1999.
Brian's Winter. Delacorte, 1996.
Call Me Francis Tucket. Delacorte, 1995.
Canyons. Ember, 2011.
The Car. Harcourt, 2004.
Christmas Sonata. Delacorte, 1994.
The Cookcamp. Orchard, 1994.
Dogsong. Simon & Schuster, 1985.
The Glass Cafe. Wendy Lamb, 2003.
Guts. Delacorte, 2001.
Harris and Me. Harcourt, 1993.
Hatchet. Simon & Schuster, 1987.
The Island. Orchard, 1988.
Lawn Boy. Wendy Lamb, 2007.
Masters of Disaster. Wendy Lamb, 2010.
Mr. Tucket. Delacorte, 1994.
Mudshark. Wendy Lamb, 2009.
Nightjohn. Delacorte, 1993.
The Quilt. Wendy Lamb, 2004.
The Rifle. Harcourt, 1995.
The River. Delacorte, 1991.
Soldier's Heart. Delacorte, 1998.
Tent. Harcourt, 1995.
Time Hackers. Wendy Lamb, 2005.
Tucket's Gold. Delacorte, 1999.
Tucket's Home. Delacorte, 2000.

Tucket's Ride. Delacorte, 1997.
The Voyage of the Frog. Orchard, 1989.
The White Fox Chronicles. Delacorte, 2000.
Winter Room. Orchard, 1989.

WILLO DAVIS ROBERTS

The Absolutely True Story. Atheneum, 1994.
Blood on His Hands. Atheneum, 2004.
Buddy Is a Stupid Name for a Girl. Atheneum, 2001.
Caught. Atheneum, 1994.
The Girl with the Silver Eyes. Aladdin, 2011.
Hostage. Atheneum, 2000.
Jo and the Bandit. Atheneum, 1998.
The Kidnappers. Simon & Schuster, 1998.
The One Left Behind. Atheneum, 2006.
Pawns. Atheneum, 1998.
Rebel. Atheneum, 2003.
Scared Stiff. Atheneum, 1991.
Secrets at Hidden Valley. Atheneum, 1997.
Twisted Summer. Atheneum, 1996.
Undercurrents. Atheneum, 2002.
The View from the Cherry Tree. Atheneum, 1988.
What Could Go Wrong? Atheneum, 1993.

RON ROY

The Absent Author. Random House, 1997.
The Bald Bandit. Random House, 1997.
The Canary Caper. Random House, 1998.
Deadly Dungeon. Random House, 1998.
Detective Camp. Random House, 2006
The Election Day Disaster. Random House, 2008.
The Empty Envelope. Random House, 1998.
Falcon's Feathers. Random House, 1998.
Fireworks at the FBI. Random House, 2006.
The Haunted Hotel. Random House, 1999.
Invisible Island. Random House, 1999.
Jaguar's Jewel. Random House, 2000.
The Kidnapped King. Random House, 2000.
Lucky Lottery. Random House, 2001.
Mayflower Treasure Hunt. Random House, 2007.
Missing Mummy. Random House, 2001.
Ninth Nugget. Random House, 2001.
Panda Puzzle. Random House, 2002.
Quicksand Question. Random House, 2002.
The Runaway Racehorse. Random House, 2002.
The School Skeleton. Random House, 2003.
The Talking T. Rex. Random House, 2003.

A Thousand Pails of Water. Knopf, 1978.
Unwilling Umpire. Random House, 2004.
Vampire's Vacation. Random House, 2004.
White Wolf. Random House, 2004.
Yellow Yacht. Random House, 2005.
Zombie Zone. Random House, 2005.

JON SCIESZKA

The Good, the Bad, and the Goofy. Viking, 1992.
Hey Kid, Want to Buy a Bridge? Viking, 2002.
It's All Greek to Me. Viking, 1999.
Knights of the Kitchen Table. Viking, 1993.
Me Oh Maya. Viking, 2003.
The Not-So-Jolly Roger. Viking, 1995.
Oh, Say, I Can't See. Viking, 2005.
See You Later, Gladiator. Viking, 1993.
Seen Art? Viking, 2005.
Spaceheadz. Simon & Schuster, 2010.
The Stinky Cheese Man and Other Fairly Stupid Tales. Viking, 1992.
Summer Reading Is Killing Me. Viking, 1998.
The True Story of the 3 Little Pigs. Viking, 1999.
Tut, Tut. Viking, 1996.
2095. Viking, 1997.
Your Mother Was a Neanderthal. Viking, 1993.
Viking It and Liking It. Viking, 2002.

GLORIA SKURZYNSKI

Buried Alive. National Geographic, 2003.
Cliff-Hanger. National Geographic, 1999.
Deadly Waters. National Geographic, 1999.
Escape from Fear. National Geographic, 2010.
Ghost Horses. National Geographic, 2000.
Goodbye, Billy Radish. Bradbury, 1992.
The Hunted. National Geographic, 2000.
Minstrel in the Tower. Random House, 1988.
Night of the Black Bear. National Geographic, 2007.
Out of the Deep. National Geographic, 2002.
Over the Edge. National Geographic, 2002.
Rage of Fire. National Geographic, 2010.
The Revolt. Atheneum, 2005.
Running Scared. National Geographic, 2002.
Spider's Voice. Atheneum, 1999.
Valley of Death. National Geographic, 2002.
Virtual War. Simon & Schuster, 1997.
Wolf Stalker. National Geographic, 1997.

ZILPHA KEATLEY SNYDER

Bronze Pen. Atheneum, 2008.
Cat Running. Delacorte, 1994.
The Egypt Game. Atheneum, 1976.
The Ghosts of Rathburn Park. Delacorte, 2002.
Gib and the Gray Ghost. Delacorte, 2000.
Gib Rides Home. Delacorte, 1998.
The Gypsy Game. Delacorte, 1997.
The Headless Cupid. Atheneum, 1983.
Libby on Wednesday. Delacorte, 1991.
The Magic Nation Thing. Delacorte, 2005.
The Runaways. Delacorte, 1999.
Season of Ponies. Atheneum, 1964.
Spyhole Secrets. Delacorte, 2001.
The Treasures of Weatherby. Atheneum, 2007.
The Trespassers. Delacorte, 1995.
The Unseen. Delacorte, 2004.
The Witches of Worm. Atheneum, 1972.

JERRY SPINELLI

The Bathwater Gang. Little Brown, 1990.
Blue Ribbon Blues. Random House, 1998.
Crash. Knopf, 1996.
Dump Days. Little, Brown, 1988.
Eggs. Little, Brown, 2007.
Fourth Grade Rats. Scholastic, 1991.
Knots in My Yo-yo String. Knopf, 1998.
Library Card. Scholastic, 1997.
Loser. HarperCollins, 2002.
Maniac Magee. Little, Brown, 1990.
Milkweed. Knopf, 2003.
Night of the Whale. Little, Brown, 1985.
Stargirl. Knopf, 1990.
There's a Girl in My Hammerlock. Simon & Schuster, 1993.
Tooter Pepperday. Random House, 1995.
Wringer. HarperCollins, 2010.

MILDRED D. TAYLOR

The Friendship. Dial, 1987.
The Gold Cadillac. Dial, 1987.
The Land. Phyllis Fogelman, 2001.
Let the Circle Be Unbroken. Dial, 1981.
Mississippi Bridge. Dial, 1990.
The Road to Memphis. Dial, 1990.
Roll of Thunder, Hear My Cry. Dial, 2005.
Song of the Trees. Dial, 2003.

The Well: David's Story. Dial, 1995.

THEODORE TAYLOR
Billy the Kid. Harcourt, 2005.
The Bomb. Harcourt, 1995.
The Cay. Doubleday, 1969.
Have Dragon, Will Travel. iUniverse, 2009.
The Hostage. Delacorte, 1987.
Ice Drift. Harcourt, 2005.
Lord of the Kill. Blue Sky, 2002.
The Maldonado Miracle. Harcourt, 2003.
Maria: A Christmas Story. Harcourt, 1992.
The Odyssey of Ben O'Neal. Harcourt, 2004.
Rogue Wave. Harcourt, 1992.
A Sailor Returns. Blue Sky, 2001.
Sniper. Harcourt, 2007.
Sweet Friday Island. Harcourt, 1994.
Teetoncey. Doubleday, 1974.
Teetoncey and Ben O'Neal. Doubleday, 1975.
Timothy of the Cay. Harcourt, 1993.
Trouble with Tuck. Doubleday, 1981.
Walking Up a Rainbow. Harcourt, 1994.

BARBARA BROOKS WALLACE
The Barrel in the Basement. Aladdin, 2005.
Can Do, Missy Charlie. Aladdin, 2000.
Cousins in the Castle. Aladdin, 2006.
Ghosts in the Gallery. Aladdin, 2001.
Hello, Claudia. Aladdin, 2000.
The Interesting Thing That Happened at Perfect Acres, Inc. Aladdin, 2007.
Julia and the Third Bad Thing. Aladdin, 2005.
Miss Switch Online. Atheneum, 2002.
Palmer Patch. Aladdin, 2000.
Peppermints in the Parlor. Aladdin, 1985.
The Perils of Peppermints. Aladdin, 2005.
Secret in St. Something. Aladdin, 2003.
Sparrows in the Scullery. Aladdin, 1999.
The Trouble with Miss Switch. Aladdin, 2002.
The Twin in the Tavern. iUniverse, 2006.

BILL WALLACE
Beauty. Holiday House, 1988.
Blackwater Swamp. Holiday House, 1994.
Coyote Autumn. Holiday House, 2001.
Danger in Quicksand Swamp. Holiday House, 1989.
A Dog Called Kitty. Holiday House, 1980.

The Dog Who Thought He Was Santa. Holiday House, 2007.
Eye of the Great Bear. Minstrel, 1999.
Ferret in the Bedroom. Holiday House, 1986.
The Flying Flea, Callie, and Me. Pocket Books, 1999.
Journey into Terror. Pocket Books, 1996.
Never Say Quit. Holiday House, 1993.
No Dogs Allowed. Holiday House, 2004.
Pick of the Litter. Holiday House, 2005.
Red Dog. Holiday House, 1987.
Skinny-Dipping at Monster Lake. Simon & Schuster, 2005.
Snot Stew. Holiday House, 1989.
That Doggone Calf. Holiday House, 2009.
Totally Disgusting! Holiday House, 1991.
Trapped in Death Cave. Holiday House, 1984.
True Friends. Holiday House, 1994.

BETTY REN WRIGHT
Christina's Ghost. Holiday House, 2010.
Crandall's Castle. Holiday House, 2003.
The Dollhouse Murders. Holiday House, 1983.
The Ghost Comes Calling. Scholastic, 1984.
The Ghost in Room 11. Holiday House, 1998.
A Ghost in the Family. Scholastic, 1998.
A Ghost in the House. Scholastic, 1991.
The Ghost of Popcorn Hill. Holiday House, 1993.
The Ghosts of Mercy Manor. Scholastic, 1993.
Haunted Summer. Scholastic, 1996.
Moonlight Man. Scholastic, 2000.
Nothing But Trouble. Holiday House, 1995.
Out of the Dark. Scholastic, 1994.
The Scariest Night. Holiday House, 1994.
Too Many Secrets. Scholastic, 2002.
The Wish Master. Holiday House, 2000.

LAURENCE YEP
Angelfish. Putnam, 2001.
The Case of the Firecrackers. HarperCollins, 1999.
The Case of the Goblin Pearls. HarperCollins, 1997.
Child of the Owl. HarperCollins, 1977.
City of Fire. Doherty, 2009.
Cockroach Cooties. Hyperion, 1977.
Curse of the Squirrel. Random, 1987.
Dragon Road. HarperCollins, 2008.
Dragon's Gate. HarperCollins, 1997.

The Earth Dragon Awakes. HarperCollins, 2006.
Mountain Light. Harper, 1985.
The Rainbow People. Harper, 1989.
Sea Glass. Harper Trophy, 2002.
The Serpent's Children. Harper, 1984.

Spring Pearl: The Last Flower. Pleasant Co., 2002.
Sweetwater. HarperCollins, 2004.
Thief of Hearts. HarperCollins, 1995.
Tiger's Blood. HarperCollins, 2005.
The Traitor. HarperCollins, 2003.

Index

About the Author

NANCY J. POLETTE is professor emeritus at Lindenwood University in St. Charles, Missouri. She is the author of more than 150 professional books, including Libraries Unlimited's *Stop the Copying, Wild & Wacky Research Projects*; *Teaching Thinking Skills with Fairy Tales and Fantasy*; *Books Every Child Should Know: The Literature Quiz Book*; *Whose Tale Is True? Readers Theatre to Introduce and Research 49 Amazing American Women*; *Literature Lures: Using Picture Books and Novels to Motivate Middle School Readers*; *Mysteries in the Classroom*; and *Gifted Biographies, Gifted Readers! Literature Activities to Excite Young Minds*. She is the winner of the Texas Legacy Award for her book on the gifted, *Gifted or Goof Off: Fact and Fiction of the Famous* and the winner of the 2012 International Mom's Choice Award Gold Seal for *The Spy with the Wooden Leg*.

CPSIA information can be obtained at www.ICGtesting.com
Printed in the USA
BVOW06s0556180214

345240BV00003B/35/P